FAILED JUSTICE

THE CRAIG AND BENTLEY CASE REVISITED

FAILED JUSTICE

THE CRAIG AND BENTLEY CASE REVISITED

M J TROW

PEN & SWORD
TRUE CRIME

An imprint of
Pen & Sword Books Ltd
Yorkshire - Philadelphia

First published in Great Britain in 2025 by
Pen & Sword True Crime
An imprint of
Pen & Sword Books Ltd
Yorkshire - Philadelphia

ISBN 978 1 39903 767 9

A CIP catalogue record for this book is available from the British Library.

Typeset in INDIA by IMPEC eSolutions
Printed and bound in England by CPI (UK) Ltd.

The Publisher's authorised representative in the EU for product safety is Authorised Rep Compliance Ltd., Ground Floor, 71 Lower Baggot Street, Dublin D02 P593, Ireland.
www.arccompliance.com

For a complete list of Pen & Sword titles please contact

PEN & SWORD BOOKS LIMITED
47 Church Street, Barnsley, South Yorkshire, S70 2AS, England
E-mail: enquiries@pen-and-sword.co.uk
Website: www.pen-and-sword.co.uk

or

PEN AND SWORD BOOKS
1950 Lawrence Rd, Havertown, PA 19083, USA
E-mail: uspen-and-sword@casematepublishers.com
Website: www.penandswordbooks.com

MIX
Paper | Supporting responsible forestry
FSC® C013604

Contents

Introduction

I was given a rather belated birthday present when I was 3. Auntie Glad, a family friend, had bought me a gun. It was plastic and bright red with a yellow trigger and hammer. I loved that gun because, like any other boy (and many girls) in the 1950s, I was wrapped up in a make-believe world of cowboys and Indians. Every cowboy had his six-shooter and I had mine. I played with it most days over several years until it fell in half and then I had *two* guns to play with.

But I nearly did not get the gun at all. At the time, the media was full of the latest crime – the murder of a policeman in Croydon in November 1952. The media's banner headlines said it all. In one of the most outrageous examples of Fleet Street hyperbole, designed to sell newspapers, the *Daily Mail* read, 'Chicago Gun Battle in London. Gangsters with Machine-Gun on Roof Kill Detective, Wound Another. "Sidney Street" rages an hour then hand-to-hand fight. Armed Police Shot Back.'

No wonder my horrified parents were reluctant for me to have that six-shooter. The fact was, of course, that virtually everything about the *Mail*'s account was nonsense. Chicago in its bloody 1920s heyday – of Prohibition gang wars and Al Capone – had no comparison with Britain in the 1950s. And the 'gun battle' took place not in London, but in Croydon, Surrey. Whether or not the miscreants – Christopher Craig and Derek Bentley – could genuinely be termed 'gangsters' is open to debate, but nobody carried a machine gun. The Sidney Street analogy refers to a police stand-off by anarchists in the East End of London in January 1911 when terrorists were cornered by both the Met and the City forces and a contingent of the Scots Guards. A Maxim gun, a howitzer and the Royal Horse Artillery were all brought to standby by an over-the-top Home Secretary (Winston Churchill). The result was the restoration of order after the burning of a house and the deaths of two anarchists. There was no 'hand-to-hand fight' in 1952 and the only armed policeman to 'shoot back' was Detective Constable Frederick Fairfax who fired twice and missed both times.

The fact that sensation headlines like the *Mail*'s (and they were by no means unique to that publication) could be written, printed and believed is proof of how rare such cases were in the 1950s. We have become sadly hardened to gun and knife violence in London in recent years, but such things were virtually unheard of in 1952.

Fast forward to the summer of 1988. That was when my wife took an intensive driving course (we consciously avoided the term 'crash course'!) Within an hour she was back, complete with instructor. I thought the worst – 'she's pranged the car; he's refusing to go on with the tuition'. In fact, my wife had told him I was a crime writer (I had three novels under my belt by that time) and he had said, 'Have I got a story for you!'

The instructor's name was Raymond Pain and his father, PC 241Z Claude Pain, had been on that Croydon rooftop during the infamous gun battle. What neither of the Pains could understand was why Claude had not been called to give evidence at the Old Bailey, in one of many 'trials of the century' as the press called them, at which Derek Bentley's life was at stake. And it had dawned on Pain senior that that was because his recollection of events that night did not accord with the prosecution allegations nor the evidence of his colleagues in Z Division. Did I want to know more?

The case of Regina v. Craig and Bentley was regarded from the start as one of the utmost importance. The killing of a policeman, rare as it was, was regarded with particular horror by police and public alike. And when Bentley was found guilty and sentenced to hang, the 'three-quarter witted boy' who had gone to Croydon that night 'just for a ride', became a cause célèbre right at the heart of the capital punishment debate and ever-present risk of miscarriages of justice.

Yes, I wanted to know more. I met and interviewed Claude Pain, long since retired from the Met and his account of events was at once shocking and appalling. It led to my book *Let Him Have it, Chris,* published by Constable in 1990 with a foreword by that indefatigable campaigner for justice, Ludovic Kennedy.

Pain's account forms Chapter One of this long-overdue revisiting of the case. Read it and weep.

Chapter 1

'Now, the Story is this …'

The chapter title comes from the opening speech for the prosecution, delivered by Christmas Humphreys, at the trial of Craig and Bentley that opened on 9 December 1952. I used it in *Let Him Have It* to outline the official version of events, which did not accord with Claude Pain's memory of it. Here I use it to outline that memory. Pain never gave evidence in court. If he had, it might have sounded something like this:

2 November is the day the Italians call the 'Day of the Dead'. In Britain, there is nothing sinister about it. It was a routine Sunday evening and Constable Pain had been to his regular photography class in South Norwood. There was not time to get home before his night shift started at 9.45 p.m. so he checked in half an hour early at the Fell Road police station, his camera still in his pocket. It had been raining, although that had eased by now and Pain was still wearing his galoshes when a routine call came in from John Ware, a resident of Tamworth Road in Croydon.

Ware told the switchboard that his wife, Edith, in the process of putting their 9-year-old daughter, Pearl, to bed, had seen two men loitering on the pavement across the road from the ware house at No. 74. It was 9.15 and the confectionery warehouse of Barlow and Parker was closed and in darkness at that time. What had struck Mrs Ware was the suspicious behaviour of the men. Each time a car or bus passed, they turned to the wall and pulled their trilbies down over their faces. Then the shorter of the two climbed an iron gate that led to an alleyway to the left of the building and the taller one followed soon after. Edith called her husband, and he went in search of a phone.

Few households had phones in 1952 and it took John Ware a few minutes to organize himself. He put his boots on (he was a tree-feller by trade, which must have been rather niche in built-up Croydon) and ran past the Robert Peel pub to the nearest police box.

Dotty Kitchen had taken his call at Fell Road police station and she passed the information to the desk sergeant, Danny Watson. Routine calls like this one were handled by whoever was on duty.

'Pain,' Watson said, 'are you ready? Get the van out. Suspects on the roof at Tamworth Road.'

Neither of the Wares had mentioned the rooftop of Barlow and Parker, but it was clear when the police got there, that that was where the men had gone. Alongside Pain at the station was Allan Beecher-Brigden, an old mate, and both officers hurried to the garage. On the way, they bumped into a plainclothesman, Detective Constable Frederick Fairfax. 'What have you got?' he asked.

'Intruders on the roof at Tamworth Road,' Pain told him.

'Right,' said Fairfax. 'I'll hop in with you.' Technically, there was no need for the CID to get involved in what was likely to be a minor situation. Beecher-Brigden was a police driver, usually in a car with a two-way radio. The van was probably decided on because of the need for a larger vehicle to accommodate at least two felons.

It took four minutes for the three officers to reach Tamworth Road and a minute or two later, a police car turned up, driven by PC 550Z Sidney Miles with PC 528Z James McDonald as his wireless operator. There was already a small crowd outside the warehouse and people were leaning out of windows, pointing to the roof and shouting to the police. The men on the roof were shouting too, and gesturing. Beecher-Brigden saw the glint of metal in the hand of one of them as he got out of the car and he thought it was a gun.

In the darkness and confusion, there was no police plan. The senior man was Fred Fairfax, but Pain had lost sight of him, unaware that he too had hopped over the 6ft expanding gate and vanished into the dark of the alley. When shots rang out a moment later, Beecher-Brigden got back to the van and radioed Fell Road that the men on the roof had guns. This was 2 November and Danny Watson laughed at him over the phone; it was probably just kids letting off fireworks. He told Beecher-Brigden to have another look. He did and his worst fears were confirmed. The shouting – and the shooting – was still going on. He radioed again and this time Watson got the message and promised firearms and reinforcements.

Claude Pain was a heavy man, 6ft tall and two years away from retirement. The only way up to the roof was via the gate to the side, but he was not sure it would take his weight. Somebody tapped him on the shoulder. 'I've got an old ladder,' the man said, pointing to his house nearby. 'It's up to you. If you want to risk going up there, you can.'

Pain jumped at the chance, only to discover that the ladder was anything but heaven-sent. It was wobbly, with two rungs missing and it only reached part way up the warehouse wall. Nothing daunted, up he scrambled. There was a metal rail that ran all the way around the roof. At the trial that followed five weeks later, the rail was described as 2ft 6in high. Pain grabbed this and hauled himself up, for a moment or two a perfect target for the gunman.

The roof ahead, he could see on that cloudy night, was about the size of a tennis court. Directly ahead from the corner he had reached, he could make out a brick wall with a sloping roof. This was the head of a staircase to the offices below, marked with a letter 'B' on the plan by PC Bernard Beard, who made a scale drawing of the area the next day. Feet to the right of that, diagonally ahead of Pain, were four rooflights, like miniature greenhouses. Beard measured these as 2ft 3in at the sides and 4ft 6in at the apex. Because the premises were still in darkness, there was no light in these.

To his horror, Pain heard his ladder being scraped away from the wall. He had no idea how to get down now. Then the shooting started again and it was coming from a pale upright extension, over 11ft high, which was the head of a lift shaft ahead of him. Clearly, the men on the roof had not found a way into the building. To Pain, it seemed the shots were totally random, fired perhaps across the neighbouring gardens to keep police away. In common with all uniformed officers that night, Pain's only weapon was his wooden truncheon, Metropolitan Police, for the use of.

Pain hit the ground – at 6ft, he presented too much of a target and he crawled forward, making for the most obvious point of cover – the staircase head. He nearly gashed his hand on sheets of glass, probably left lying around by workmen. Behind the wall, he was relatively safe, but he could not see anything and made the decision to dash the 8 or 9 feet to the nearest rooflight.

By the time he was in this position, both the miscreants were hiding behind the lift-head (referred to as 'the stack' during the trial) and Fairfax, already on the roof before Pain, had shouted out 'I am a police officer. Come out from behind that stack.' Pain did not hear this. Neither did he hear the reply from one of the men, 'If you want us, fucking come and get us.' He did hear someone – and it had to be Fairfax – as the only other copper on the roof at this time – shout, 'Keep your heads down. There's shooting. There's shooting.'

In fact, Fairfax himself had been shot already. A bullet had grazed his right shoulder and he was struggling with the taller of the two men, the one who had not pulled the trigger. Fairfax hit him and dragged him behind another rooflight, the one in front of Claude Pain about 15 feet away. Now, despite the wailing of police sirens and the bursts of gunfire, Pain could hear all the conversation. The tall man had blond, wavy hair and was probably still in his teens. If he had once had a hat, it had gone now and he was hysterical and crying.

Fairfax realized that he was still in the line of fire of the other man. At the trial, he testified that the shooter was circling the roof and reached a position where he had a clear shot at Fairfax, Pain and his friend, now firmly in police custody. Why he did not fire was never explained. The plainclothesman dragged the teenager behind the staircase head and, according to him, had to help PC McDonald up onto the roof from a drainpipe he was standing on.

Seconds later, the door of the staircase crashed open as Sidney Miles's boot hit it. Silhouetted against the dim light from the stairs, Miles was a target from heaven. As he moved imperceptibly to his left, another shot rang out. Instinctively, Miles raised his hands to his head and pitched forwards onto his face, 8 or 9 feet from Pain. As Pain described it to me years later, 'I crawled forward into the open space and saw three darts protruding from his trouser pocket.' Sid Miles was an old mate, a darts fanatic – he never went anywhere without his arrows. 'He must have been rushing up those stairs,' Pain remembered. 'His blood must have been pumping. He looked like a pig.' Claude Pain would remember that swollen head and the blood for the rest of his life.

By this time, Fairfax and the taller lad had been joined by McDonald and Constable 463Z Robert Jaggs. Pain dashed back to the rooflight having helped to drag Miles's body out of the firing line. Constable 192Z, Norman Harrison, had been directly behind him on the staircase and he had leapt over Miles, throwing his truncheon and a milk bottle he found on the ground at the gunman, who fired back at him.

The decision was made to get the boy down the stairs. All the policemen present, using him as a human shield, got inside the stairwell and took him down. Pain stayed where he was, with Miles's body feet from him. He was still unarmed, except for his truncheon, and he was alone.

A couple of minutes must have passed and Fairfax was back. He had been given a .32 automatic by a colleague on the ground and behind him were Harrison, McDonald and Jaggs. 'Drop your gun,' he shouted from inside the staircase head. 'I've got a gun now.' The boy shouted back, 'Come on then, copper, let's have it out. Are we going to have a shooting match? It's just what I'd like.' Fairfax ran forward, circling around to avoid another bullet and fired twice. Both shots missed. The lad held his gun in the air, shouted, 'See, it's empty!' and dashed to the corner of the roof.

To Claude Pain it looked as if he fell, but there was little doubt that the boy was trying to kill himself. 'Give my love to Pam!' he shouted and he crashed down, 30 feet, onto the roof of a greenhouse, bounced off and lay groaning on the ground.

Once the hoo-ha was over, ambulancemen clattered up the stairs with a stretcher. Barlow and Parker's was now ablaze with lights and Pain helped the crew load Miles's body onto the stretcher and came down with him. There was a huge crowd at street level, ambulances, fire engines, cars, all flashing lights and chaos. A total of forty-four policemen had been called to Tamworth Road, but it looked like more. Various newspapers reported over two hundred.

In a patrol car, Sergeant Edward Roberts was sitting with a revolver, painted black, in his hand. 'That doesn't look very nice, does it?' Pain said, in one of those pointless statements people in shock often make.

'You'd better make your way to the station,' Roberts said.

And that is what Pain did. At Fell Road, he made notes of what had just happened in his pocket book. He copied them in longhand on the official form. And he never saw either the book or the form again.

When Claude Pain told me this story, he was nearly 80 years old. His mind and his memory were clear and sharp – not just in my view, but that of experienced television journalists who interviewed him and a Scotland Yard superintendent who spoke to him at length shortly after my book came out. His story did not fit the prosecution case. It did not chime with the statements and the court testimony of the other officers on the roof.

So I asked for clarification. I contacted Bill Waddell, an ex-policeman and curator of Scotland Yard's Black Museum. He invited me to meet him there on a miserable wet February day. My taxi took me past the 'real' Yard, architect Norman Shaw's opera house that was never used as such and was the Metropolitan Police headquarters in 1952. We went on to the grim, faceless monolith that is today's HQ, outside of which the triangular sign turns for ever. In the hallway, full of very tall policemen of various ranks, an eternal flame burned, to commemorate the long list of officers – Sidney Miles among them – who died in the course of duty. The Roll of Honour Ledger, beautifully inscribed in copperplate, was open at the day's date – 13 February – recording the murder of Constable Nathaniel Edgar in Southgate in 1948.

I was struck by the hallowed atmosphere here. Everybody talked in hushed tones and it felt like a church. Waddell was a heavy-set man with dark eyes. He took me up to his office many floors up and we sat facing each other. The Black Museum – properly the Metropolitan Police Crime Museum – is not open to the public, because it contains gruesome relics of crimes past: hangman's rope; death masks; murder weapons. There too was the gun, the knuckleduster and the two knives carried that November night in Croydon in 1952, but Waddell made no offer to show me any of them. Instead, in a hectoring tone, he lectured me for ten minutes on exactly what he thought of authors who came out with theories based on supposition and innuendo.

'A lot of shit has been written about this case,' he told me. 'And most of it has come our way.'

He had a file on his desk relating to the case of R. v. Craig and Bentley. Though no one on that rooftop in Croydon knew those names at the time, everybody knows them now because the hanging of Derek Bentley for a crime he did not commit has gone down as one of the worst miscarriages of justice in British history. I had no idea what the file contained and Waddell's offer to show me was very half-hearted. He was busy and I was getting the bum's rush. I asked if I could see the weapons and reluctantly he took me through a side door. There was a group of the specially invited here being shown the exhibits and Waddell pointed out what I had hoped to see. The gun, universally referred to at the time and in court as a Colt

.45 is actually an Eley .455 calibre revolver, with a six-shot chamber. Christopher Craig had sawn off the barrel so that it would fit more neatly in his pocket. The sawn-off section, which, unaccountably he carried that night in Croydon, was lying alongside it. There was the knuckleduster, made in a workshop by Craig and found in Bentley's pocket on the night in question by Fairfax who frisked him. By comparison with the vicious weaponry available in the 1980s and still more so today, the knuckleduster with its 'murderous' spike looks pretty tame. At the trial, the judge, Lord Goddard, made great play of this – 'Have you ever seen such a horrible weapon?' he asked the jury, even though no one used it that night and it remained in Bentley's pocket until Fairfax found it. I handled one of the spent bullets, wondering which of the many fired by Craig this was. Then, Waddell made it clear, it was time to go.

Bill Waddell approved of the 'hang 'em and flog 'em' Lord Goddard, the Lord Chief Justice, one of the most pernicious men ever to hold office. He approved of hanging and no doubt lamented the abolition of the death penalty in the UK in 1965. So distorted was his view of British justice that he believed it was the job of defence counsel to prove Craig and Bentley innocent, rather than for the prosecution to prove their guilt. My visit to the Yard made me realize, perhaps for the first time, exactly what I was up against.

My next step was to try to locate Christopher Craig. He had been found guilty of murder in January 1953 and had spent ten years at Her Majesty's pleasure before being released into the community. One source told me that he had changed his name to avoid undue publicity, had married and had two daughters. He had become a plumber, although how much work he could have got when he was ex-directory is difficult to say. He had applied for emigration papers to New Zealand to start a new life, but was turned down.

I knew that he *had* given interviews to the leftie publisher Victor Gollancz on his release in 1963 and he had spoken to David Yallop who wrote *To Encourage the Others* in 1971. In 1989, as I was writing *Let*

Him Have It, the pop star Elvis Costello performed *Let Him Dangle*, the lyrics of which I included in my book and the media were suddenly interested. On 4 June 1989, *The People* newspaper tracked Craig down (the Met could not find him in 1971) and wrote a double-page spread. By this time, I had found Iris Bentley, Derek's sister, who spent the rest of her life fighting for justice for her dead brother and when I saw *The People* article, I rang her. I spoke to her daughter Maria and could hear Iris screaming in the background. She had seen the paper too and there was Chris Craig, fat, bald, bearded, but, unlike Derek, very much alive. I managed to get his address in Clophill, Bedfordshire and wrote to him. I got no reply, probably because he no doubt received a lot of unwelcome mail as a result of *The People* piece.

So I tried the police themselves, the four men who were 'conspicuously brave' and had won medals for their courage in the darkness of the Barlow and Parker rooftop. I knew that James McDonald and Robert Jaggs were dead, but Harrison and Fairfax might still be able to explain Claude Pain's account. In both my letters, I explained who I was and what I wanted to know. Fairfax wrote to me, on 8 December 1988, 'Thank you for your letter dated 6th inst. I wish to inform you that I am neither prepared to meet you or to discuss the case with you.'

End of. Norman Harrison did not reply to me directly but via April Goodey, the Yard's Press Officer who contacted me on 17 December:

> I received a reply to your request from a former PC Norman Harrison who declines to participate in any way with your book.
>
> He has also asked me to pass on a warning to you that he is prepared to sue if the publication contains any inaccuracies 'factual or otherwise'.
>
> I am sorry to pass a message of this kind to you in these circumstances and can assure you it was most unexpected, as

obviously an officer in the case could help where accuracy is concerned.

Really? Ms Goodey was of the new school, trained in openness and honesty and, in dealing with the press, used to nuances and walking on eggshells. Norman Harrison, for all his youth in 1952, was probably old school, a dinosaur of the Bill Waddell/Lord Goddard mindset. I had not mentioned Claude Pain to either Fairfax or Harrison; what, therefore, did they have to hide?

I widened my net. Fell Road police station has long gone, but Croydon is still home to Z Division. I wrote to them and received no reply at all. My enquiries with Waddell had got nowhere. All paperwork relating to the Craig and Bentley case, the Yard told me, was housed at the Public Record Office (today The National Archive) at Kew, specifically in the file numbered MEPO 2/9401. These would not be available until seventy-five years after the current date, 2047.

So I tried the Directory of Public Prosecutions (now the Crown Prosecution Service) asking to borrow the trial transcript. Volume 81 of the *Notable British Trials* series, edited by barrister H. Montgomery Hyde, had been published in 1954, but I had no way of knowing whether this was a full, unedited version. I learned later from John Parris, Craig's counsel, that the *Notable British Trials* series is a sanitized, edited version of events. My correspondent at the DPP wanted to know more about me and what my specific interest was. I provided that information by letter and received no further reply.

In desperation, I wrote to Croydon Magistrate's Court in case something of the original charges against Craig and Bentley were still lodged there. All depositions, I was told, would have been passed to the Central Criminal Court at Old Bailey as Croydon were only obliged to keep records for three years. The Old Bailey never acknowledged my enquiry.

Back I went to Kew, asking specifically for information regarding the statements of Pain, Beecher-Brigden and James Alderson, three policemen who were there on the night in question and were referred to by David Yallop as the 'three monkeys' because, officially at least, their voices were never heard. Again, I got the same stonewalling. Kew passed me back to the Yard and the Yard regretted to say, 'we are unable to disclose any information from a closed file.' When Iris Bentley asked to see the relevant file in 1987, she was told by the Home Office that they could not be released because of 'sensitive material' (whatever that is supposed to mean).

I rang the Yard's Press Office to ask for information on the careers of Z Division men prior to the rooftop shooting, assuming, in my naivety, that such information would be readily available. I heard a man say to a colleague, cupping his hand over the receiver as he answered my call, 'There's some bloke here wanting to know about old crimes. That's peculiar, isn't it?'

I then had to explain to the Press Officer who Craig and Bentley were and, in a nutshell, what happened in Croydon all those years ago when one of their own was murdered and another wounded.

In talking to the Press Office, I realized that too many years had intervened. Witnesses were dead, others had gone to ground. And today, well over a quarter of a century on from those fruitless enquiries of mine in the late 1980s, the world of Craig and Bentley – and of Claude Pain – is like another planet.

Chapter 2

The Violent Playground

The children who lived through the Second World War, according to psychologists, sociologists and historians, formed the most disturbed and delinquent generation in British history. 'The day war broke out,' to quote the radio comedian Rob Wilton (3 September 1939), Derek Bentley was 6; Christopher Craig was 2. When the war ended, Bentley was 12, approaching school-leaving age, and Craig 9. Their formative years were spent in an atmosphere of anxiety, tension and deprivation. Today, such things are taken into consideration in the context of law-breaking and criminal sentencing; in 1952, they were not.

According to the account given by William Bentley, Derek's father, in *My Son's Execution* (1957), the baby was lucky to survive the trauma of his birth. He was a twin (this had not been detected during Lilian Bentley's pregnancy) and the sibling died two hours after birth. Derek himself contracted bronchial pneumonia and had to be rushed to an oxygen tent at Guy's Hospital, where a blood donation from his father (the first of many) saved his life.

The Bentleys then lived in Blackfriars, a slum in a deprived area in the teeth of the Depression in the years after the Wall Street crash. Derek's elder sister Joan was farmed out (a common occurrence) to a grandmother and Derek was brought home to the two-roomed flat to share with his parents and sister Iris, two years his senior.

At the age of 3, Derek fell off a parked lorry and landed on his head. Back in Guy's again, doctors told the Bentleys that the boy had had an epileptic fit as a result of the fall and such fits would continue, especially if there were blows to the head. This happened spectacularly when he was 6, the year war began, and he was rushed to Lambeth Hospital. William Bentley was an ARP warden now and Iris and Joan were terrified when they first saw him in his gas mask; Iris thought it was the devil and locked herself in the lavatory. Like many other terrified and distraught mothers, Lilian Bentley refused to let her children be evacuated. They got as far as the departure point, the school playground, and she took them back home.

On 10 September 1940, Derek's Nan's home was hit in a night-time bombing raid and William Bentley was one of the rescue team. One of the bodies he carried out was that of his daughter, Joan. Most of her head had been blown off and he only recognized her by her clothes. Derek became withdrawn and constantly frightened as a result. Night after night, he would snuggle up to Iris and ask, 'What's going to happen, Sis?'

By August 1941, William had got his family out of London, at least as far as Edgware, where the Bentleys had friends. A year later, Lilian gave birth to another son, Denis (with one 'n' because he was named after the doctor who delivered him). Hours after his birth, Edgware experienced its first ever air raid. Camrose Avenue School was harsh. Iris hated it and Derek became the target of bullying and name-calling, by teachers as well as other pupils because he was often absent and even when present, seemed away with the fairies.

On 1 January 1943, the dreaded brown envelope hit the Bentley's doormat – William had been called up. Derek hid under the loose floorboards, desperate for his dad not to go. But Mr Churchill had other ideas. The later phases of the war saw the arrival of the V1 and V2 rockets – the doodlebugs with their deadly whine punctuated by silence. One of them demolished twelve houses in a row in Edgware – the Bentleys' among them – on 5 October 1944. William Bentley was home on leave and he pulled strings to get the family rehoused in Elephant and Castle. They were back in the slums again, made worse by the debris and wreckage of the Blitz. There was no bath, no electricity and the bedroom was composed of rickety bunks shared with another family.

In September, another flying bomb hit the Bentleys. Derek had been ill with headaches and a blueness of the skin that the family doctor, Dr McManus, could not explain. The ceiling came down on the 8-year-old as he lay in bed, but he was unhurt.

Bentley's education, or lack of it, should have become central to the 1952 murder case, although, as we shall see, the trial judge, Lord Goddard, would have none of it, objecting to defence counsel's attempts to introduce it as mitigation at the Old Bailey. At John Ruskin School in Walworth, where Derek was sent at the age of 11, it was obvious that he was totally illiterate. Thousands of children, with schools closed and fathers away in the armed forces, were in a similar position. Even today, without the excuse of a world war, nearly 3 million adults in Britain are illiterate too. When Derek was examined by Dr James Munroe, head of Psychological Medicine at Guy's, in 1949, he believed the problem to be innate, not, in fact, caused by intermittent school attendance. Dr McManus continued to believe that the war was responsible.

In 1945, the Bentleys moved to Norbury and Iris and Derek both attended Norbury Manor School. It was here that Derek met Christopher Craig and the Bentleys were, as at Edgware, like fish out of water. The school itself was typical of the time. 'We use the cane,' Mr K.R. Bonnetto, the headmaster, told the press in 1952. 'If a boy kicks over the traces, then he should be made to realize that the punishment is going to be quick and automatic.' Rather like a hangman's rope.

By May 1946, Derek's truancy (and his continued fits) was causing serious problems. Lilian gave birth to another son, Roger, who was born with what today is called Down syndrome but was then known as mongoloidism. When Derek, not 13, had a particularly bad fit, the doctor gave him phenobarbitone, which was regarded as a panacea for just about everything at the time, but added to the boy's distance. When little Roger died in November, Iris was with him. Derek took his little brother's death very badly, as did his mother, folding and unfolding the baby clothes for months afterwards.

When investigator David Yallop wrote *To Encourage the Others* in 1971, he interviewed two of the staff at Norbury Manor School. Both of them put Bentley's situation down to that old chestnut of over-indulgent parenting. That kindly headteacher, Bonnetto, referred to him as 'a great lump of lard, an utterly worthless piece of humanity'. He would probably – and rightly – lose his job for that today.

In early March 1948, Lilian Bentley opened the door to two uniformed policemen. They had Derek with them, still not yet 15. He and another boy had been arrested for stealing bus tickets and trying to break into a shop. It was almost a blueprint for Croydon four years later. Bentley told his father he had done it for a dare so that people 'might stop taking the rise'. At Croydon Juvenile Court, both boys were bound over for two years with a £2 fine. His father confined him to the house for three months.

In July, having attended nine schools in twelve years and having been ignored by the authorities in all of them, Derek Bentley left education. While looking for work and getting nowhere because of his illiteracy, he was again in trouble with the law, charged (again with another youth) with stealing tools. The magistrate asked him to spell 'fluorescent' (which William Bentley couldn't do, either). Reports were filed (which David Yallop could not find in 1971) and Derek was sent for a three-year stint at Kingswood Approved School in Bristol. Here, as a result of an IQ test, he rated 66 with a reading age of 4½. Such evaluations have changed over time, but in 1950, 66 would place Bentley in the 'feeble-minded (Educationally Subnormal)' category. David Yallop agonizes over the various definitions of this, but in fact, he had no need. All the evidence of Bentley's behaviour on the Croydon rooftop points to an amateur burglar, suddenly out of his depth and terrified. There is nothing 'feeble-minded' about it.

According to the official information now available at The National Archive, on 24 June 1949 Bentley was examined by Dr Munroe at the Sir Charles Simmonds Clinic. He was uncooperative, but Munroe accepted that the epileptic fits probably were the result of head trauma in childhood. William Bentley wanted Derek home, but Munroe sent him back to Kingswood. 'There is no doubt that Derek is very backward intellectually and that most of this is the result of congenital lack of intelligence.' Mr Fido, Chief Warden at Kingswood, suggested a history of petit mal (epilepsy). The family doctor in Norbury, Doris Reynolds, described Derek as 'mentally backward'.

On 11 February 1952, Bentley was examined for National Service, a legacy of the need for fit, articulate young men for the armed forces which was deemed necessary after the war. His right eye was impaired and he was only fit for grade IV, restricted service on account of subnormal intelligence. Psychiatric treatment was considered necessary.

What is fascinating is the family history which emerges in these papers, which David Yallop probably never saw. His account of Bentley's childhood (like that of Benedict Birnberg, the family solicitor) is based largely on Iris's recollections. Nowhere does it say, other than in the official report, that William Bentley had four convictions for larceny. In February 1931, he was given three months' hard labour 'as a rogue and vagabond for loitering with intent'. Despite the Victorian phraseology, this attitude to law and order seems just as relevant to Croydon as Derek's IQ.

Kingswood came to an end in July 1950 and between July of the following year and February 1952, Derek worked as a furniture remover in Norbury. He was paid £3 10s a week and his work was satisfactory. From May 1952 until July, he worked as a dustman on £6 15s a week, but proved unsatisfactory here and was demoted to roadsweeper before being dismissed for bad timekeeping.

Derek Bentley undoubtedly had problems all his life – very few of them of his own making. But his real problem was Christopher Craig.

'Everyone knew Christopher Craig in Norbury,' Iris Bentley remembered years later (*Let Him Have Justice* 1998). 'He hung around street corners wearing a black coat and a trilby hat … He fancied himself as a little Al Capone. He was known as the Kid or Kiddo, the little gangster, because he was only 15.'

The official 'antecedent history' of Craig in The National Archive records that he was born on 19 May 1936 in Croydon. He attended Norbury Manor Secondary School between September 1947 and July 1951, in the B stream, described as 'top class of Inferior Group'. The headmaster, Frederick Glogg, quoted from Craig's reports that he took no interest in work whatsoever; had he done, he could have been average. He was a persistent truant and his parents covered for him – 'a general lack of home discipline' (which no doubt explains his older brother Niven, who would go on to do a twelve-year sentence for armed robbery). He was mentally stable and could read without understanding. He once ran away from home and was found wandering in Hove. His one outstanding ability was athletics, especially swimming.

Craig's father, Niven Matthew, was a bank teller, although various accounts have promoted him to manager, which fits the man's pomposity. A little bizarrely, he appeared before Croydon magistrates' court in July 1943 and was fined £5 for possessing a Browning automatic pistol. As an officer in the First World War, he was used to firearms.

Craig's mother, however, was a different proposition. Between 1931 and 1937, she was committed *four* times for shoplifting. Today, this is seen as an example of psychological aberrant behaviour; in the 1930s it was plain, old-fashioned larceny.

Craig's brother Niven similarly had four counts against him, for store-breaking, office-breaking, stealing ammunition, possessing firearms and larceny up to 30 October (three days before the Croydon shoot-out) charged with 'armed robbery, robbery with violence and possessing firearms with intent'. The other children, one son and four daughters, apparently led exemplary lives.

When Christopher left Norbury, he worked for two weeks as a storekeeper at a motor engineers in Thorston Road, Croydon and left of his own accord. He then worked briefly as a welder. Shortly before the raid on Barlow and Parker's, Craig worked as a fitter in a garage in SE5 for £2 a week, where his work was described as satisfactory. He was 'willing and hardworking'. Roughly a year before the Croydon shoot-out, Christopher Craig was found guilty at Hove Borough Juvenile Court (where he had run away) with Graham Pleasants, aged 12½, of possession of a firearm – a .45 Webley revolver with two rounds of ammunition and nine rounds of 9mm. Pleasants carried a Luger.

One night, when Iris was on duty selling tickets at the Astoria cinema in Norbury, Craig sauntered up in his gangster outfit, talking in that mid-Atlantic drawl that he thought made him sound like the actor James Cagney. 'If I put a gun up to the cash desk, would you hand the money over?'

'You'd have the biggest shock of your life if you did.'

If we compare the murder rate in Britain pre- and post-war, the figures are remarkably similar, both in terms of numbers and killers and victims. Motive does not change much either – domestic violence is by far the most common. What *is* different is a marked increase in firearms as the weapon of choice – twenty as opposed to seven. This was because of the number of guns available on the streets, many of them brought home by 'Tommies' returning from various theatres of war. My father brought a Luftwaffe flare gun which we kept hidden away for years. There is a ridiculous scene in the otherwise excellent movie *Let Him Have It* (1991) in which a harassed teacher demands that the boys in his class hand over their guns – at least twenty of them clatter onto his desk. Christopher Craig was different. A police search of his house in Croydon revealed at least forty guns and ammunition, and Craig was in the habit of carrying a pistol wherever he went. His headteacher called this a 'harmless hobby' and was much more concerned with knives. On my third visit to the Black Museum at the Yard, I was able to handle the knuckleduster, but not the gun, even though its chamber was empty.

How much the war, and its disruption, explains the mindsets of Craig and Bentley is difficult to say. The *Sunday Pictorial* in September 1942 carried an article which tried to advise anxious parents – '[magistrates] know as well as you do that Tom is not really bad at heart; they are there for your child, not against him.' The term 'juvenile delinquency' dates from 1817 at a time when Britain was trying to readjust after twenty-two years of warfare against Revolutionary and Napoleonic France. After 1945, it was back again, in the form of the 'cosh boys' referred to contemptuously by Lord Goddard at the trial.

In fact, although the war cannot have helped, there is ample evidence that the crime rate among 'young persons' (teenagers, as we would say today) was already rocketing in the depressed 1930s. Commissioner of the Met, Philip Game, went so far as to blame shops for showing off alluring produce, which smacks horribly of the 'she was asking for it' mentality common to rapists. The law got tough; in 1951 over 500 birchings (beating with twigs tied together in a bundle) were handed down by magistrates who, the *Pictorial* said, wanted to be the children's friends.

Every major city had its gangs of young tearaways (although Francis Selwyn's attempt to create a 'Craig and Bentley gang' in his *Gangland* – 1988 – is woefully wide of the mark). Christopher Craig was undoubtedly a charismatic leader of weaker lads. 'Compared to him,' William Bentley wrote in 1957, 'my son was like water.' Technically, but not in law, both boys were children in 1952. Neither of them could vote, yet both had been at work (or out of it, in Bentley's case) since they were 15. But, despite kind interpretations of juvenile behaviour, mostly from the Labour Party, the law waded in harshly. The 'hang 'em and flog 'em' attitude was by no means confined to dinosaurs like Lord Goddard.

Child psychologists like John Mays of Liverpool University have written on the need for children to lead dangerous lives, to live in a world of adventure without any real idea of the consequences. 'For the slum boy ... the side of the warehouse is his mountain chasm ... Nightwatchmen, patrolling police and shopkeepers are worthy antagonists to test his steel against.' Except, of course, that on 2 November 1952, it all went horribly wrong.

Terence Morris used Croydon as the focus of his study *The Criminal Area* in 1957. He poses the obvious – but interesting – question of whether criminal behaviour is passed on from one generation to another in such areas. Ray Pain, the son of the policeman who features in Chapter One and whom we shall meet again, was the same age as Christopher Craig. His memory of Croydon gangs was of lurking on street corners, in 'kipper' ties, trying to impress the girls. From time to time, the police would raid the cinemas (like the Astoria where Iris Bentley worked) and turf out the under-aged couples from the back rows of the 'one and nines'. It may be that Ray's experience was modified by his father being a 'bobby', but his friend Terry was often on the fringes of trouble and had an uncle who was an old lag.

As in all history, change is constant and often rapid. Craig and Bentley lived in a strange limbo between the war and the 'Teddy Boy' violence of the Rock 'n' Roll era, where American influences were strongly felt for the first time and lads walked around Croydon, as elsewhere, in suede 'brothel-creepers' or 'winkle-pickers', ludicrously tight denim jeans, and with DA (Duck's Ass) haircuts in an attempt to emulate Elvis Presley and Tony Curtis. Both Ray Pain and Terry remembered Fifties Croydon as being safe, but already the gangs were loitering near toilets on Tamworth Road to menace and beat up 'queers' out in search of rough trade. By the mid-1950s, they extended their targets to include the tiny immigrant community – 'Paki-bashing'. Derek Bentley died eighteen months before the movie *Blackboard Jungle* was released (no doubt Iris saw it) and it became forever associated in the public mind with flick-knife violence to the thumping Bill Hailey tune of *Rock Around the Clock*.

The delinquents were a subculture, anti-society for the hell of it and usually working class and low income. Occasionally, boys from richer backgrounds, like Christopher Craig, were drawn into this culture, although of course, in Craig's case, he was pivotal to it. If he had a gang at all, it was made up of Bentley, grammar school misfits like Norman Parsley and Frank Fazey and a couple of 13-year-old girls. Lord Goddard, because he was a snob of the old school, did not doubt that Craig came from a good background. His father had been a captain in the Great War and was chief teller at his bank. Goddard did not, presumably, know about the captain's illegal ownership of a gun. Fenton Bressler, the lawyer who wrote a smarmy biography of Goddard in 1977, says that the robbery that Craig took part in on 1 November 1952 was carried out with another boy 'whom it is not now necessary to name'. His name was Norman Parsley.

'Now, let us put out of our minds,' said Goddard in his outrageously biased summing up of the case, 'any question of films or comics or literature of that sort. Those things are always prayed in aid nowadays.' If there was any doubt about the mental acuity of the Lord Chief Justice, this last phrase surely proves that he should no longer have been sitting on the bench.

Approximately two hours before he shot and killed Sidney Miles, Craig went to the pictures to see *My Death is a Mockery*. This was a black and white 'B' feature starring Donald Houston as a fisherman who takes to smuggling and gets involved in a shoot-out with the police. Perhaps, given the screening times on that Sunday, Craig did not stay to the end. Had he done so, he would have seen Houston face the hangman. This film was not mentioned in court (although there was a reference to it in the 1991 *Let Him Have It*) but it seems to me to be absolutely crucial. I can still clearly remember coming out of cinemas as a youngster, blasting away with an invisible and imaginary six gun at anything that moved on the street. Did Christopher Craig do the same thing, but with an actual gun? Today, *My Death is a Mockery* seems tame indeed, but Craig was never exposed to today's 'video nasties' as a boy and there is no doubt that Goddard was wrong about the pernicious effects of trashy, violent movies. The average cinema goer (like the average juror) has an IQ which is equivalent to what is now an 'ungraded' GCSE. They have no interest in acting techniques, clever lighting, believable dialogue, but they do get a message and it is often the wrong one.

The American gangster movies of the Thirties, which were still being made and shown in Craig's day, often centred on criminals, men who had nothing but contempt for authority – Cagney, Bogart, Raft all personified this type. This was why Craig swaggered around in trench coats and trilby hats, talking in a cod-Chicago accent, with a gun in his pocket. Craig went to the pictures three or four times a week; he lived and breathed this sort of mindless violence.

Comics were probably less of an influence. Both Craig and Bentley were functionally illiterate, so the graphic images of comics were perfect for them. 'I think the only books he [Craig] knows anything about are the books of Enid Blyton that he gets other people to read to him,' Niven Craig senior told the court, casting a wholly false light on his malicious son. Some of the gangster comics that Craig liked were banned from Britain in 1955. Child psychologist Dr Fredric Wertham wrote 'hostility and hate set the pace of almost every story'. By contrast, Bentley's favourite reading matter was the *Beano*, the *Dandy* and *Rupert Bear.*

Derek Bentley had been medically assessed several times by the time of the Croydon shoot-out, but it was the report of Dr J.C.M. Matheson, Principal Medical Officer at Brixton prison, on 5 December 1952 that makes the most interesting reading. This was four days before the 'trial of the century' at the Old Bailey and it says a great deal that Matheson was not called upon to testify. That was because his role was merely to determine whether Bentley was sane, fit to plead and fit to stand trial. He decided that he was all of the above, but only after a hostile and biased piece of reporting. Matheson had read the previous medical reports, interviewed Bentley daily, talked to his father and the prison officers who were in regular content with him.

The doctor's summation, that Bentley was 'arrogant [and] boastful' does not sound remotely like the confused and limited young man everybody else saw. Of course, there are two sides to everybody and no doubt the quiet, reclusive, dutiful son of the Bentley family was nothing of the kind on the street. 'He was lairy,' Christopher Craig told Thames Television years later. Craig would not have tolerated him otherwise.

The same Dr Matheson produced a report on Craig two days before Bentley. Craig's birth was normal, he was a good baby and easy to rear. He wet his bed until he was 12 (one of the conspicuous signs of serial killers) and was spoiled rotten by his older siblings. Craig clearly enjoyed the limelight. Matheson found him to be below average intelligence and his 'word blindness' (which we would call dyslexia today) was the result of laziness. He was not interested in the opposite sex (any more than Bentley was) – girlfriends like 'Pam', whose name he called out as he leapt off the Croydon roof, were arm-candy, nothing more. Matheson found Craig immature and unstable, but, like Bentley, sane and fit to stand trial.

The other point about Craig was the influence of his brother, Niven. The man had a criminal record going back to the war years and had only been released from military prison in 1950. In September 1952, he was charged with the armed robbery he had committed the previous March. In sentencing him to twelve years in October, Mr Justice Hilbery said:

> You are not only cold-blooded but from my observation of you I have not the least hesitation in saying I believe you would shoot down any police officer who was attempting to arrest you … I think you would do it absolutely coldly, utterly regardless of the pain you might inflict.

With a blueprint like that, a brother who drove a flashy American car and carried wads of cash, how could Christopher Craig have turned out differently?

And so, on Sunday 2 November 1952, Craig and Bentley took a bus to Croydon 'just to have a look round'.

Chapter 3

The Thin Blue Line

In November 1952, journalist Kenneth Allsop spent a week with a typical Metropolitan Police division, giving his *Picture Post* readers a flavour of what front-line policing was like in the post-war years, still the age of austerity. He did not specify the division but he refers to 'a markedly brutal and tragic incident' that had recently occurred and one careless photograph clearly shows the 'Z' on a constable's shoulder tab. The title of his article was 'Fear in the Suburbs' and letters in the same edition of the *Post* demanded that the 'cosh boys' causing the problem should be flogged.

The statistics that Allsop used proved conclusively that teenaged crime was falling by the end of year, but the public, trustful of most of the media, were already wary of government figures. A local barmaid believed the police should be armed, American-style. Sales of chains and padlocks trebled. Nobody answered their doors after dark. It would not be Christopher Craig or Derek Bentley standing there, but how many more lads were like them?

Most of us see the police – especially the Met, the 'most public institution in the world' – through the eyes of fiction. 'If you want to know the time,' the Music Hall song went, 'ask a policeman.' He was caricatured by artists like Lawson Wood in the 1920s and 1930s as an avuncular buffoon, red-faced, moustachioed, overweight and flat-footed. Such caricatures showed men far too old for the active service on the streets. Traditionally, they gave people directions, directed traffic on roads without the automatic light systems we have today, helped old ladies cross the road and if they caught little boys scrumping apples, gave them a clip around the ear before taking them home to Dad who would give them another one. It was all very idyllic and comforting and it was a lie.

But there was another fictional image that existed alongside this one. Satirical magazines like *Punch* and *Judy* lampooned London's police for their ineptitude. So deep did this criticism run that it was taken up by most of the public. 'Mr Plod', Enid Blyton's hapless copper in the Noddy books, was a name given to any bobby on the beat. In 1888, the year of the Ripper, *Punch* was particularly vitriolic about both London forces (the Met and City) because they failed entirely to catch the Whitechapel murderer dubbed by the press Jack the Ripper. They referred to the Met as the 'defective force' after Queen Victoria herself had criticized their handling of the case.

As crime fiction itself became more popular, so broadsides against the *real* police increased. There was hardly a mention of the Met in 1878 when the CID was set up, but by 1901, criticism was everywhere. In part, that was because Sherlock Holmes had arrived (in 1891) an *amateur* detective of genius who ran rings around the men paid to catch criminals. When I wrote my first detective fiction novel, nearly a century after Holmes' debut, I put Inspector Lestrade (one of Conan Doyle's Yard men) centre stage. *He* was the crime solver and Holmes merely a drug-addicted, interfering busybody.

In fiction, private detectives are popular because they are not bound by red tape, procedure or even the law. Edgar Wallace's *The Four Just Men* (1905) were only just in the sense that their ends were met. They always got their man, but their means were highly debatable, involving every underhand trick and crime in the book. This lawless, vigilante world has been copied thousands of times over the years and the genre remains popular today.

As a little boy in the 1950s, I was brought up to believe in British justice and to trust policemen. It did not occur to me that a bobby could be uncaring, inept or – shock, horror – corrupt. Such things were not possible. Compulsory Saturday night television viewing was *Dixon of Dock Green* on BBC when kindly, avuncular Sergeant Dixon, aka Jack Warner, appeared on the screen with a little homily, acted honourably and cleverly in a half hour black and white programme and saluted us all in uniform at the end, reminding us to mind how we went and to 'look after dear old Mum'. Cringeworthy though it is today, it is worth noting that it and Scotland Yard's *No Hiding Place* were pretty well the only cop shows on television. We had no other yardstick. These were the images that made the Americans and others around the world believe that our police were wonderful.

Interestingly, the George Dixon character came from a movie, *The Blue Lamp*, which I did not see until several years later but which was made in 1950. The film was made at Ealing Studios the previous year with the approval of the Met's Commissioner Sir Harold Scott and the uniforms, equipment and locations were all provided by the force itself. The central tenet of the story, of kindly old Dixon being shot dead by a tearaway, was based on the 1948 murder of Y Division officer Nathaniel Edgar (Y807) by an army deserter, Donald Thomas. The case was fairly open and shut but Thomas did not hang because the government was debating the issue of capital punishment at the time and the sentence was commuted to life imprisonment.

What very few people have noticed is that the *Blue Lamp* killer, a very young Dirk Bogarde, says to a friend concerning the shooting, 'I had to let him have it; he was coming for me.' The phrase 'let him have it' was to hang Derek Bentley, but, as we shall see later, it had been used before, and not by Ealing Studios.

At the criminal-catching end of police fiction was the detective – trench-coated, trilby-hatted, pipe-smoking and tough. Again, it was a characterization based on the real detectives of the time – Ted Greeno, Reg Spooner, Bob Higgins, George Hatherill and, above all, Bob Fabian. So famous had Fabian become, catching all but one of twenty-three murderers, that a television series was made, which was introduced by him and told the stories of some of his cases. *Scotland Yard*, narrated by criminologist Edgar Lustgarten, covered others, although they became less authentic as the series developed.

In the late Fifties, with Derek Bentley dead and Christopher Craig in prison, the image of the polite, powerful, unruffled detective who referred to villains as 'chummie' still persisted. John Mills hunted a fugitive in *Tiger Bay*. Nigel Patrick was looking for a murderer in *Sapphire*. Stanley Baker was handling damaged teenager David McCallum in *Violent Playground.*

It was not until the late 1960s and 1970s that 'realistic' cop shows were made in this country. *Z Cars* and *The Sweeney* took the lid off police forces. Coppers swore as frequently as the riff-raff they were catching. They drank to excess. They beat up women, even their wives. They took bribes, lied in court and were, occasionally, guilty of murder. *The Sweeney* in particular was responsible for fact aping fiction. I once spoke to a serving Met officer who told me that before John Thaw and Dennis Waterman reached our television screens, policemen used conventional language. Afterwards it was 'get the guv'nor on the blower', 'get the wheels out', use 'shooters'.

What about the real thing? What was life like for the men (and handful of women) who faced the 'cosh boys' of the 1950s?

When Claude Pain joined the Met, it was 100 years old. Formed in 1829, 'Peel's bloody gang' was the brainchild of one of the most dedicated and innovative Home Secretaries of the century. So closely did the new force identify with Robert Peel, that policemen in London came to be known first as 'Peelers', then by the altogether more friendly 'Bobbies'.

London was divided into seventeen police districts and the idea was to have men in uniforms who looked nothing like the army 'aiding the civil power' and to carry out a preventative policy; merely the sight of a Peeler patrolling the streets would deter crime. In 1921, the last of the divisions – Z – was set up to cover the Croydon and Norbury area. For all the cheerful Lawsonesque imagery of policemen in the early twentieth century, the reality was very different. A series of scandals had been uncovered and were widely reported in the national press.

The detective branch at Scotland Yard, created in 1843, was dismantled in 1877 over the trial of several officers involved in the turf war scandal and bribe-taking on an unprecedented scale. In the year that Pain joined Z Division, Sergeant Goddard (no relation to the later Lord Chief Justice) was similarly found guilty of taking bribes from Kate Meyrick, a West End night-club owner and of turning a blind eye to what went on in her establishments. Goddard was with what would later be called the Vice Squad and earned £6 a week. Odd then that he had two bank accounts, one with £12,000 in it, owned a £2,000 house in Streatham and drove a flash Chrysler car.

Police pay – or the lack of it – had always been a problem. Of the 3,000 Peelers recruited in 1829, nearly all of them had been removed within three years for drunkenness and bribe-taking. 'The police society', wrote Mike Seabrook in *Coppers: an Inside View of the British Police* (1987) 'has a very long collective memory. Officers talk about the police strike of 1919 as if it is a personal memory, though most of their fathers were unborn when that strike took place.'

One of Claude Pain's first memories of the job came very early on, when his 'parent' colleague showed him how to hitch his overcoat belt to park railings and have a quiet nap while pretending to be on duty. Lord Birkenhead, a high court judge in the 1920s wrote, 'There is no finer, no more honourable, no more honest and no more courageous force of men in the world.' One wonders who he was talking about.

The 1930s saw a shake-up in police procedure, if only to alleviate the monotony of beat patrols, where officers, singly or in pairs, prowled an allotted number of streets day and night, to check that all was well. Foot patrols continued, but were backed up by the 'Dr Who/Tardis' style blue police telephone box such as the one that John Ware used to call for help on 2 November 1952 Increasingly, cycles, motorcycles and cars (the latter equipped with radios) were being used to stay one step ahead of criminals who were always ready to exploit the latest technology. The mobile units of 1919 morphed into the Flying Squad in 1935, a unit known to the Underworld as 'the Heavy Mob'.

For all its attempts at modernity, however, 'it remained,' in the words of David Ascoli (*The Queen's Peace*, 1979) 'an ultra-conservative, artisan institution, still wedded to a hierarchical structure ... The police service [note the use of the new term] with its lack of incentives, still attracted brawn rather than brains.'

By the 1950s, times were, once again, 'a-changing'. It was the age of angry young men to the generation of John Osborne and playwrights of his time. 'The new society,' Ascoli wrote, 'with its vision of a synthetic Utopia, its appeal to materialism, its tolerance of indiscipline and its politics of envy, has much to answer for.'

It was a violent age, too, a disjointed society that would never settle back to pre-war norms, a time when the natural precepts of freedom had vanished under a crippling bureaucracy, one in which central government assumed an ever-larger role in the lives of everyday people. John George Haigh, the acid-bath murderer, was busy trying to dissolve Olivia Durand-Deacon in a tub of sulphuric acid in 1949. The dashing fantasist Neville Heath was torturing Margery Gardener three years earlier before killing her and hiding her body in Branksome Chine, near Bournemouth.

Government itself was going through a seismic experience. The coalition cabinet of the war years was dissolved. Winston Churchill, the hero of the hour, was dismissed by the electorate as being out of touch with the brave new world that he himself had done much to create. The new government was the most reforming of the century, with Clement Attlee at the helm. The National Health Service was set up by Aneurin Bevan, who had called the Hendon Police College that trained the Met a Fascist institution.

For the police, there *was* light at the end of the tunnel. Sir Harold Scott was appointed Commissioner in June 1945, the first ever civilian to hold the post. Ever since Rowan and Mayne in 1829, it was assumed that only military men could do the job. Pay was increased in 1946 and service conditions improved. Read the memoirs of famous detectives like Robert Fabian, Albert Webb, George Spooner and George Hatherill and you will be struck by the grimly austere accommodation and regulations of young officers of their generation. In May 1949, a constable's basic pay was £5 5s a week (Derek Bentley got more than that as a council refuse collector). The following year, the Oaksey Commission lifted this to £340 a year. Change came too fast for some people and not fast enough for others. Use of police cars saw flat caps in use for the first time, as opposed to the bobby's helmet, itself based on the infantry's Home Service pattern of the 1880s. Officers occasionally patrolled in shirt sleeves at the height of summer and the upright collars of the still-Victorian tunics vanished, replaced with modern lapels. In the press photographs of Constables Harrison, McDonald and Jaggs in January 1953, they all wear the new pattern. They are shown shaking hands with the commissioner, the man who oversaw the creation of six-men tactical teams which the Met still uses. A Police Cadet Corps was set up in 1951, with 1,000 applicants in the opening month (one of these was Claude Pain's son, Ray).

One problem in the Met that had never been addressed and may provide a clue to what *really* happened on that Croydon rooftop, was the (sometimes open) hostility between the uniformed branch and the CID. By 1922, it was possible to regard the plainclothesmen as, in David Ascoli's words, 'a privileged elite, whose plain clothes could cover, in the interests of crime detection, a multitude of sins. [It] had become a thoroughly venal private army.'

And Commissioner Hugh Trenchard, himself an RAF man, was talking rubbish in 1934 when he wrote 'the state of jealous rivalry … which has so long existed between the CID and the uniformed branch is gradually being put to an end and the two branches integrated into one harmonious whole.'

'There were some funny things going on in those days,' Claude Pain told me. 'If seven or eight superior officers tell you something, you start to believe it.'

In the last chapter we looked at the backgrounds of Craig and Bentley. Now, let us look at Claude Pain's. The photograph that he showed me was taken in his first year when he was in J division in Stepney. The tunic is Victorian, complete with the whistle and chain that replaced the wooden rattle in the 1890s, and the white metal collar badges stand proudly – 330J. By the end of November 1936, he was with H Division in Whitechapel, with its associations with the Ripper murders of 1888. Because of the chaos when the Crystal Palace burned down in Sydenham, he was one of several officers drafted out of the area to cope. It was the end of an era – the Crystal Palace was never rebuilt.

When the war broke out, Pain was in Selsdon and Croydon as PC 241Z. There were more men in police uniform during those years than at any time in history. These were reserve forces to back up the regulars and they all had to learn a raft of new legislation designed to tighten up on security by a government driven to paranoia by the exigencies of the moment. Dockyards had to be guarded, ration books checked. Pilfering became a new crime. And of course, the Fifth Column were everywhere, shady men and women intent on undermining morale, carrying out acts of sabotage and spying in general. The seventh edition of the police 'Bible' (*Police Law* by C.C.H. Moriarty) published in 1941 contained an extra fifty-two pages of concentrated text, all of which had to be learned by long-suffering constables.

The first bomb of the Blitz fell on Addington near Croydon on 19 June 1940. Between September of that year and July 1941, there were 1,000 alerts, 23,000 deaths and more than 40,000 injuries (one of these was little Derek Bentley). On 11 May 1941, there was a direct hit on Scotland Yard. The Black Book compiled in top secret by the Secret

Services in Berlin complained that the British police were steady and reliable and not likely to break ranks to aid a foreign power like Hitler's, poised to invade. In 1944 and 1945, 2,341 flying bombs hit London, killing 7,988 and injuring 20,783 (Derek Bentley again). Despite this large and unprecedented pressure, police morale had never been higher. By the end of the war, 276 medals had been presented, but in terms of sheer numbers, the force was at its lowest for sixty years, at 12,231 men and women, for no very clear reason.

For most of this time, Claude Pain had a living-out beat in Selsdon. One of his many duties, in an age before lollipop men and women, was to supervise the road crossings at Selsdon Secondary School. It was important for the children in particular to experience as much normality as possible. And everybody trusted a bobby.

Pain's family had been evacuated to the safety of Wales. His wife, Anne, still had a trace of the old Merthyr Tydfil accent when I met her years later and she spent most of the war working at the Arsenal in Bridgend, packing parachutes, one of those many jobs that had once been done by men.

In the 1940s, when dog fights over London were commonplace, Pain worked closely with the RAF. More closely connected with the locality, bobbies like Pain, especially on bikes, were able to get to crash sites quickly. He pedalled furiously after a Spitfire spluttering and trailing black smoke one day near Featherbed Lane, but the aircraft hit the ground at Hartland and the pilot was dead before Pain could get there. He received commendations from the bench, as on the occasion when he and Sidney Miles chased a housebreaker across London by bus!

In *Let Him Have It, Chris*, I left one page (81, in fact) blank to represent the appalling lack of information on the policemen who faced Christopher Craig's gun on the rooftop. Unless an officer chooses to write his memoirs, the official record is one of silence. From the late nineteenth century, a handful of detectives, like Maurice Moser, John Littlechild and Walter Dew, went into print to describe their careers.

Their efforts were universally frowned upon by their superiors, although a number of commissioners and assistant commissioners also told their own stories. In all cases, the result is unsatisfactory. Even when highly able officers like Robert Fabian went into print, they were often writing years after events and always without contemporary notes.

Inevitably, Sidney Miles is a walking eulogy by men who did not know him, like the Archdeacon of Croydon who wrote, 'He was a man who was absolutely fearless. The courageous part he played in last Sunday's shooting affray was typical of him.' Miles was born in Eastry near Sandmill in Kent and had been a gardener before he joined the Met. He was commended three times for gallantry, the last time in 1941 where his work in air raids was particularly impressive. The police were often the first to reach scenes of devastation, even before the fire brigade and ambulance services got there. Inevitably, the trauma of such situations took its toll, but Miles soldiered on. He played football and cricket for Croydon Police Athletic Club and lived at Tower View, Shirley, with his wife Catherine. They had no children. On the football pitch, he was an immaculate full back and never fouled another player in his life. Between 1926 and 1929 he had served with the Royal Army Medical Corps, which is why he was so useful in air-raid emergencies.

'On a quiet Sunday,' Archdeacon Tonks said at Miles's funeral, 'we lost one who we could ill afford to lose ... He was an excellent member of a team, a man whom others were glad to have at their side in a critical situation.'

His brother walked with Catherine behind the coffin, which was draped with the Union Flag and topped with his helmet, belt and a wreath of chrysanthemums and violets. 'He was a man with a ton of guts,' a colleague remembered. 'He had a terrific energy in tackling any and every kind of job. There was no particle of fear in his body.'

Ironically, Sidney Miles should not have been on that rooftop that night; he had stepped in to help a colleague at the last moment.

Frederick Fairfax was the only CID officer there that Sunday. As such, in the congratulatory photographs that followed the case, he is smiling at the camera. But in Croydon, not everyone remembered him fondly. When David Yallop's *To Encourage the Others* was being made into a dramatized documentary by the BBC, he was played by Michael Sheard, whose best-known role, the deputy head Mr Bronson in the long-running series *Grange Hill*, lay in the future. I got to know Michael well, working on a series project that, sadly, never came off. He told me that on more than one occasion when he and his fellow actors were enjoying a pint in a Croydon pub, he heard locals at a nearby table sneer, 'There's that bastard Fairfax.' There is no doubt that he was a bully. He lived across the road from Claude Pain and once ticked off 16-year-old Ray for canoodling in his own lounge with a girlfriend. It was none of his business, of course, and certainly not against the law, but Fairfax was the kind of policeman who gave the Met a bad name.

Another of his ilk was his boss, DCI John Smith. He spoke to the *Croydon Advertiser*:

> [Fairfax] is a well-trained officer, a pretty good boxer and generally knows how to look after himself. But that doesn't count when you're dodging bullets … a man who faces bullets from that [referring to Craig's gun] with a wound in his shoulder, as Fairfax did, is a remarkably brave man. No effort should be spared in paying tribute to him.

Fairfax joined the Met in 1936 and was a qualified ABA judge in amateur boxing around Croydon. He was married with one son, who joined the Met in due course. His hobby was mechanics and he had been commended six times for gallantry, mostly for arresting burglars and shopbreakers. Both David Yallop and Fenton Bressler interviewed the man in subsequent years and their questions never ventured beyond the immediacy of the case. As we have seen, he refused to talk to me at all and was not interested 'in the views of some twerp who wasn't there'.

Mrs Beecher-Brigden, the widow of one of the three wise monkeys along with Pain who were not called to court, told me that her husband spoke highly of Fairfax. Claude Pain clearly did not. Fairfax wore his sling prominently for the media's benefit after the shooting, but Pain saw him surreptitiously remove it to hand crank his car along their street. The Commissioner gave Fairfax the George Cross for his valour and he was promoted to Detective Sergeant First Class. On leaving the force, he tried to run a shop but, a former colleague told me, 'People knew him for what he was and no one would go in there.' His private enquiry agency is, by definition, a closed book and I have no idea how successful that was.

Of the three other officers who faced Craig's bullets in Tamworth Road, there is virtual silence. The youngest was Norman Harrison, 27, with blond hair like Derek Bentley's and a fresh complexion. I was able to find a former ex-colleague who remembered him fondly as a 'good, honest copper', conscientious and kind. Why, then, was his attitude so hostile when I tried to contact him, threatening to sue me for any inaccuracies?

James McDonald died while I was writing *Let Him Have It, Chris*, on 13 December 1988. Other than DS Shepherd, Smith's Number Two in the Fell Road CID, he is the only officer whose name appears in another context in the local press. The week before the Tamworth Road shoot-out, he was Constable D. Day's wireless operator who gave chase after three men were disturbed breaking into a wine merchant's. The crooks' car hit two walls and a post before screeching to a halt in Drummond Road, North End. Day and McDonald dashed after the three on foot and McDonald threw his torch at one, Frederick Miller, before feeling his collar.

The last policeman on the roof was Robert Jaggs. In the awards ceremony, he has a shock of wavy dark hair and appears older than the others and not very well. This may be due to the benefit of hindsight, because Jaggs became an alcoholic and was found dead in Balham High Street in 1978.

If the policemen I contacted back in 1989–90 had had the courtesy to meet me and talk over details of the case, I would probably never have written *Let Him Have It, Chris.* As it was, their reticence – and the silence of the official record – made me suspicious. And sadly, the record of the Metropolitan Police in recent years has done little to change my mind.

Chapter 4

The Trial of the Century

How many of them have there been? The innumerable 'trials of the century' at which tickets changed hands for an obscene amount of money? The cliché belongs, of course, not to the judiciary or the police but to the media and we shall look at the record of the 'fourth estate' in the Craig and Bentley case in a later chapter.

On Monday, 3 November 1952, while Christopher Craig was lying in Croydon General Hospital, his every word recorded by a string of policemen, including Claude Pain, Derek Bentley appeared in Number One Magistrates' Court, Croydon. Both local newspapers referred to him as a well-built youth, wearing a 'highly coloured shirt, with no tie and a sports jacket'. The 'uniform' of teenaged tearaways has changed considerably over time, but the 'Crombie' coat, with its wide shoulders and pastel colours was generally frowned upon by anybody over 40. And what kind of lout appears before a magistrate without a tie? The court described him as an electrician, probably because he did odd jobs in his father's radio repair shop. It gave a ludicrously false impression.

The only witness called was DCI John Smith, in charge of the investigation, who, according to what Bentley told his family, had already kicked him in the head during the interrogation. He told the magistrate:

> At 5.30 a.m. today, I saw accused detained at Croydon Police Station. I said to him, 'I am a police officer and I have just seen the body of PC Sidney George Miles at Mayday Mortuary lying dead. As a result of inquiries I have made, I am going to charge

> you with being concerned with Christopher Craig in murdering him at Tamworth Road about 9.30 p.m. yesterday.'
>
> I cautioned him and he said, 'Craig shot him. I have not got a gun. He was with me on the roof and shot him then, between the eyes.'
>
> He was charged and again cautioned and he made no reply. On that evidence, I ask for a remand in custody until next Monday.

O. Milsom, the Clerk of the Court, had read the charge and Bentley answered, 'Not me, sir.' B.W.N. Still, Chairman of the Court, asked Bentley if he had any questions for Smith. He did not. 'Do you still want legal aid?' Still asked. 'I will see my father,' Bentley answered. At this stage, Bentley had no counsel and almost certainly no knowledge of procedure of the courts. The family sat as close to him as they could and Iris played a lip-reading game with Derek that they had done since childhood. He told her he wanted a cigarette! After six minutes, he was led via an underground passage to the police station and then driven to Brixton prison.

Two days later, the inquest on Sidney Miles opened at the coroner's court. This was a centuries' old tradition, carried out by a royal servant, the crowner, to determine the cause of death, especially where foul play was concerned. Catherine Miles, pale but stoic in her widow's weeds, gave evidence in 'a quiet, steady voice'. She just nodded her head slightly when asked if she had identified her husband's body.

There were nine men on the jury, picked at random from the local citizenry and coroner J.W. Bennett told them:

> You have been called in connection with the death of PC Sidney Miles, who served in the Metropolitan Police Force in this borough and who, according to the reports I have received, was

> carrying out his duties last Sunday evening when he met his death from a gunshot wound to the head.

Dr David Haler, the pathologist, testified that the cause of death was indeed a gunshot wound. Watching proceedings was the ubiquitous DCI Smith and the somewhat irrelevant F.G. Piper, welfare officer to Z Division.

John Parris, the barrister who would go on to defend Craig, wrote (in *Most of My Murders*):

> Coroner's inquisitions, when a trial is pending, serve no useful purpose and, in the circumstances of this case, to require Mrs Miles to identify her husband's body and then speak of it in public was an agony which she might well have been spared. The only result was to increase public indignation against the two accused and possibly prevent them receiving an impartial trial.

According to the usual rules, the inquest was adjourned *Sine Die* (date to be decided).

Long before the Clean Air Act, cities like London experienced what are called atmospheric inversions – bitterly cold air trapping rising smoke from the polluted city to produce a massive build-up of sulphur dioxide. On 5 December, people walked into lampposts and buildings with a visibility of less than 5 yards. Motorists, far fewer then than now, of course, were stranded, trying to find telephone kiosks to reach the AA. Patrolling policemen wore life jackets, in the days before hi-vis and the River Police worked overtime hooking out victims who had fallen into the Thames. Animals choked to death. By 9 December, an astonishing 4,000 people had died and 2,000 had been hospitalized. Today, a catastrophe of this sort would be blown up out of all proportion by the ever-hysterical media. The Meteorological Office would revel in their few hours of fame. In 1952, a people hardened to the Blitz and the doodlebugs just shrugged and got on with life.

Four men who had done so were the barristers briefed to prosecute and defend Craig and Bentley at the Old Bailey. The Central Criminal Court had been established in 1834, moving in 1901 to the site once occupied by the debtors' prison of Newgate, which itself had been the scene of umpteen hangings in the days of the 'bloody code', a vicious judicial regime that routinely whipped prostitutes at the cart's tail and hanged 9-year-old children for stealing a loaf of bread.

The Bailey, with its famous dome topped by the gilded figure of justice, scales in one hand, sword in the other, had been restored after severe bomb damage in 1940–41. The Dickensian interiors were gone and jury and counsel now sat, in all five courts, on plush leather seats. Microphones had been set up so that witnesses could be called from adjoining rooms and the jurors had all the mod-cons of a brave new world – a creche, restaurant, cloakroom and retiring room.

A capital case like that of Craig and Bentley would take up to two years to come to trial today (no doubt accompanied by the current trend of podcasts on a daily basis). In 1952, the case opened on Tuesday, 9 December (thirty-seven days after the death of Sidney Miles). That was partly because the court's calendar was the busiest it had been for years – 101 people stood trial in that session – and partly because the judge in the case, the Lord Chief Justice Lord Goddard, was an old man in a hurry with an agenda of his own.

Outside, in the bad weather along the Old Bailey, touts, still sporting their wartime moustaches and trilbies, haggled with the throng of spectators round the block. Some tickets changed hands for £30 (just over £900 today). The Bentleys turned up on foot. The Craigs swanned up in a Rolls Royce provided by the *Sunday Pictorial*'s Harry Proctor, who watched the family like a hawk, having coughed up £350 (£10,000) to keep them loyal to the paper. Mr Craig, ex-captain and bank teller, looked tall and imposing. Mrs Craig had been crying, reflecting the emotions of her broken family. Their daughter Lucy was the focus of the cameramen. In her twenties, with raven hair and smart clothes, she turned heads wherever she went.

John Parris, for Craig, arrived on foot too, struggling with a red bag and briefcase. He was dismissive enough of the court's proceedings and judges generally in his 1960 book, but in his second, *Scapegoat* (1991) the shackles of litigation were off and he tells it like it was. An outsider, from the northern circuit in Leeds, he was not part of the cosy public school and Oxbridge-educated cronies of the capital. They resented his presence and made sure he knew it.

Parris's book ought to be a blast of fresh air in the stultifying world of wigs and windbags, but, in reality, *Scapegoat* is not only riddled with errors of fact, but Parris is clearly obsessed with how little he was paid. When I met him, months before he went into print a second time, he ran his own publishing house and lived in a large, over-the-top house once owned by the Earl of Clarendon, the adviser to Charles I *and* Oliver Cromwell *and* Charles II. 'There was no legal aid in those days [1952],' Parris moaned, 'and counsel were expected to appear for those without funds for a fee of three guineas [£290].' The original idea was that Parris would be second chair to Derek Curtis Bennett, one of the most famous criminal lawyers of his day, but the man was not available and Parris was on his own.

Parris had been selected because he had successfully defended a villain who was a friend of Niven Craig junior and word of mouth got him the gig. This did not happen until Tuesday, 2 December (via a letter to Leeds) and the trial was due to start two days later. At his own expense (there is that word again) Parris caught a plane to London and met Lord Goddard in his chambers along with Frank Cassels, defending Bentley, and the lead prosecutor, Christmas Humphreys. Parris complained, quite rightly, that he had insufficient time to present his case. 'Well, he's got no defence,' Goddard said, rather pre-empting what a jury might decide, so, in essence, what was Parris worrying about? Only when Parris threatened Goddard to go to the press with this brazenly partisan attitude, did the judge back down and grant an adjournment until the 9th (which of course, still did not allow enough time for defence counsel to do their job properly).

Parris met his client in Brixton prison two days before the trial opened. 'The outstanding impression' of Christopher Craig was 'one of femininity. He had dark brown eyes, soft bow-shaped lips and a smooth skin that would have passed as attractive on any girl and his voice and manner were diffident and gentle.' Perhaps it was this, Parris reasoned, that made Craig adopt the swagger of a tough-guy, so that his peers would not laugh at him. This was the same 'diffident and gentle' boy who had killed one policeman and wounded another, as well as telling umpteen police officers that he wished he had killed more of them.

Craig's hero was his older brother Niven, who had been sentenced to twelve and a half years in prison for armed robbery by Mr Justice Hilbery. In *Scapegoat*, Parris raises the real possibility that this too was a miscarriage of justice, which explains the younger Craig's attitude to the police and to the law. The lawyer knew that Craig's flash clothes and crepe-soled shoes would cut no ice with a jury and told him to get his father to buy something 'quiet and conservative' for court.

Craig told Parris that five of them – Craig himself, Bentley, Dulwich College boy Norman Parsley, Frank Fazey and another lad Parris does not name were out on the town of Croydon that night. The plan was to rob a butcher's shop where Bentley had done some part-time delivery work. He had stolen the shop keys and the keys to the safe, but when they reached the place, there was a light on – the butcher was probably doing his books prior to the week's work. At some point, the others wandered away, leaving Craig and Bentley to saunter down Tamworth Road in search of another target. Throughout the trial, there was talk of a third boy on the Barlow and Parker rooftop. I asked John Parris when I met him who it might have been and he told me, 'Frank Fazey, of course,' but he could not prove it.

The 'trial of the century' began at 10.30 a.m. on Monday, 9 December, the smog still enveloping London. The original jury comprised ten men and two women; both women were challenged by Parris. In these hysterical 'Me Too' days, that challenge would raise eyebrows, but the defence was perfectly entitled to their choice. 'Where there is a crime of violence, women become so blinded by their horror of the crime,' he wrote, 'that even if they entertain doubts about the accused's guilt, they give the benefit of the doubt to the prosecution.' He was afraid they would identify overmuch with the widowed Catherine Miles.

Presiding over the court was Rayner Goddard, who, as Lord Chief Justice, dominated the legal system and bullied everybody in sight. Winston Churchill called him 'Lord God-damn', but the cronies of the legal profession smarmed around him, another senior judge, Lord Denning, being very impressed by his imposing upper lip. He was a product, as were all judges in those days, of public school (Marlborough) and Oxbridge (Trinity College, Oxford). He had no affinity whatsoever with the Craigs and Bentleys of this world and today's weak, liberal Bench probably can barely believe that such a dinosaur literally held the power of life and death in his hands. Lord Denning, who wrote the foreword to Fenton Bressler's gushing biography, said, 'All respected him. Some feared him. None dared scorn him,' – although, by his own account, John Parris did his level best. What no one has commented on was Goddard's age. In 1952, he was 75 years old and today we might query whether dementia did not play a part in the man's behaviour at the Old Bailey. He ranted because Dr Jazwon had been brought 'all the way from Manchester' to give evidence. He cradled Craig's knuckleduster, calling it a horrible weapon and smashed the wood of his own lectern with it, even though the implement was in Bentley's pocket the whole time on the rooftop and had no relevance to the case whatever. Throughout the trial, he interrupted 104 times, 102 of them to bail out the prosecution when he thought their case was failing.

Goddard was a repellent figure, as will become apparent throughout this book. One of his favourite jokes involved his sentencing of three men to be hanged at Winchester Assize. Outside in the street, a barrel organ was playing the *Eton Boating Song* – 'Swing, swing together' – which Goddard found hysterically funny. Most revolting of all was the story told to John Parris by Goddard's clerk, Arthur Smith, who used to provide the judge with a spare pair of trousers because Goddard would frequently ejaculate as the black cap was placed on his head. If this is anything but gallows humour of an embittered court official, Smith should have reported it and Goddard should not only have been removed from office but subject to psychiatric treatment. As Ludovic Kennedy points out in *Thirty-Six Murders* (2002), 'I find it hard to believe that at [Goddard's] age his ejaculation was spontaneous and can only conclude that, with the bench protecting his lower half from the eyes of the court, he did his business unseen, a repetition perhaps of nights in the dorm at Marlborough.' Quite so, M'Lud.

Christmas Humphreys led for the prosecution, with John S. Bass in the second chair. It did not help the fraught atmosphere of Number Two Court that John Parris had inadvertently walked in on Humphreys dismissing him to a colleague. 'Oh, he's some young chap who hasn't been called [to the Bar] long. I suppose he got the brief because he's related to the Croydon solicitor.' In fact, Parris was in no way connected with Parris and Co – that was merely a coincidence.

Humphreys' opening for the prosecution was detailed and clear, made all the more so by a plan of the rooftop drawn by PC Bernard Beard who was the first witness called. A series of photographs of the same area provided by Chief Inspector Percy Law (the second witness called) was less helpful. Five were taken and all of them are still present in the relevant files in The National Archive. They were widely available at the time and at least one of them has appeared in virtually every book on the case. The first photograph, of the alleyway beside the Barlow and Parker warehouse, although it shows six drainpipes which gave the police access to the roof, does not show the rooftop at all. One photograph shows the shattered greenhouse into which Craig plunged after the shoot-out and one is taken from this area looking up to the roof level. In terms of the positions of the participants, it shows nothing at all.

The two remaining photographs show the roof as it would have been seen from Claude Pain's position, with the staircase head to the left (door open) and the roof lights and lift-head 'stack' ahead and slightly to the right. There is no photograph taken from Craig's position, nor that of Norman Harrison (see below) and in one particular instance, as we shall see, clarity is wholly lacking in the evidence of DC Fairfax.

Humphreys' father was a judge and his mother a Justice of the Peace, so the law ran through his veins. He was a Buddhist who became a judge and increasingly eccentric in his later years (he died in 1983). Educated at Malvern and Cambridge, he continued the public school/Oxbridge tradition that was the norm in those years. By sheer coincidence, Humphreys prosecuted in the three murder cases that did most to end capital punishment in Britain – those of Derek Bentley, Timothy Evans and Ruth Ellis.

John Stuart Bass is altogether vaguer, if only because he was dead by 1954. He was trained at Lincoln's Inn, but the war disrupted his career and he ended up as a brevet major. He was second chair at the Bailey by 1950 and worked as an additional judge at the Mayor's and City of London Court until his untimely death.

Frank Cassels is a different proposition. Without his wig he looks a bull-necked thug. John Parris, so happy to attack Goddard and the judiciary generally, expresses outrage that both David Yallop and I have little good to say about Cassels. On his own admission, Parris had a conference with Cassels – after all, in a sense the lawyers were on the same side – and Cassels spoke 'with considerable venom' and said, 'I think both little fuckers ought to swing.' In the way that lawyers have of protecting each other, Cassels told Yallop in 1971 that the word he used was 'bastards'. Parris in turn had softened this still further in 1960 with 'little beggars'. 'The implied suggestion,' Parris wrote in 2002, 'of both these authors [Yallop and me] that Frank did not do his best for his client is a grotesque slur on the memory of an honourable man and shows a total ignorance of the ethics and obligations of the Bar.'

What *is* grotesque is that, whatever actual words he used about Craig and Bentley, the *defence* attorney believed them guilty and that they should die for it. Christopher Craig, at 16, was too young to hang and Derek Bentley was under arrest at the time of the shooting, effectively in police custody and did not even carry a gun that night, still less use one. My argument in 1990 was 'If [Cassels really meant those words] then surely there is at least room for the question: how hard did he try?' As we shall see in a later chapter, Cassels' appeal on Bentley's behalf was shambolically incompetent.

At the Old Bailey on that first day, having heard the location evidence of PC Beard and Inspector Law, Niven Craig senior was called, bizarrely, as a prosecution witness. The purpose of this was merely to establish young Christopher's age, but it gave Parris the opportunity to grill Craig senior on the family's propensity for gun ownership. He referred to the father's conviction for firearms possession until Lord Goddard made the first of many interruptions implying that this line of questioning was irrelevant. It was, of course, germaine to the whole cosh-boy gun culture of homes shattered by war, but, like the addiction to comics and films, Goddard would have none of it. How much the jury bought Parris's attempts to portray the younger Craig as a choirboy, with his Enid Blyton books and his membership of a Bible class at a Streatham church, is open to debate. Cassels, of course, had no questions. Humphreys re-examined, at pains to point out the extraordinary range of ammunition that young Craig had hidden at home. His father denied all knowledge.

Next came Edith Ware, whose daughter had seen two men loitering with intent across the road from her house. Interestingly, *both* men wore trilbies, although the police found Bentley's at his home hours after the shooting. Neither Cassels nor Parris made anything of this.

Then came perhaps the most important prosecution witness, DC Frederick Fairfax. His testimony, which was not perhaps as clear as it ought to have been, is virtually a verbatim rehash of the statement he made within hours of the shooting – the statement I had not been allowed to see. By the time of the trial, Fairfax had been awarded the George Cross, the highest award for gallantry in the police, been promoted to Detective Sergeant and transferred to C Division.

Fairfax told the court that he had got to Tamworth Road in a van with Harrison and 'other officers' (no mention of Claude Pain, his near-neighbour), had climbed over the gate alongside the warehouse and scrambled up the second drainpipe to the roof. Visibility up there was limited, above street light level, and clouds obscured the moon. Fairfax had no torch.

The detective saw Craig and Bentley standing between the stack and the roof lights. Goddard wanted clarification on this and Fairfax confirmed that both boys ducked behind the stack. Fairfax called out, 'I am a police officer. Come out from behind that stack.' Craig shouted back, 'If you want us, fucking well come and get us.' 'All right,' Fairfax said and duly obliged, grabbing Bentley and pulling him into the open. While holding him, Fairfax went after Craig but Bentley broke away and shouted, 'Let him have it, Chris.' Then the first shot was fired. It hit Fairfax's shoulder and the impact knocked him off balance. At Humphreys' request, Fairfax pointed to the point of impact, using the phrase 'through there', implying a penetrative wound. Forensic evidence, from a pathologist and ballistics expert, would later pour doubt on this. According to Fairfax, he was 6 feet from Craig when the gun went off.

The lads now split in different directions and Fairfax, though injured, grabbed Bentley again. He knocked the boy down with his fist and pulled him in front of him, as a shield. Fairfax frisked him and found no gun, but did find the knuckleduster in Bentley's right-hand coat pocket. This was odd in itself, because Bentley was left-handed. Neither defence counsel raised this point.

Fairfax found Bentley's knife too, described in court by the emotive word 'dagger' with its sinister implications. As a boy in the 1950s, much younger than Derek Bentley, I routinely carried a knife, as did most of my friends. There was nothing sinister or criminal about it. 'That's all I've got, guv'nor; I haven't got a gun.' Fairfax hauled Bentley to the safety of the staircase head, putting two brick walls between them and Craig. But Craig, according to Fairfax's testimony, circled the roof to a point (marked with '90' on Beard's plan) where he had Fairfax in direct view, yet he never fired a shot.

At this point, PC James McDonald was scrabbling up a drainpipe, but he was older and heavier than Fairfax and could not make the final climb. With a wounded shoulder and with Bentley standing alone and perfectly capable of running to join Craig or even trying to make an escape, Fairfax hauled his colleague onto the roof and they talked tactics behind the staircase head. McDonald asked what sort of gun the shooter had and Bentley replied, 'He's got a .45 Colt and plenty of bloody ammunition too.'

Both policemen heard scrabbling inside the staircase head. Fairfax shouted out that he was round to their left. This was a clear misdirection. Common sense, as well as the evidence of Fairfax and McDonald, dictated that they were to the *right* of the men on the staircase. No one raised this crucial issue until my book *Let Him Have It, Chris* in 1990.

An officer, Sidney Miles, dashed out of the door. Because he had kicked it open, he gave Craig ample time to guess his movements and Fairfax heard another gunshot. Miles fell pole-axed and another shot drove the detective back from the body as he tried to recover it.

After Miles went down, PC Harrison dashed out of the door, joining the others behind the staircase head. They decided to get Bentley out of the way and again, using him as a shield, muscled him through the doorway – 'They're taking me down, Chris.' At the bottom of the stairs, Fairfax handed Bentley over to other officers and somebody gave him a gun, a .32 automatic. Back on the roof, Fairfax told Craig that he had a gun too and the lad fired at him as he re-emerged onto the roof. Fairfax ran forward in a semi-circle, firing twice as he did so. Craig jumped off the roof.

Parris's cross-examination exposed anomalies in Fairfax's account. The bullet that had gone through the detective's shoulder had fallen out of his braces in Croydon General Hospital. In other words, it had hit the officer a glancing blow that had 'scored' the skin, not broken it. A .45 calibre bullet, it was explained by Lewis Nickolls of the Metropolitan Police laboratory at Scotland Yard the next day, would have shattered the shoulder if fired directly at Fairfax's 6ft distance, or left a large exit hole. This had simply not happened. Craig's contention, which Parris got out of him on that second day, was that he had fired at the ground as a warning shot and that the bullet had ricocheted upwards and caught Fairfax a glancing blow. Parris also scored excellent 'Brownie points' by eliciting from Nickolls that with the gun barrel shortened and the wrong calibre ammunition for the weapon, the whole thing was a lottery. The image we still have is that a shot (to Miles) between the eyes is the work of an expert marksman with the deliberate intent to kill. Craig was not a marksman at all and the *intent* to kill, which alone make the charge one of murder, was not proven. Such technicalities were beyond the jury – and, because of his gross bias, the judge. Craig had made his hatred of the police very clear and no one in court could doubt that he had murder in his heart.

Constables McDonald, Harrison and Jaggs all gave their testimony on that first day. None of their original statements, now in The National Archive, was made available to me in 1990, even though I had asked for them and they related to a case that had happened nearly forty years earlier. McDonald was pulled onto the roof by Fairfax; everything else followed the Fairfax pattern. Norman Harrison had got to Tamworth Road in the police van (no mention of Claude Pain). Unlike the others, he got round to the back of the warehouse in Upper Drayton Place and over a fence into the garden of No. 26 before climbing onto the sloping asbestos roof of the warehouse. From there, Harrison had a clear view of the flat roof, referred to, confusingly, in Beard's plan as Nos. 27, 28 and 29.

From that position, he should have clearly seen both Craig and Bentley, even if they were hiding behind the stack, but he saw no one. He did see Fairfax, however, scrabbling up the drainpipe and onto the roof. He spoke to him, meaning that the conversation took place in the open between two men 60 to 70 feet apart. Yet Fairfax had made no mention of this. Harrison saw Fairfax grab Bentley and pull him towards the staircase head. Bentley broke away and shouted 'Let him have it, Chris.' Then Harrison heard two shots from the stack direction and he saw Fairfax fall.

Harrison tried to edge his way along the gutter, lying on his back and completely exposed to Craig's bullets had the lad decided to turn his gun to his left. In fact, he did, firing one shot in his direction. It was now that Harrison dropped his torch (it was found by officers the next day lodged in the roof gutter) and he edged his way back, Craig firing at him once more. Once down on the ground, Harrison joined Miles and other officers and dashed up the stairs to the roof.

When Miles went down, just ahead of Harrison, the young constable saw Craig standing with a smoking gun in two hands. He threw his truncheon at him in desperation, as well as a milk bottle and a block of wood lying on the ground. 'I am Craig,' the gunman yelled. 'You've just give my brother twelve years. Come on, you coppers. I'm only 16.' Harrison helped the others get Bentley down the stairs and heard Craig shout, 'Are they hurting you, Derek?' and he fired again. Harrison was still on the staircase when Fairfax rushed back past him with a gun in his hand and he saw him fire twice.

Under Parris's cross-examination, Harrison had difficulty explaining exactly where Fairfax, Craig and Bentley were on the roof, which *may* be explained by the shock of events or the passing of time or both. In pointing out that McDonald's testimony differed from Harrison's, Parris unleashed another interruption by Goddard, effectively the third prosecution chair in the court. 'You need not tell us,' the judge said, 'whether one man is right or wrong,' thereby negating the whole point of giving testimony at all. Parris pressed Harrison in a rather fatuous way – 'I suggest he [Craig] was never there at any time when any shots were fired at all.' David Yallop would make much of this in 1971. Rather lamely, Harrison riposted, 'Well, he was, sir.'

Jumping all sorts of guns under cross-examination by Frank Cassels, Harrison had the impudence to say, 'I heard Bentley call upon Craig to fire as he walked away.' But *no one* said that Bentley had called on Craig to fire, in that 'let him have it' could mean 'hand over the gun'. This is the crux that everybody remembers about the Craig and Bentley case – the exact meaning of the phrase. For those thoroughly familiar with the rooftop incident, Derek Bentley denied using those words; so did Christopher Craig. James McDonald heard the words but could not see who had said them. Claude Pain did not hear them at all. Robert Jaggs was not there at the time. Only two officers swore that Bentley had used the phrase – Fairfax and Harrison. But, as we shall see, in 1952, a lot of Metropolitan policemen had read those exact words before, in an incident many miles away from Croydon.

As Sergeant Edward Roberts told the court after Harrison's evidence, Bentley was handed over to him outside Barlow and Parker. Roberts cautioned him but could not remember exactly what Bentley said in reply. This earned him a mild reproof from the judge – 'Do you not remember without your notes, officer?' Roberts went back to Tamworth Road and was there when PC Wells found Craig's gun in the smashed greenhouse.

Parris had no questions for Roberts, but Cassels did. He ascertained that with Bentley and Roberts in the car to Croydon police station were Constables Stephens and Alderson, both from another station. Cassels clearly found Bentley's spontaneous blurting out 'I knew he had a gun, but I didn't think he'd use it. He has done one of your blokes in,' unlikely. According to Roberts, this was not in response to a question. Indeed, according to Roberts, no questions were asked. 'I suggest to you,' Cassels said, in lawyer-speak for 'you're a liar', 'that this remark which you have attributed to Bentley … never in fact was said?' 'Yes, it was,' Roberts sulked, 'certainly.'

In cross-examination, Christmas Humphreys wanted confirmation of the availability of PC Alderson. As far as I am aware, his statement, now in The National Archive, was never used and for reasons unknown, he was not called to court. He is, consequently, one of David Yallop's three wise monkeys.

PC Stuart Lowe was next. He had got to Tamworth Road at about 9.45, shinned up a drainpipe and down again, having seen Miles's body and was back on the ground in time to see Craig sitting on the roof rail with his gun pointing at the staircase head. Lowe rattled off a disjointed list of Craig's words, which more or less corroborated what other officers had said. When Craig jumped, Lowe was the first to reach him. He pinned him down, although the boy was clearly hurt, dazed and in no position to struggle. 'I wish I was fucking dead. I hope I've killed the fucking lot.' Lowe found a sheath knife in Craig's belt.

The last policeman to be called from the rank and file who were there was PC Henry Stephens who had driven Bentley, Alderson and Roberts to the station. He agreed with Roberts that Bentley's statement was spontaneous and that he was not asked any questions. In fact, Roberts had said, 'I should not make any other statement now.' Odd that Roberts himself did not mention that.

Dr Nicholas Jazwon was based at Crumpsall Hospital, Manchester by the time of the trial, but on the night in question he was Casualty Officer at Croydon General. Parris went straight to the point, eliciting from the doctor that Fairfax's wound had merely grazed the skin and was consistent with a bullet trajectory going upwards and over the shoulder – in other words, a ricochet shot unless Craig was lying on the ground, which he was not. Fairfax's '6 feet' distance was established as 39 feet.

Goddard, sensing a loophole in the prosecution case, leapt in. 'I do not know why the doctor has been brought from Manchester to say that.' With fitting sarcasm, Parris shot back, 'I thought the jury might like to appreciate it.' When Parris pushed the idea of a ricochet shot, Goddard again intervened. 'The doctor is here to give medical evidence, not to speculate on the flight of bullets.' But, in cases of shooting, a doctor's testimony is not speculation but hard evidence. For Goddard to dismiss the man as an incompetent bystander was disgraceful. He bullied Jazwon – 'Well, are you competent to answer such a question?' 'No,' Jazwon mumbled, 'I think not, really.'

Dr David Haler was called to give evidence in the context of Sidney Miles. His practice was in Weymouth Street, W1 and he had performed the post-mortem on Miles in Croydon Borough Mortuary. The fatal wound had entered the forehead above the left eyebrow and the exit was 15 degrees over the midline, running horizontally through the head. In other words, this was a direct shot and could not possibly have been a ricochet. Neither Cassels nor Parris had any questions of Haler, although in the light of the theories of David Yallop in 1971, the doctor found himself in more of the limelight.

Dr Douglas Freebody was summoned to explain the injuries to Craig. He had a fracture of the seventh dorsal vertebra (spine) and a fractured dislocation of the manubrium sternum (breastbone) as well as a fracture of the left wrist. According to some sources, a number of policemen had manhandled Craig over a wall, which cannot have helped his injuries; needless to say, none of this emerged at the trial.

There was discussion, especially between Freebody and Parris, of the drugs given to Craig in hospital. Presumably the defence was trying to place doubt in the minds of the jury in the context of any incriminating remarks Craig may have made during the days after the shooting. The list of painkillers was already in Parris's possession and is still to be found in The National Archive, together with dates and times when they were administered. 'What bearing,' Goddard wanted to know, 'have the drugs got on this case?'

Dr Gordon Hatfield, medical officer at Croydon General, was brought in to testify about all this. Presumably, Goddard had no objection because the doctor only came a short distance to give his evidence. Parris was not going to let Hatfield off lightly. He pointed out that pentathol, which had been administered to Craig, was known in the United States as the truth drug and that it had the side effect of making people more talkative and removing inhibitions. Rather pathetically, bearing in mind his calling, Hatfield said that 'I would not like to say anything about that. I cannot.'

Again, Goddard realized where this line of questioning was going and he was at pains to get the doctor to stipulate how small the dose was. Parris countered with a reminder to the jury that pethidine caused elation in some people, no doubt in the context of Craig's boasting of his prowess on the rooftop.

After the flurry of medical witnesses, the police were back. Stanley Shepherd was a detective sergeant in Z Division who saw Craig in hospital at about 11 p.m. on 2 November. He reported the lad's conversation, such as it was and the fact that his boss, DCI Smith, arrived half an hour later and officially charged Craig with murder. It was Shepherd who went to the Craig home in Norbury and found the cache of bullets he owned stashed under the floorboards of an attic.

He also interviewed Bentley at Fell Road, at 4 a.m. 'Are you in charge of this case, guv'nor?' Bentley asked. Shepherd lied and told him he was. It was now that the most controversial part of the prosecution case was called into question. Bentley made a statement under caution and did his best to sign his name. In the event, he missed the second 'e' out of Derek. Humphreys asked Shepherd to read it out. Bentley had been at home watching television. There was only one channel available in

1952 – BBC. All programmes were in black and white and broadcast time was limited to evenings only, ending at 11 p.m. with the national anthem. Many people were in the process of buying their first set (9in screens only) to watch the coronation of Elizabeth II. As a repairer of radios, William Bentley was among the first to own the 'one-eyed monster' that would revolutionize a nation's lifestyle.

Craig called at the Bentley house between 8 and 9 p.m. but Lilian told him her son was not at home, unhappy as she was with the lad's character. Minutes later, Norman Parsley and Frank Fazey called and again, Lilian sent them away. Bentley ran after them, however, and the three of them met Craig. Parsley and Fazey left and Craig and Bentley took the bus to Croydon. At Tamworth Road, Craig hopped over the gate alongside Barlow and Parker's and Bentley followed suit. He also followed Craig up a drainpipe.

At some point, Craig saw a flashlight beam. This had to be Constable Harrison's, because Fairfax was not carrying a torch. 'It's a copper,' Craig said. 'Hide behind here,' and they ducked behind the stack. The rest of the statement followed events largely as described by the police. Obviously, Bentley did not know any names, so Fairfax was 'a plainclothes man'; Miles was 'a policeman in uniform' (which even John Parris got wrong in *Scapegoat*).

One of the many odd things about this statement was that it had a kind of PS – 'I should have mentioned that after the plainclothes policeman got up the drainpipe and arrested me, another policeman in uniform followed and I heard someone call him "Mac".' At the end, Bentley tried to sign the document – 'This statement has been read to me and it is true.'

Parris, in cross-examination, attempted to solicit some sympathy for his client, but Shepherd was not having any of it. 'He was distraught with pain, was he not?' 'I could not say, sir,' Shepherd shrugged. 'He appeared quite normal.'

When Cassels pointed out to the court that Bentley was illiterate, Shepherd's reply was 'So he says.' In the next encounter, he admitted that Bentley had difficulty writing his name. The sergeant had no idea of Bentley's limitations. Neither he nor DCI Smith asked any questions. This was pursued aggressively by defence counsel and it has formed a central plank in the various books that have been written – mine included – about the case. Goddard, of course, was there to help Shepherd out. All the sergeant had done was to read the last sentence back to Bentley because he seemed hesitant. Cassels told the court that he was not making 'any complaint about the way the statement was taken', but he should have. There were – and are – strict rules about the taking of statements and, bearing in mind Bentley's educational limitations, little of what Shepherd read out rings true.

In 1974, in a very different case which related to Irish terrorism (see Chapter 11) 17-year-old Carole Richardson, a known confederate of the Guildford Four, gave a statement to the police who, notoriously, had arrested the wrong men. Of this, she later said, 'The statements which I wrote were virtually dictated to me and I wrote down what they said and suggested to me ... I was forced to go along with what was happening because I was terrified of them and what further treatment I would get.'

Carole's interrogation was carried out by officers of the Surrey police, but the methodology was the same in the Met. The Judge's Rules, which cover statement-making are very clear – questions could not be asked, except to clarify the meaning of what an accused has said. It is very obvious that Bentley's statement was in response to questions and why make a prominent point of the policeman called 'Mac'?

The court was then subject to another parade of policemen. James Ross, PC of Z Division, was in Drayton Place behind the warehouse, getting there at about 9.55 and saw Craig dive off the roof. Guarding the lad in hospital, Ross heard him say, 'I got the gun from a house in Purley. There are plenty more where that came from.'

Constable Vincent Denham was with Craig in hospital too and the boy had asked him whether Miles was dead. Unlike Shepherd, Denham recalled that Craig was in great pain and not behaving normally as a result. Constable John Smith reported that Craig boasted of killing Miles. 'I'm all right,' he had said. 'All you bastards should be dead.' PC Thomas Shepherd had made no reply to any questions that Craig asked him. 'What do you get for carrying a knuckleduster? Bentley had mine ... Did you see the gun I had? It was all on the wobble, so I took it to work and sawed two inches off the barrel.' This, of course, made it *less*, not more accurate as a weapon. PC Ernest Brown reported that Craig had said, 'That night I was out to kill because I had so much hate inside me for what they did to my brother.'

The last prosecution witness on the first day was PC James Gordon who testified that he had recovered a spent bullet (Exhibit 8) inside the doorway at the top of the stairs.

The second day, Wednesday, 10 December, began with Humphreys' examination of DCI John Smith, who, unlike Shepherd, *actually* headed the investigation. The man had had a busy night on 2 November. He went to Barlow and Parker's, then to Mayday Mortuary to look at Miles's body. Next he checked on Fairfax at Croydon General and finally cautioned Craig and charged him with murder. The next day, he interviewed Bentley at Fell Road and was present while he made his statement to Shepherd. At 5.30 a.m. on 3 November, he charged Bentley with Miles's murder. Later that morning, he was on the warehouse roof as spent bullets were recovered and he attended Dr Haler's post-mortem on Miles. He had also handled Craig's gun. There were four spent cartridges and two misfires. Smith handed over the gun and ammunition to Lewis Nickolls of the Police Laboratory and was present at Croydon Magistrates' Court as we have seen.

Cassels prodded Smith on Bentley's intelligence and the inspector conceded that it was below average. Like Shepherd, he denied that any questions had been asked of Bentley during the making of his statement.

Humphreys tried to put words into Fairfax's mouth, contrary to his testimony in court, concerning the trajectory of various shots. Inevitably, Goddard saw the problem and casually dismissed the whole thing with, 'I do not think it matters one way or another.'

Lewis Nickolls, the ballistics expert, was called next. His problem was that the fatal bullet was not found. Parris elicited from him the information that sawing off the gun barrel and filing the bullets to make them fit the chamber would make the gun wildly inaccurate, a degree of 6 feet at a range of 39 feet, the distance between Craig and Miles at the time of the fatal shot. Parris went for the jugular, calling Nickolls's competence into question – 'The truth is you are not a ballistics expert?' The gun, referred to by Nickolls himself as a Colt .45 was actually an Eley .455, although manufactured by the Colt company. Goddard leapt to his rescue. 'This revolver, if it is fired off … is quite capable of killing people? No matter whether it is accurate or inaccurate.'

Humphreys had his knuckles rapped by the judge because he realized that Parris had an opening with Nickolls's unsatisfactory answers. Goddard assured him that that would not happen 'if that defence is run, I shall tell the jury that that is no defence at all.'

The prosecution had called twenty-four witnesses, all but six of them policemen. The defence called just two, Craig and Bentley. When I raised this imbalance in *Let Him Have It, Chris*, John Parris came back with the lame and fatuous retort that it was not the job of counsel to provide defence witnesses. One wonders, then, whose job it was. Certainly, the police were not going to widen their enquiries; one of their own had been killed. They had no intention of helping his killer to get away with it. What of the solicitors acting for Craig and Bentley? Other than appoint barristers, they did nothing.

Contrary to what was becoming usual practice, Bentley had to stand throughout the proceedings. Craig, because of his injuries, was allowed to sit. Parris quizzed his client about his interest and ownership of guns. He had first fired an antique cap and ball pistol and altogether owned between forty and fifty firearms. At each admission, Lord Goddard saw fit to interrupt, as if to make it clear to the jury what a double-dyed villain Craig was. At one he asked the boy if he knew that firearms could kill people. When Craig admitted that he did, Goddard mumbled, 'Let us get on to something that matters.'

Craig confessed to Parris that he liked gangster films and saw a lot of them. On the night in question, he had fired *at the ground* to scare off Fairfax (which was wholly consistent with the detective's shoulder wound) and at no time did anyone say 'Let him have it, Chris.' Goddard was anxious to establish that Craig reloaded his gun, as this again put him in a bad light. The boy contended that he never intended to hurt anyone, yet by the same token, the gangster films he loved were full of such violence. The world of movies has moved on since 1952. Grisly death by gunfire as in Arthur Penn's *Bonnie and Clyde* (1967) were not portrayed graphically. The actual (and horrific) consequences of a bullet were never seen on the big screen.

Craig's first memory on recovering in hospital was of someone (clearly a policeman) hitting him in the mouth and calling him a murdering bastard. Needless to say, no police testimony mentions this. Craig denied that he had made any statements to his police guards during this time, which was clearly nonsense. Apart from the evidence given in court and quoted above, we have detailed statements in the Archive from Constables Ross, Pain, Riding, Kennedy and the unfortunately named Archibald Bastard. He was particularly malevolent to Claude Pain – 'I would like to sew your fucking heart up with a long knitting needle' and 'What wouldn't I give for my .45 gun.'

Christmas Humphreys cross-examined him, pressing the relationship between Bentley and Craig. Craig said their paths only crossed occasionally and he did not remember him from school, which was Bentley's testimony. The gun from Purley used in the shooting actually came as a result of a swap with another friend, Martin Vincent.

It was now that Goddard's obsession with the knuckleduster became obvious. He wanted to know why Craig had made it at all and why there was the 'dreadful' spike at one end. Having examined this weapon myself, the spike is actually blunt and very short, perhaps half an inch long. To call it 'dreadful' is pushing the envelope considerably. Craig's evidence was that Bentley did not know that he had a gun, despite Bentley's evidence to the contrary – 'I told the silly bugger not to use it.' Craig only told his oppo about the Eley when they were on the roof. Goddard became exasperated when Craig's response to one question was 'I do not know.' What he would have made of the PACE (the Police and Criminal Evidence Act) legislation in 1984 and the criminals' irritating response of 'no comment', I can only imagine.

Humphreys tried to pin Craig down on 'Let him have it.' 'Three officers heard it in the darkness from different points of the compass. Are you saying he did not say it?' 'I am only saying I did not hear it and if they heard it they have better hearing than mine.'

Both Humphreys and Goddard challenged Craig on his taunts to the police on the roof. 'Come on, you brave coppers. Think of your wives.' It was Craig's contention that this was meant to frighten them away, not threatening to make their wives widows.

The Lord Chief Justice again acted as prosecution counsel when he dismissed Craig's explanation for his hospital statements – 'I was hardly conscious at the time, sir.' Hardly conscious!' Goddard sneered. 'Don't talk such nonsense.'

In *Scapegoat*, John Parris goes through the trial testimony with a fine-tooth comb. He examined Craig without putting the defence case so that he could address the jury after the prosecution's summing up. The law is such an ass (see Chapter 10) that because the defence called no other witnesses, it gave Parris a chance to talk to the jury *after* Humphreys' closing argument, which would lessen the impact of the prosecution. He had told Craig to be truthful and was generally impressed by a limited 16-year-old's ability to hold his own against the most powerful jurist in England (not to mention the most biased). What particularly narked Parris was Goddard's introduction of Niven Craig's crime – 'guilt by brotherhood' as Parris calls it.

Then, it was Bentley's turn. Virtually all the evidence you have read in this chapter so far comes verbatim from the *Notable British Trials* series, Vol. 81 edited by barrister H. Montgomery Hyde and published by William Hodge in 1954. The series goes way back to Mary, Queen of Scots, who was tried for treason in 1586. No one would seriously expect *that* trial to be a verbatim account, given the passage of time, deterioration and loss of original documents and so on. But we *do* have a right to expect that a trial held in 1952 would be reported accurately. *But that is not the case*. In a throwaway line, John Parris (who was, of course, present in court) says that Bentley's breaking away from Fairfax was brought out in cross-examination, but is not in the edited edition. We are therefore entitled to ask what else is missing.

One thing that certainly is is Bentley's performance in the dock. All independent witnesses, in the gallery and with the press, were struck by how confused, shell-shocked and limited Bentley's responses were. None of this is apparent in Montgomery Hyde's version. In response to Frank Cassels' questions, Bentley did not name either Norman Parsley or Frank Fazey as the boys who called at his home on the night in question and Cassels did not press him.

Having got to Croydon on the 109 bus 'just to look around', Craig slipped the knuckleduster into Bentley's pocket. He had no idea, despite the continued pressure from Goddard, why he followed Craig over the gate alongside Barlow and Parker's. Not until he saw his mate shinning up a drainpipe did he realize, in Cassels' phrase, 'he was up to something'. Interestingly, Bentley testified that he had difficulty climbing the pipe. According to Iris, his sister, he had no head for heights and would have found this climb as mountainous as clearly Constable McDonald did moments later.

According to Bentley, he still had no idea that Craig was armed when Fairfax grabbed him. He did not struggle or offer any violence and he did not break away from the plainclothesman. He did not say, 'Let him have it, Chris.' He denied telling the officers on the roof what sort of gun Craig had because he did not know one from another. It was Craig who had shouted that he had a .45 Colt. He saw Miles drop from the shot that killed him, his head 'smothered in blood'.

Bentley denied most of the conversation in the police car on the way to the station and, most relevantly, contended that his statement at Fell Road was given in response to questions rather than as an uninterrupted monologue. Everybody who knew Bentley said that he was incapable of stringing words together in that way.

In his cross-examination, Christmas Humphreys purred empathetically that he did not understand people like Derek Bentley. 'Look at your statement, Exhibit No, 15, will you?' 'It is no good my looking at that, sir.' Even an out-of-touch dinosaur like Goddard stepped in with 'He cannot read it.' Humphreys was well and truly on the warpath by the time he came to an end of his cross. He ranted:

> I see – still thinking of your own skin [not wanting to be shot]. In other words, you were prepared to assist Craig by such hitting with knuckledusters, or stabbing with daggers, or shooting with a revolver at the police as would enable you to escape if caught in the crime that you were committing?

These were 'other words' indeed and they were Humphreys'. The knuckleduster and the knife had nothing to do with the murder of Sidney Miles or the wounding of Frederick Fairfax. The knife was a common 'Boy Scout style' sheath knife, not a 'dagger' with all its Machiavellian undertones, and the inference that Bentley was prepared to shoot police officers when he carried no gun and was in police custody when Craig fired was laughable. Did Cassels object, as he had every right to do? No, he merely said, 'My Lord, that is the case for Bentley.'

Goddard sent the jury off for lunch, during which he discussed a point of law with counsel. Parris was arguing the issue of Craig's intent. Goddard dismissed this with his usual avoidance of justice and common sense. English law is based on custom and precedent (which I believe is a dangerous practice) and Parris had done his homework. He cited the case of Rex v Appleby in 1940 (which was to come back to haunt the police in the years ahead) and of the 1873 decision by Mr Justice Brett, who had laid down that if a police officer was killed in the line of duty, the charge could be one of manslaughter if actual intent could not be proved. Interestingly, in this duel of wits, it was Parris who was protesting and Humphreys and Goddard denying his contention. Cassels, whose client faced the noose, said nothing.

In his closing summary, Humphreys had the gall to quote the Appleby case:

> Where two persons engage in the commission of a crime with a common design of resisting by violence arrest by an officer of justice, they have a common design to do that which will amount to murder if the officer should be killed in consequence of resistance. If, therefore, an officer of justice is killed in such circumstances, both persons are guilty of murder.

Then, Humphreys came out with a centuries-old 'escape clause' which was, as we shall see, still being trotted out by the law lords in 1998. He noted that the police evidence was not exactly the same. Some heard one phrase, others another:

> You might think that is inevitable in the course of a gunfight in the dark, with the consequent excitement … You will take the

> evidence of all those police officers and see if you can believe for one moment that virtually every one of them can be wrong.

Humphreys knew perfectly well that he was muddying the waters here. The crucial line was 'let him have it, Chris', a clear incitement by Bentley for Craig to shoot. Other statements, in the car and the hospital after the shoot-out pale into insignificance. But it was not 'all those police officers'. It was only two of them – Fairfax and Harrison. The third, McDonald, was not on the roof at the time and could not say who actually said it. What we have, then, is a stand-off – two policemen with one version; two tearaways with another. And, given the mindset of the public in 1952 and the extraordinarily biased summing up the jury was about to hear from the Lord Chief Justice, guess which way the verdict went!

John Parris's defence summation was excellent. He reminded the jury of the importance of the oath they had taken. He admonished them – actually, a waste of time – to ignore the furore about the case in the press (see Chapter 5). He painted a picture of Christopher Craig as a troubled boy, who felt inferior because he could not read and who carried weapons as bravado, not with intent to kill or even hurt. 'Think back,' Parris said to the all-male jury:

> Did you not, on occasion, carry the most sinister-looking knives? Would you not have been delighted to get your hands on a revolver that really worked? … Think back to the days when you played games of cops and robbers and highwaymen and Bow Street runners or perhaps cowboys and Indians.

Parris pressed home the noxious influence of gangster films, especially on a lad who was illiterate.

Even Craig's rooftop yelling was merely an example of his bravado. He had been caught, armed and trespassing on private property, with a probable intention to burgle. Some boys (Bentley was one) would have stood there meekly, terrified. Others would have burst into tears. Craig went into full Jimmy Cagney mode – 'Come on, then, coppers! Let's have it out.' 'Come on, you brave coppers, think of your wives!' … 'Are we going to have a shooting match? It's just what I like.'

Parris pointed out that the forensic evidence supported Craig's story. Fairfax's shoulder wound was consistent with a ricochet shot from about 30 feet away, not the 6 feet that Fairfax claimed, and not directly into his shoulder. Similarly, the bullet mark found near Constable Harrison's position on the sloping roof behind the stack was *nowhere near* the man and is in keeping with a wild shot intended to deter the police.

Goddard obviously thought that Parris's summation would sway the jury in Craig's favour because he stepped in. 'Mr Parris, I think it is only right that I should tell the jury that what you are saying to them now [the accident/intent distinction] is not the law.' When Parris cited the Appleby case, Goddard told him he had misread it. Parris ended by reminding the jury that Craig had a clear shot at Fairfax when he was only 3 feet away and did not take it. He pushed for a verdict of manslaughter.

Cassels' defence of Bentley also highlighted the problem of accurate reportage on the Croydon rooftop. He pointed out, however, that everyone agreed that at no time did Bentley try to resist the police presence or break away, perhaps to rejoin Craig, not even when Fairfax was otherwise engaged helping McDonald onto the roof; and not when Fairfax and McDonald were dragging Miles's body out of the line of fire. Cassels hit the nail on the head when he said, 'You know, you come into that jury box not leaving your common sense behind you.' But because of their slavish adherence to the letter of the antiquated and straitjacketed law, that is exactly what *all* counsel in the court had done and most especially the judge. Cassels at least had the foresight to describe Humphreys' 'murderous dagger' correctly as a 'small sheath knife', and reminded the jury that Bentley could have used it on Fairfax during their scuffle, but did not. Defence counsel also pointed to the holes in conflicting police testimony which Humphreys had already tried to plug; McDonald cited Bentley saying, 'I told the silly bugger not to use [the gun]' of which Fairfax, less than 2 feet away, had no recollection.

Cassels also pointed out that when Bentley told Craig that he was being taken down, only one of three policemen there at the time remembered a shot being fired directly afterwards. The inference was that Bentley's phrase was again intended to be an incitement for Craig for fire.

Only when it came to Bentley's statement did Cassels hint at the boy's limitations, going so far as to suggest that 'it may be, and possibly is, his own fault'. There is nothing about his IQ, his inability to understand situations and people. Nobody, in 1952, had any interest in that. Defence did point out, however, that the statement is disjointed, full of non sequiturs and points to answers to police questions. Even then, Cassels waters down his attack – 'Do you think there was not some little jogging along, some little questioning – I do not say improper – by the police officers?'

The court was adjourned until the third day.

As John Parris makes clear, Goddard's summation, beginning at 10.30 a.m. on Thursday, 11 December, 'was, as all his charges to juries were, not an impartial summing up of the evidence but a vicious speech for the prosecution'.

In the eleven pages of the judge's summing up, I counted nineteen errors of fact and/or interpretation. Because of the protocol of the legal system, no one was allowed to interrupt or query what Goddard was saying. To be fair to Parris, he did correct him on a point of fact, the numbers of shots fired. Goddard's response? 'I do not know that it very much matters.'

In claiming, as he did, that Craig had a motive – his brother's being sent down for armed robbery, which gave him a hatred for the police

– he was exceeding the facts. That information came from the police; Parris had challenged it and Craig had denied that he said any such thing. Goddard made no reference to that. Goddard reiterated his interpretation of the murder/manslaughter debate that he had already gone through with Parris. Clearly, the defence counsel's argument had not moved the judge one iota – he trotted out the same prejudicial view he had expressed earlier; in other words, Craig was guilty of murder. He had the gall to say to the jury, 'Now, you know, because I sit on the Bench and you sit in the jury box, it is not necessary that we leave our common sense at home.' Cassels had raised the same thing earlier in the trial and here was the old dinosaur, a man with no common sense at all, at it again. He invented conversation between Craig and Bentley on the rooftop – 'It's all right. I've got a revolver with me.'

Goddard then spent several minutes pointing out how ghastly the knives and knuckleduster of the miscreants were – the weapons that did not feature in the crime and which stayed in the lads' pockets the whole time.

In the context of the already infamous 'Let him have it, Chris,' Goddard, inevitably, defended the police. 'Are you going to say they [Fairfax, Harrison and McDonald] are conspicuous liars?' as well as being, in the judge's words, 'conspicuously brave'. As John Parris points out, 'this was a complete *non sequitur*; bravery has nothing to do with truthfulness. It invited the jury to believe that if they found Craig guilty of manslaughter or acquitted Bentley, they would be accusing three brave officers of perjury.'

Goddard's defence of Bentley was reduced to four lines in an eleven-page summation – and that for a 19-year-old who was facing the death penalty. The edited Montgomery Hyde account quotes the judge as saying, 'if you find grounds for convicting them, it is your duty to do so.' According to Parris, *who was there*, he actually said, 'Unless you can find grounds for not convicting them, it is your duty to do so,' which has a different slant altogether.

As the jury was being sent away to deliberate, the foreman asked to see Fairfax's coat and waistcoat. Goddard reminded them that the issue was the murder of Miles, not the wounding of Fairfax, but in Montgomery Hyde's flat, ironed-out version, there is no hint of the fact that Goddard blew his stack at this, smashing the woodwork of his bench with the knuckleduster so hard that the damage was there for years and he screamed at the foreman. And in case John Parris should be accused of hyperbole, another lawyer, Anthony Samuelson, sitting in the public gallery, witnessed the same ludicrous outburst.

It took the jury one and a quarter hours to return guilty verdicts on both boys, with a recommendation to mercy in Bentley's case. Arthur Smith placed the black cap on Goddard's head (whatever state his trousers were in by this time) and he passed the death sentence – 'Take him down.' Christopher Craig was to be 'kept in strict custody until the pleasure of Her Majesty be known.'

Chapter 5

Print the Legend*

'On behalf of the Prosecution, I ask you to forget everything you have read about this case up to the moment.' This was the quite proper advice given to the jury by Christmas Humphreys early on in his opening statement at the trial. In his closing argument, John Parris said the same thing. 'You had read the newspapers and probably you had discussed it with your neighbours in the "local" … you may have seen pictures in the newspapers which portrayed [Craig] as a young thug.'

The tragedy is that both counsel were wasting their time. Advance knowledge of a case via the media and the opportunity for a jury to make up its mind before it is even called to court is one of the many glaring weaknesses of the British legal system (see Chapter 10). Today, with what has amounted to a media revolution and rapidly expanding technology, the press is more intrusive than ever in our lives, so called 'social' media perhaps more so. It was not quite like that in 1952, but even so, the fourth estate, as the press has been called, did considerable damage to the cause of justice at the time.

The Metropolitan Police, as an organization, has worked with the press for decades. In 1888, when the Whitechapel murderer caused such a furore in London's East End, the Met briefed journalists and had no real objection to their hanging around police stations and murder sites in search of a story. The City of London force, by comparison, gave no interviews and no cooperation to the press at all. And if information was not forthcoming, the gentlemen of the press just made it up, writing pure speculation and gibberish, often with garishly unlikely 'crime scenes' to frighten people over their breakfast tables. The grittiest publication (although there were many nearly as bad) was *The Illustrated Police News*, whose title gave the wholly false impression that it was an official police publication; it was not.

In the Victorian period, 'orrible murder' sold papers. Prevented by the mores of the time, not to mention the obscenity laws, sex could not be reported graphically. Crime, however, was fair game. By 1952, the mores had changed and scandal sheets like *The Sunday Pictorial* and *News of the World* pushed the boundaries continually.

We have already read the *Daily Mail*'s banner headlines about the Croydon shooting, but its detailed article went on to make ever more assumptions and mistakes. The article contended that Craig and Bentley were *inside* the Barlow and Parker warehouse, rather than on the outside of it. One of the 'bandits' (what an odd phrase for 1950s Britain) fired a Sten-gun. Sidney Miles was said to be in plain clothes (he was not) and a *detective* constable (which he had never been). Frederick Fairfax, however, was a DC, not, as he was wrongly designated, a PC, and both he and Miles reached the roof via a fire escape (there was no fire escape at Barlow and Parker's). The *Mail* claimed that 200 police were there (the statements in The National Archive suggest 44) and that 30 of them were armed. In reality, only Fairfax fired a gun; a second *may* have been the one that Claude Pain saw in the hand of DS Roberts (although equally, that may have been Craig's Eley). There is no evidence at all that anybody was firing at ambulancemen and firemen, as the article claimed. And the whole thing, over in less than twenty minutes from the police arrival, lasted, the media said, for an hour. The villains had 'an unlimited supply of ammunition' and 'Sten gun bullets hit the streets'. That same Sten-gun was 'flung into the face of three officers facing the gunman'. There was 'a chase over the rooftops'. As David Yallop wrote in 1971, 'the staff reporters should have got some kind of inverted Pulitzer Prize for a historic piece of misreporting.'

The attitude of the media could not be better summed up than by looking at the involvement of Harry Proctor. John Parris had known the man when he was a journalist in Leeds and had twice got him off drink-driving charges. Since many hacks' stories, then as now, were obtained from chats in pubs, this was presumably an occupational hazard. Proctor rang Parris to tell him that the *Pictorial* had 'bought' the Craig family for £500 and that he and his assistant Madeleine McLoughlin were to 'manage' them, complete with a Rolls Royce for getting about. Proctor wanted Parris to get him into Brixton prison for an interview. 'You can always tell them I'm your clerk.' Quite rightly, Parris refused, but Proctor got in anyway by some other subterfuge. He interviewed Craig twice and he proudly showed his articles to the family. This is surprising, because one of them said:

> What a handsome youth! I thought. And then he grinned and broke the spell. As I saw the lip curl and the impudent flicker creep into his eyes, I knew I was watching just another of those brass-faced little hooligans of which this post-war world is so bitterly ashamed. A lazy, cowardly, selfish young lout.

Thanks, Harry! I am sure the Craigs were delighted.

Proctor's article was what the British public expected to see in 1952 – the 'cosh boys' were everywhere and a menace to society. He asked Craig if Bentley had used the words 'Let him have it' and Craig resolutely denied that he did. This was *before* the trial at which the words became so ominous and central to the prosecution's case, yet Proctor did not include this interview testimony until several years later.

The *Pictorial* wanted more and pressed Proctor to produce an article in which Niven Craig senior condemned his son. Proctor wrote it all, including snippets from Niven taken out of context and his editor Fred Redman called it 'a brilliant human document'. The fact that it was a work of fiction was irrelevant in the cut-throat world of Fleet Street.

Niven agreed to sign off the articles as long as the whole thing was not sensationalized. But this was the *Sunday Pictorial* – what hope was there of that? True to form, the paper's banner headlines read 'My Failure: By Craig's Father'. Niven Craig broke off all contact with Proctor after that, but the damage was already done.

As John Parris wrote in 1991, 'Harry Proctor was an exponent of the journalistic principle "Make it fast, make it up".' Proctor had form in this context. He wrote a 'front-line story' about the bombing of Dover during the war without having been there. He later made up some nonsense about a body found floating in the flood waters of the East Anglian coast, using a photograph, taken on the Thames near Blackfriars Bridge at low tide, of an anonymous child suitably wrapped like Moses. According to Parris, Proctor had numerous affairs (and illegitimate children) including one with a 14 year-old pupil at his Christian Science Sunday School.

While the Craigs were effectively kidnapped by Proctor in the expensive Angel Hotel in Shepperton, the screen actor Alan Ladd was staying there, making the war film *The Red Beret* for the studio. Mrs Craig got his autograph. On the night that the Old Bailey jury found their son guilty of murder, the Craigs were wined and dined at the lavish Prospect of Whitby pub along Execution Dock on the Thames' north bank. According to John Parris, Proctor tried it on with Lucy Craig back in the hotel before nipping out of the window at the arrival of her father.

With the verdict against Craig in the bag, Proctor – and the media generally – moved their attention to the Bentleys, as we shall see later.

If the Craig family were effectively removed from any direct approach by the *Sunday Pictorial,* the Bentleys and the case in general was wide open to all other outlets. The media in the 1950s was experiencing something of a revival. The war years saw the heavy hand of Churchill's paranoid government – 'careless talk costs lives' – and editors were constrained to 'keep Mum' about all sorts of goings on. Newspapers were reduced in length too, with limited space for news items and editorials. Moriarty's *Police Law* outlined the need for strict press regulation in wartime. With the disappearance of all that, there was a newfound freedom which sometimes got out of hand.

As early as 1928, John Gore had referred to Britain's newspaper capital as 'a street of hasty judgement and elastic morality' and, since the advent of W.T. Stead's 'new journalism' three decades earlier, provincial papers had followed suit. From South Wales's *Western Mail* via the *Leicester Evening Mail* and as far north as Lanarkshire, the provincials carried the Craig and Bentley story, especially as the trial got underway.

Just as Harry Proctor had got his hooks into the Craigs, so Len Cotton of the *Sunday Dispatch* targeted the Bentleys. Once the trial was over and Bentley was facing a death sentence, William Bentley was trying every avenue to keep his boy alive. He told Cotton that he had visited the police to lodge a complaint about Craig a week before the shooting. He had been told that, in the absence of an actual crime, there was nothing they could do. Cotton did not have the journalistic flair of Proctor, but his article, purported to be written by William Bentley, put the blame on Craig.

In the middle of all the press hoo-ha, Lucy Craig got married (accounts appeared in virtually every paper) two days after the trial ended. Various questions were raised in the media, extending to the House of Commons, of the links between school truancy, illiteracy and crime. *Reynolds News* reminded everybody how little police widows like Catherine Miles got for their husbands putting their lives on the line. The woman got a measly £2 16s a week. The widow of PC Nathaniel Edgar, murdered in 1948, received a huge sum, but that came from private donations, not the government. James Dow, writing in the *Sunday Chronicle*, raised the issue of the lenient sentence handed out to Craig, who may well have been out in five years. He believed that the younger boy, as the instigator and ringleader should have been hanged and the parents of such wrong-doers should be punished for their part in producing such delinquents. Lord Goddard must have been delighted.

Beverly Nichols was incensed that 'the young brute with the knuckleduster [Craig] should be given pentothal while his wrist was being set'. As tax-payers, Nichols ranted, 'you and I pay for that pentothal.'

What was totally lacking across the media spectrum was any doubt, still less outrage, at the fact that Derek Bentley was going to hang for a murder he did not commit.

The duplicity of the press is shown by various papers' response to the film *No Orchids for Miss Blandish* released in 1948. It was a British thriller in what today we might call the 'noir' genre. The *Daily Herald* advised the Plaza cinema in London to 'take it off at once'. The *Daily Mirror* found it as 'fragrant as a cesspool'. The *Star* wrote, 'Without doubt it is one of the most undesirable pictures ever turned out by a British studio.' *The Times* said it should have a 'D certificate for disgusting'. The *Observer* found it 'repellent. All the morals of an alley cat and the sweetness of a sewer.' So much for the moral high ground. Four years later, every one of those publications was happy to brand Craig and Bentley as vicious killers before the trial had even started. Incidentally, the crowds flocked to the Plaza in droves (perhaps *because* of the adverse press reaction) and the manager reported no complaints at all.

*The title of this chapter comes from a John Ford western, *The Man Who Shot Liberty Vallance*, ten years after the Craig and Bentley case. The hero, James Stewart, is a successful senator but his fame really rests on the mistaken belief that he killed a vicious outlaw (Lee Marvin). It is *that* that people are impressed by, not his political achievements in later life. So, in the case of Craig and Bentley, everybody who read a newspaper bought into the lie of the Croydon rooftop gun battle and drew their own conclusions. The guilt of Fleet Street is inescapable.

Chapter 6

The Appeal

The Bentley family had expected to be called to the courtroom, as Niven Craig had been. In the event, they spent agonizing hours in the corridors of the Old Bailey, waiting and hoping. William had squeezed his way into the packed room to hear the death sentence on his son. Lilian, Iris and little Denis were in a café across the road, unable to bear the tension.

'Well, Will?' Lilian was still sitting in her coat on that cold Thursday, hardly able to read what was etched on her husband's face.

'They've found him guilty,' William told her, 'but it will be all right. The jury recommended mercy.'

The women cried.

Uncomprehending, Denis said, 'Is it bad, Dad?'

Somehow, William managed to smile and ruffled his boy's hair. 'Not so bad, son. It could have been worse.'

Nobody remembered getting home later. William called the doctor who brought sedatives and the man of the family now had the unenviable task of taking on the power and the indifference of the state.

Derek was housed in the grim condemned cell at Wandsworth, a 'reformed' prison opened in 1851 on the plan of the model Pentonville. When I visited it (I was not allowed in) it still had a depressing, dismal frontage, despite the new electronic sliding gate and the fact that no executions had taken place since 1965. It was chilling to be told that, even in 1990, the execution shed was still in position, in case parliament did the unthinkable and brought capital punishment back. Two of the Victorian cells had been knocked into one so that family visits of the condemned could take place. There was a glass partition up to eye level and there was to be no touching. The most the Bentleys could do was to press their hands against Derek's with a pane of glass between them.

The family came every day, the awkward silences filled with determination once it was decided that the sentence would be contested. There are surprisingly few letters from the public in The National Archive, but one from Mrs W. Corry of Ladbroke Grove, dated 4 January 1953 sums up the attitude of the Goddard school. The *Sunday Despatch* had carried a story about Bentley laughing and joking with his warders (this was before the Appeal). 'Normal meetings,' said the article, 'between condemned men and relatives are tearful affairs. But in the case of Bentley, they are more like impromptu parties with everybody laughing.'

Incensed, Mrs Corry wrote to the police commissioner. The piece was:

> The most disgraceful piece of journalism I have ever had the misfortune to read. It makes light of the Death Sentence – also makes out that the warders are laughing and joking – while one of their colleagues lie murdered – and a widow weeps. I hope Derek Bentley pays the full penalty and you will deal with the libel on your warders by the Sunday Dispatch and make them refute it publically [sic].

Catherine Miles, on the other hand, had told the press that she did not think that Derek should die. In the book that was ghosted for him four years later, William wrote, 'But to Mrs Miles goes the honour of rising above a deep personal sorrow to express the opinion that Derek should not die.'

They all passed a ghastly Christmas. The Bentleys bought a basket of fruit for Derek, but they were told he could not accept it by the warders. The family took it home and it stayed untouched on the sideboard as the days seemed to fly by.

Today, in courts of law in this country, there is an automatic right of appeal for anybody on the spurious grounds that you keep going until you get the verdict you want. The Court of Appeal itself was set up in 1907, specifically to test the validity of trials involving capital punishment. Beyond that, as the Bentleys discovered, was the House of Lords, then the highest court in the land. More recently, still further layers have been added – the unelected Court of Human Rights in Strasbourg and the fatuous and unnecessary Supreme Court, an American invention which ought to have no place in the British legal system.

The Bentley appeal was heard on 13 January 1953 before the judges, David Croom-Johnson (a crony of Goddard), Roger Ormerod and Colin Pearson. In John Parris's view 'the last two were reasonable men; the presiding judge [Croom-Johnson] was a bastard.' Parris himself could hardly have brought an appeal on behalf of Craig – his guilt, even allowing for intent, was apparent for all to see. That was not the case for Bentley, and Cassels went to work.

Defence counsel made the point in his opening remarks that Craig's name had become a 'household word in this country' (thanks to the media, of course). Croom-Johnson was clearly a man in a hurry. 'We have all read these papers. We are fully aware of the circumstances of the case and the point is quite a short one, is it not?'

It was. Cassels said, quite rightly, that Goddard had failed to put Bentley's case during his summing up. It only ran to two lines of printed text. This amounted to a misdirection on Goddard's part. Cassels pointed out that Bentley's contention that he had not used the words 'Let him have it', had not fired a gun or incited Craig to do so, and was effectively under arrest after the first shot (which wounded Fairfax) was fired. Miles was killed by the sixth or seventh shot, by which time Bentley was firmly in police custody and took no part in the rooftop 'battle'. In fact, as Cassels pointed out, Bentley was not being physically held at the time and could have broken away to rejoin Craig but did not do so.

Cassels explained to the judges that Goddard's summation of the conversation in the police car when Bentley was being taken to Fell Road included only the police testimony and not Bentley's refutation of that. Bentley's testimony had been given twenty-four hours earlier – Goddard's version of events only minutes before the jury was sent away to deliberate.

The next argument that Cassels raised was Bentley's statement and exactly how it was delivered. Was it a continuous stream of consciousness (of which Bentley was incapable) or was it a result of police prompting (which might well have made it inadmissible). Croom-Johnson airily dismissed this as occurring in a number of cases, as if illegally obtained statements were commonplace and therefore acceptable. He went further. 'Surely, it is for the learned judge to decide what he is to lay before the jury.' This will be discussed in a later chapter, but it effectively gives biased dinosaurs like Goddard carte blanche to say what they like to a jury. When Parris had challenged the judge at the time, Goddard shut him down. 'I shall tell the jury that that is no defence at all.'

Cassels was at the end of his tether. Croom-Johnson was highly dismissive of the man and his arguments. We can just see Cassels, through clenched teeth, saying, 'I would suggest, with the greatest possible respect.' And Croom-Johnson slipped up when Cassels said, 'but the Chief Justice went into the version of the police officers,' with 'Of course he did.' In other words, Goddard was a bigot and Croom-Johnson would probably have done the same thing. He constantly contended that Goddard must be allowed leeway, which again opened the door to incompetence and/or bias and brings into question the role of judges under the law.

When Cassels had finished, it was Christmas Humphreys' turn and he essentially repeated what he had said in the original trial. All members present had printed copies of the transcript and were able to refer to relevant questions and answers. 'That was the case for the Crown and is today.'

Cassels came back with a point of fact. When Bentley had shouted 'They're taking me down, Chris' there had been no shots fired (even though Humphreys, in his summing up had said there were). Fairfax's testimony was that no more shots were fired until he got back up on the roof. Croom-Johnson added that he was confused about the shooting on the rooftop – 'I am afraid I gave up,' which hardly inspires confidence in the workings of the law.

Unsurprisingly, Croom-Johnson, as leading judge, summed up in Goddard's favour. He could find nothing wrong with his friend's summing up, consistently maintaining that it had all been up to the jury and that they had made up their minds. In this context, on 13 October 1991 *The People* Sunday newspaper quoted Vic Waller, who was a juror in the original case. He said that the jury made up their minds not on the evidence but 'one what they believed to be an instruction from the trial judge that both were guilty'. Could there be a more damning indictment of Goddard and the system he represented? 'In the opinion of the Court, the idea that there was a failure on the part of the Chief Justice to say anything short of what was required in putting that sort of case to the jury is entirely wrong.' Croom-Johnson raised an interesting point in relation to when the 'joint felonious enterprise' came to an end:

> It is a little difficult for Mr Cassels because his own client was asked specifically at the hearing whether he was under arrest at the time when this shot which killed Miles was fired. He would not have it. He said he had not been arrested, that he was not under arrest that the police officer [Fairfax] had not detained him.

This was an important point and no one addressed it. At no point did Fairfax or any other policeman say 'You are under arrest' or even the more usual, 'You're nicked, son.' There are many instances, especially in riot situations, when the police grab a miscreant, but laying hands on someone is not automatically affecting an arrest. Someone with

Bentley's limitations would not have understood the subtleties and merely gave the court a factual account of his being held by the police (at various times not physically at all). The point at issue is that from the moment Fairfax dragged Bentley away from Craig, frisking him for weapons, the joint enterprise (ludicrously referred to in court as an 'adventure') was over. Whatever happened after that, for example Craig's murder of Miles, was not remotely Bentley's fault.

John Parris referred to me as a 'schoolmaster who knows nothing about the law'. As we shall see in a later chapter, the law is designed to protect itself and its own more than the average citizen. Cassels did not go far enough in his criticism of Goddard because the system would not let him. He would have been held in contempt by Croom-Johnson and his own career would have been in jeopardy.

'In our opinion,' Croom-Johnson pontificated, 'this is nothing more than an ordinary appeal in a murder trial, an ordinary appeal which is, in our judgement, without foundation and which is accordingly dismissed.'

This time, the Bentleys were in court. This was not the Old Bailey but in the warm grey buildings at the Fleet Street end of the Strand, near the newspaper offices that had howled in protest at the killing of a policeman and had bayed for blood. Derek Bentley was there too, complete with warders from Wandsworth. Iris knew that all the debate went right over his head. In her own book, *Let Him Have Justice* (1993) Iris made a comment about the silence of PC James Alderson who had sat with Derek on the ride to Fell Road. The appeal judges compounded Goddard's error on this, claiming that Alderson's statement was available for the court to see. 'Not true,' said Iris. 'Nothing from Alderson was ever filed in the court.' To this day, nobody has seen the notes Alderson made that night and it was not until December 2023, in research for this book, that I was allowed to read his statement for the first time. I had asked for it thirty-three years earlier.

Little Denis made the meeting with Derek after the appeal's dismissal just about bearable. He rabbited away as though any minute

Derek would be home. But he would never come home. And this was the last time that Denis would see him.

Now, the deluge started. While the media sat on the fence, hundreds of people wrote letters and sent telegrams to the Bentleys. In the days before the Internet and social media, it was the only way for ordinary voices to be heard. Today, the white noise would be unbearable. Flowers were sent from as far afield as France and Holland. The Bentley vases could not cope and the kitchen sink was used to house them; the bath was full of correspondence. A few were vicious, glad the 'justice' was being doled out. Most were adamant that Derek must not die. The phone rang day and night, Iris and William fielding all the calls because Lilian could not cope and Denis was too young.

There were other letters too, written to the prime minister, Winston Churchill, the Attorney General Lionel Heald and above all, David Maxwell-Fyfe, the Home Secretary, the 'man who rations mercy'. The Bentleys' MP, Reader Harris, met William and Iris but told them that because Derek had been found guilty he must be and that nothing could be done. With that in mind, the Bentleys never voted Tory again and the grand old man who had led Britain during the war was going through his least 'finest hour'. The debate over capital punishment became a simplistic party political one.

Other MPs were more positive. Aneurin Bevan, the Welsh firebrand who had set up the National Health Service, met the family in the Commons and was kind and supportive. Sydney Silverman, the back-bencher pushing for the permanent abolition of capital punishment, pressurized to get Bentley's case debated in the House. The Lords turned down the appeal on 22 January. Since long before the constitutional clash of 1911, the Upper House had been on borrowed time. Unable to dismiss or even delay finance bills since then, it nevertheless remained the highest court in the land – over 600 unelected dinosaurs of the same social class as Goddard, holding their titles because of who daddy was. Hereditary peers had no concept of what the family of a 'three-quarter witted boy' was going through; the last member of the House of Lords to die by execution was Lord Lovatt in 1747.

Petitions were mounted to let the government know that *they* worked for the people, a message all too easily (and regularly) forgotten. Celebrities like the actors Peter Ustinov and Diana Dors added their names to the lists. The journalist Kenneth Allsop saw a mood of ebullience around the country that he likened to Dunkirk, thirteen years earlier. Mass prayer meetings were held in Hyde Park, 'Bentley' stickers were plastered over public buildings.

Derek's bedroom was a shrine. Lilian went in there every day and changed the bed once a week, although no one slept in it. His clothes were there, the toys and comics of his childhood in the bottom of the wardrobe. On the day that the Lords turned down the appeal, William at last knew that all hope had gone:

> I jumped from my chair to shake off the horror. Then I lost my grip on my own identity. I did not know who I was. The familiar articles of furniture in the sitting room seemed strange. I went into the kitchen and filled a kettle to make tea. It was as if someone else was doing it and I was watching him from outside. I came back, as it were, in flashes and with those lucid moments came the certainty that my son would be hanged. I can never hope to describe the horror; it was terrible beyond words.

The human-interest angle had now reached America which was facing its own battle with teenaged delinquents. Reporters from all over the world jostled William and Iris and they took two parcels of petitions, a fraction of what had been delivered to them, to the Home Office in Whitehall, cameras flashing. The elder Bentley had a letter drafted by a solicitor with eight points which Goddard and the Court of Appeal should have answered and had not.

Then, a cruel and extraordinary hoax happened. Among the mail the Bentleys had received was a box containing a note that read, 'Your son will need this.' And the box contained a noose. But it was the telegram from Sarah Bartley of Southend which grabbed William's attention. She was the sister of Maxwell-Fyfe, the Home Secretary – 'I have written to him, asking him to spare your son's life. Have no fear, Mrs Bentley. Derek will not die.'

Mrs Bentley was housebound, so William hired a car and drove to see her. He spent over an hour with the woman, finding her very intelligent and fully familiar with the Craig and Bentley case. But David Maxwell-Fyfe had no sister; he was an only child. William Bentley went to his grave believing that she was sincere. We have to assume that she was just another of those ghouls that high-publicity criminal cases drive out from under their rocks.

The Bentleys never got to meet Maxwell-Fyfe. To some, he was the hero who had prosecuted Herman Goering, head of the Luftwaffe, at Nuremberg in 1946, but a man who could not prosecute Goering had no right to be a lawyer at all. Others had the measure of him. The future prime minister, Harold Macmillan, rightly dismissed him as 'stupid' and got rid of him from his cabinet in the 'night of the long knives' in 1962. When Maxwell-Fyfe complained that he had been dismissed with less notice than he would give a cook, Macmillan countered that it was easier to get another Lord Chancellor than a good cook, which squarely put the ennobled Lord Kilmuir firmly in his place. Winston Churchill told John Parris, 'Of course, the man was a complete bloody fool. But he was a loyal and servile bloody fool. Every government needs people like that to keep it going' – which does not say much for Churchill's government or governments in general, come to that. Fellow lawyer Harry Hylton-Foster QC wrote, 'The nearest thing to death in life, is David Patrick Maxwell-Fyfe.' He was among the 1,200 mourners at PC Miles's funeral, flying the police flag as all good Home Secretaries should. After that and even before it, it was downhill all the way. Sydney Silverman and Nye Bevan were among those who badgered Maxwell-Fyfe, reminding him that there had never been such public indignation over a single case before. 'All the same,' the windbag had said, '[I] feel that there is not sufficient reason [to interfere with the court's verdict]. The balance is still the other way.' How far party politics was already operating here is hard to say – Silverman and Bevan were Labour; Maxwell-Fyfe, Tory.

As Ludovic Kennedy wrote in 2002, Maxwell-Fyfe was 'a Scot whose arrogance matched his ignorance'. He told the Commons, in 1950 in connection with the wrongful execution of Timothy Evans (like Bentley, for a crime he did not commit), 'There is no possibility of an innocent man being hanged in this country and anyone who thinks there is is living in a world of fantasy.' Interestingly enough, Maxwell-Fyfe also assured the House that Evans' statement, like Bentley's, had been taken in the proper way. It had not. Evans, too, was of limited intellect. Whether he had murdered his wife and baby was a matter for the court, but there was no doubt that his statement was fabricated. In the event, Evans' landlord, John Christie, was later hanged for the murder of Beryl Evans.

On Monday, 26 January, a young reporter knocked on the Bentley's door at Norbury Road. He asked if it was true that the Home Secretary had not granted a reprieve. He was from the *Daily Express* and the paper had been briefed earlier that morning. In shock and horror, the Bentleys dived through the vast batch of letters in the bath and there it was, a brown OHMS franked letter sent by ordinary post:

> Sir, I am directed by the Secretary of State to inform you that he has given careful consideration to the petition submitted by you on behalf of your son Derek Bentley and I am to express to you his deep regret that after considering all the circumstances of

the case he has failed to discover any sufficient ground to justify him in advising Her Majesty to interfere with the due course of the law.

I am, Sir,
Your obedient servant,
F.A. Newsam

'I do not want to describe,' William Bentley wrote, 'what happened to my wife and daughter after I read the letter out to them, but I shall hear their screams as long as I live.'

Newsam's pros and cons on the hanging issue are still in The National Archive. On the 'For' side (for reprieve), arguing against the death sentence was a number of salient points which Goddard had either belittled or ignored in his summation. Bentley did not at any time attempt to use the weapons he carried. He did not attempt to break away from Fairfax after the first time. 'Although he incited Craig to shoot' (a highly dubious contention, of course) that resulted in the wounding of Fairfax, not the murder of Miles. Bentley was actually in the custody of officers (Fairfax and McDonald) when Miles was killed. Bentley did not carry a gun or fire a shot. Craig denied that Bentley made any incitement to shoot; he needed no provocation for that. Bentley was very young, although over the legal age for the death penalty. The jury had recommended mercy. Goddard saw Craig as the worse offender of the two. There were Home Office precedents (that loaded, dangerous word again) for reprieve if the prime offender (Craig) could not be executed. There was a risk that Bentley could become a cause célèbre if he were to be hanged. The 'great majority' of letters to the Home Office was in favour of a reprieve.

Newsam's note, written on 20 January, lists twelve points in the reprieve column. In the 'Against' column, in favour of the death sentence, he lists the 'bad murder of a police officer' (as if there could be such a thing as a 'good murder') 'at a time when there is much anxiety about crimes of violence'. It was this that gave rise to David Yallop's title *To Encourage the Others* and John Parris to choose *Scapegoat* for his. Hanging might act as a deterrent for wayward youth. Bentley knew that Craig had a gun and he incited him to use it. He had expressed no remorse. He made no attempt to stop Craig or dissociate himself from it (untrue, according to both Craig's and Bentley's accounts). He had 'previous' in terms of theft. He was well over 19. The precedent of an older man escaping justice because he had a younger accomplice could not be accepted. The police would approve the sentence being carried out. That made nine points against twelve.

There was no mention of the jury's recommendation to mercy. No reference to the huge outpouring of outrage that the impending execution had engendered. No evidence that Maxwell-Fyfe had any conscience at all. Of course, he did not. He believed that the all-too-fallible British legal system was so perfect that an innocent man could not hang. And he went on to sit in the House of Lords as Lord Kilmuir, another of the unelected out of touch with reality.

He himself was outraged when the news broke. 'My decision,' he wrote in his autobiography, 'brought down on my head a stream of vituperation without parallel in my career.' He had so many unpleasant phone calls, at his office and home, that the Post Office switched them off. He was bombarded with argument in the Commons and had to cancel a speaking engagement on Burns Night. The next day, however, Maxwell Fyfe was congratulating himself on the number of letters he received supporting his decision. He told himself – and the few readers who bought his book – that 'popular sympathy with "the underdog" had swung from the dead policeman to Bentley and finally to myself.' For the pompous Home Secretary to see himself as an underdog defies belief.

When David Yallop wrote *To Encourage the Others* in 1971, Lord Goddard told him that Maxwell Fyfe did not consult him or indeed anyone about the case. The Home Secretary believed that the damning phrase on the rooftop was 'Give it to him, Chris', which has a very different meaning. He also confused the number of shots fired and which hit Fairfax and which hit Miles. Astonishingly, he believed too that *Craig* had been sentenced to death and had appealed. Neither of those facts was true, as it could be presumed, had he read anything of the case at all, the Home Secretary would know.

Tellingly, in his self-serving autobiography, Maxwell-Fyfe wrote, 'In the Bentley case I had an additional question of the possible effects of my decision upon the police force, by whom the murder of a police officer is justly regarded as the most heinous of crimes.'

This issue was uppermost in Lord Goddard's mind during the trial too. David Yallop and I are in agreement that this 'sliding scale of values on human life' (Yallop) is appalling. Interestingly, it is still the attitude of the police, not just in Britain, but in the United States. When John F. Kennedy was killed in Dallas, Texas on 22 November 1963, another man, Officer J.D. Tippit, was shot dead on the same day. One policeman is on record as saying that Tippit's murder was more important than that of the president. If David Maxwell-Fyfe was kow-towing to the Metropolitan Police, with pressure on him from everyone from the Commissioner, Harold Scott, to the humblest bobby on the beat, then he should have been ashamed of himself.

What was left? Silverman's debate in parliament. On the 22nd, the MP for Nelson and Colne presented a Motion signed by fifty members of the House for a reprieve, in effect over-riding Maxwell-Fyfe's overly harsh decision. But the ass that is the law kicked in again and the Speaker, William Morrison, removed the petition from the Order Paper later that night. Silverman challenged him the next day. Fellow MP and barrister Reginald Paget spoke to support him:

> We are a sovereign assembly. A three-quarter-witted boy of nineteen is to be hanged for a murder that he did not commit and which was committed fifteen minutes after he was arrested. Can we be made to keep silent when a thing aa horrible and shocking as this is to happen?

The official line was as heartless as it was pompous and will be discussed in a later chapter. Erskine May's enormous tome *Parliamentary Practice* says, 'In any case involving a capital sentence on which the exercise of the prerogative of Mercy depends, it should not be made the subject of a question while the sentence is pending nor may the sentence itself be raised in a question while it is pending.'

In other words, the decision to hang Bentley could only be decided *after* Bentley was hanged. As Iris Bentley wrote in 1995, bagsful of telegrams were appearing in the Commons chamber, challenging Maxwell-Fyfe, the Speaker, the *system*. They came, wrote Iris, 'from people who could not believe that something like this could really happen in England. England that won the war against Hitler.'

The Bentleys made their way to Wandsworth, to say goodbye to Derek.

Chapter 7

'This Boy is being Murdered'

At Wandsworth, the regulations were clear. Bentley was watched, night and day, by two warders operating in shifts. He was allowed cards, chess, dominoes and draughts and played regularly with his guards. It is probably impossible for us to grasp the mindset of these men, knowing that they were living full-time with a limited, working-class boy who was going to hang in weeks, then days, then hours. Newspapers and books were also available, although it is doubtful that Bentley could read them. Food came from the prison canteen and a pint of beer was on offer on request. Derek did not take up the offer of a pipe, but he no doubt welcomed the ten cigarettes a day and could smoke them in his cell. The governor or medical officer checked on him twice a day and the chaplain had free access to a condemned man. The Visiting Committee decided who could visit – usually family rather than friends – and the prisoner could write and receive letters. In Derek's case, of course, he had to dictate his to one of the warders.

On the day after Maxwell-Fyfe's decision was made public, the Bentleys visited as usual. Derek was not there and they had to wait an agonizing twenty minutes for his arrival. 'Sorry I'm late,' he said. 'There was a nice man who wanted to shake my hand.' The nice man was Albert Pierrepoint, the owner of a pub, *Pity the Poor Struggler*, in Lancashire. He was also the public executioner.

Judicial murder, the government's ultimate sanction before the abolition of the death penalty, had a long and ghastly history. Until the 1860s, hangings took place in public and were always well attended. Thousands turned up to see, for example, Arthur Thistlewood and his

Cato Street conspirators 'turned off' outside Newgate, where the Old Bailey courtroom stands today. That was in 1820 and it was the last time that criminals' heads were cut off after death and displayed, blood still dripping, to the mob. The authorities always expected trouble and hundreds of policemen and soldiers waited at the crowd's edge, ready to wade in. Usually, however heinous the crime for which a man or woman was hanged, the mob's fury turned on the executioner, who had the generic name Jack Ketch for decades after the real one had died.

By the 1860s, the circus atmosphere of such events had gone and from 1868 all hangings took place inside a prison, with a black flag hoisted over the roof to let the people know the deed had been done. The first of the Victorian hangmen was William Calcraft, an amateur by anybody's standards. He was often drunk, and his MO consisted of using a standard drop, irrespective of the weight or height of the victim. That meant that death was often due to slow strangulation, rather than an abrupt snapping of the spine, with Calcraft obscenely tugging on the victim's legs in an attempt to finish him off. About the only courtesy shown to the hanged was in the case of women like the poisoner Mary Ann Cotton, whose long dresses were tied at the ankles to preserve their modesty.

The first of the modern, technically minded hangmen was James Berry in the 1880s, but even he sometimes made mistakes. In the infamous case of John 'Babbacombe' Lee, due to be executed for the murder of his employer, the trapdoor of the scaffold refused to open. The prisoner was returned to his cell and a bag of Lee's exact weight was placed on the trap. The machine worked perfectly and he was recalled. Again, the doors refused to open and Lee was sent back once more by thoroughly rattled officials and his sentence commuted to life imprisonment. In another case, Berry got the length of the drop wrong and the victim's head was ripped from his shoulders by the rope.

Albert Pierrepoint came, as was often the case, from a family of executioners. His uncles, Henry and Thomas, had been hanging people since the 1920s. Thomas executed the poisoner Jean Pierre Vacquier at Wandsworth in 1924 and Patrick Mahon in the same prison in the same year. He assisted Robert Baxter at Pentonville in the executions of the cop-killers Frederick Browne and William Kennedy in 1928 at the end of a case, like that of Craig and Bentley, that caused an outrage because a constable had been killed. Unlike the Croydon shoot-out, George Gutteridge was brought down by a bullet and then had two more fired into his eyes.

By 1934, Albert assisted at the hanging of Ethel Major for the poisoning of her husband, Arthur. This was at Hull, proving what a roving brief executioners had. The first time that Albert took the leading role (allowing for some hangings when the executioners' names were not recorded) was in the execution of Antonio 'Babe' Mancini at Pentonville in October 1941. Mancini was a Soho night-club owner up to his neck in violence and surrounded by lowlife. Just before Pierrepoint pulled the lever, checking that everything was in place, Mancini said 'Cheerio'. He followed this up in 1942 with the hanging of the 'blackout killer' Gordon Cummins, at Wandsworth. In one of the least-covered serial murderers in history (because of the preoccupation of the media with the war) we know relatively little about Cummins' vicious murder spree today and poor books on the subject have not helped.

A handful of German spies parachuted into the country or trying to operate here met their fate at the end of Pierrepoint's rope, but his reputation was really made by his hanging of Nazi war criminals after the Nuremberg trials of 1946. Pierrepoint was troubled by this. In keeping with most other executioners, he was a quiet, inoffensive-looking man, slipping in and out of prisons unnoticed on hanging days, but the execution of SS people, especially the team at Bergen-Belsen turned him into something of a national hero and he was besieged by reporters. Joseph Kramer, the camp commandant, was a huge man but hardly the gorilla 'Beast of Belsen' that the press had called him. Fritz Klein was Belsen's doctor – the first medical man that Pierrepoint had hanged. Eight other men died that day, as did 21-year-old Irma Grese. Carrying a whip at Belsen, she was responsible for about thirty deaths a day. She showed no emotion at all, except a curt command in German – 'Quick, get it over.'

The Nuremberg executions were highly professional and that professionalism continued with the hanging of the serial killer and cad Neville Heath in the same year. 'In January 1953,' Pierrepoint wrote in his autobiography, 'I had to hang Derek Bentley, the nineteen-year-old youth of retarded intelligence ... Bentley was sentenced and the execution was carried out after widespread national protest.'

Recently, people have pointed out that Pierrepoint did not 'have to' hang anybody, but that is naïve to the point of imbecility. If Pierrepoint had not done it, *someone* would have. In fact, in those days, the Home Office received at least a dozen letters a week from people offering their services. When the hangman shook Derek's hand, he was testing his strength. He knew from the prison records that he was 5ft $10^7/_8$ inches (and not the 6ft 4in that I had been led to believe he was when I wrote in 1991). He weighed 173lb.

The original date for the execution was 30 December 1952, only seven weeks after the death of Sidney Miles. Pierrepoint could not make that date, so the next day was decided on. It was moved, after the failed appeal, to 28 January.

Iris's account of the last meeting with Derek is heartbreaking, as was William's memory of it, written years earlier, when the hurt was still raw. That was the only time that Derek broke down, unable to continue the constant chatter to hide his fear any longer. 'Help me,' he said to his dad, 'Help me, please.' At that stage, the debate in the Commons was still to be heard, on the next day, but Iris shook with emotion the whole time she was there, looking at Derek through the mist of the glass partition and her own tears.

On the night before the execution, thousands of angry people crowded into Fairview Road, cheering and applauding outside the

Bentley house at the end of the terrace. There were others, moving in a body along the Thames Embankment. Still more advanced on the Home Office, Downing Street, even Buckingham Palace. The Bentleys were asked to lead a petition to see the queen and a wheelchair was on offer if Mrs Bentley, with her spinal condition, could not walk. We now know that Her late Majesty, the quintessence of constitutional behaviour, would never have gone head to head with the government and the law lords, but at the time she was young and fresh and, like Lilian Bentley, the mother of a boy herself.

Today, we are used to street protests, from anti-Vietnam marches to Extinction Rebellion and Just Stop Oil via Black Lives Matter. None of this was known in 1953 and demonstrations of this type were unheard of. Watching it all, of course, was the Metropolitan Police, one of whose number had been killed in the line of duty. We can presume that none of the officers watching would have any sympathy for this crowd at all. William and Iris Bentley were indeed at the head of the crowd, but they called for calm and order and, because this was 1953, they got it. 'My family and I,' William told them, 'Thank you from the bottom of our hearts. We shall always be grateful to you. But nothing more can be done. My son is now in God's hands.' Others were not so reasonable. There is a note in the Archive relating to a phone call made at 6.50 p.m. on the 27th – 'If Bentley dies tomorrow, the stinking sergeant and three PCs will be for it.' The Post Office was unable to trace the call and we are left wondering who was being threatened. Logically, the sergeant was Stanley Shepherd and the constables were Fairfax, Harrison and McDonald, those who had sworn they had heard, 'Let him have it, Chris.'

The next day, execution day, dawned raw and cold. At Wandsworth, a crowd of over 1,000 stood close to the huge, studded gates. As this crowd grew more restless, a Rolls Royce turned up. This was not one hired by Harry Proctor of the *Pictorial* but one owned by Mrs Violet Van der Elst, one of those eccentrics that only Britain can produce. Her father was a coal porter and her mother a washerwoman but she herself claimed descent from Julius Caesar and Nero (not altogether a good thing, perhaps). She was also a millionairess as head of a beauty treatment industry and spent a fortune on good causes, in particular the abolition of the death penalty. Clement Attlee's government, swept to victory after the war, revolutionized the country with nationalisation and the implementation of a welfare state which became, briefly, the envy of the world. Among other reforms, Attlee and his Home Secretary Chuter Ede, suspended executions and reviewed the whole process. Albert Pierrepoint, as the practitioner at the sharp end, was involved with a parliamentary committee of enquiry. It explains why, for instance, Donald Thomas, who had shot and killed PC Nathaniel Edgar in February 1948, was not hanged but serving time in gaol. Whenever sentence of death was passed by a high court judge, Violet Van der Elst would patrol the London streets in her Rolls, exhorting people via her loudhailer to pressure the government into law reform. She also had an army of men with 'sandwich boards', mingling with crowds at their busiest, like Oxford Street, Trafalgar Square and Piccadilly Circus. Inevitably, one of her most strident opponents was Lord Goddard.

There was trouble even before she arrived at Wandsworth. Scuffles broke out between the crowd and the police and prison warders on duty at the gates. The Met had to draft in more officers to contain the situation. Mrs Van der Elst banged on the prison door. 'This boy is being murdered,' she said and demanded to see the governor.

That governor, W.J. Lawton, was inside at the time with a knot of officials outside Bentley's condemned cell. It was five minutes to nine. With him were C.R. Wigan, the under-sheriff of Surrey; James Murdoch, the prison doctor; the chaplain, the Reverend Ball; two warders and a technician, along with Albert Pierrepoint and his assistant, Harry Allen. With twenty-nine seconds to go, Wigan raised his finger, the traditional sign, and Bentley's door was opened. His arms were pinioned behind his back, the belts designed by the Pierrepoints years before. No one spoke. No one shook hands. There was no quiet, measured conversation envisaged by the scriptwriters of *Let Him Have It*, the movie that lay thirty-eight years in the future. Bentley was not given brandy or anything else to drink. The wall slid sideways with a grating of steel. The execution shed had been feet away from the boy for weeks and he had no idea it was there. Bentley did not cry – his family, clinging to each other at their besieged home in Norbury, would have been proud of him. They placed Bentley's feet on the marks on the two trap doors and the mechanical mantra went through Pierrepoint's brain as it did every time. 'Draw on the white cap, adjust the noose, whip out the safety pin, push the lever, drop.' On the actual job, he would write, 'you're dealing with human flesh. You've got to get it right.'

Allen dropped to one knee, pinioning Bentley's legs in seconds. The chaplain was praying to Pierrepoint's left, the hood over Bentley's head billowing and closing as he fought for breath one last time.

The prison clock chimed for the ninth time, and the body of Derek Bentley, the 'three-quarter-witted boy' hung at the rope's end, creaking on its housings. One of his shoes, without laces in case he had tried to hang himself, had fallen off. The whole process had taken between nine and twelve seconds. No one could have been more proficient than Albert Pierrepoint.

Outside in the street, the shouts of 'Murder' died away. 'Let us be with him in his moment of need,' Violet Van der Elst said. Flat caps and trilbies came off heads among the now silent crowd. Then the reformer led them in a mournful *Abide With Me*, followed by *The Lord is my Shepherd* and *Rock of Ages.*

When a warder appeared moments later to put up the formal execution notice, however, the mood changed again. The crowd smashed the glass of the noticeboard, screaming 'Let's get the murderers!' People threw apple cores and coins at the police cordon.

Iris's version of Derek's end is different. She was not there, of course and we cannot imagine the wave of emotion that ran through the whole family at the time. According to her, Pierrepoint *did* shake

Derek's hand, *did* give him a brandy. He *was* crying and his last words were 'I didn't say it. I didn't tell Chris to shoot that policeman.'

Among the many vitriolic letters that Maxwell-Fyfe was still receiving was a typed anonymous one:

> You murdering bastards. This is the first Nazi murder in England. Your wonderful Duke of Ed. Inherits this from his Nazi uncles. He swore all the time 'Bentley must drop'. Now we swear he must drop. If he lives to see the coronation, he'll be lucky ... Don't think you can escape free. You carried out the orders. You wicked sods. Tell your Duke a short burst awaits him. There's no hurry. But he's got it coming.
>
> From Six Sworn to avenge
> Bentley

The letter was postmarked Enfield, Middlesex, dated 4 February. The DCI looking into it reported (probably accurately) that, 'the wording rather indicates a person who is mentally unbalanced.' Why Prince Philip, the Duke of Edinburgh, should be a target is incomprehensible. As to the 'six' not hurrying, that was to prove prophetic. Prince Philip died peacefully in his bed in 2021, aged 99!

Bentley's body hung for the allotted hour in the execution shed to make sure that life was extinct. Dr Murdoch and Pierrepoint lifted him down. Dr David Haler, who had carried out the post-mortem on Sidney Miles and had testified at the trial, carried out another autopsy in Wandsworth prison mortuary. Bentley's brain was 'perfectly normal' and the cause of death was 'judicial hanging'. It was all just a formality. If Pierrepoint's measurements were correct, Derek's neck would have snapped at the third vertebra and death would have been instantaneous.

'The law is a machine,' wrote William Bentley a year later, 'that grinds out life and death and good and ill. It has no heart.' He went to the prison to collect his son's clothes and was told that they had been burned. That custom was changed five months later. At lunchtime on the day of execution, Derek was buried in a cheap coffin somewhere in the prison grounds, the fate of the hanged for decades.

The day after he died, a letter arrived from Derek. It was in a warder's handwriting and Iris believed that the idea behind writing it came from Harry Proctor, anxious as ever to control the media involvement with the case. It is heartbreaking, with the fond minutiae of a man facing the end after only nineteen years, with thanks to his family and his friends. Dad mustn't go on grinding his teeth. Little Denis had better behave himself. His love for his mother, his sister, his animals and even his battered old bike, Sally, is self-evident. But one paragraph is very telling. 'I'll tell you what, Mum, the truth of this story has got to come out one day and as I said in the visiting box that day, a lot of people are going to get into trouble and I think you know who those people are.'

But nobody ever got into trouble over the death of Derek Bentley and despite victories by activists over the years, the Bentley family are still waiting for real justice.

Chapter 8

The Truth of this Story?

The first book to pinpoint the injustice of the Craig and Bentley case was the MP Reginald Paget's *Hanged – and Innocent?*. Written with fellow crusader Sidney Silverman, it was published by Victor Gollancz, himself a champion of underdogs and good causes, within months of Bentley's execution.

Silverman had pushed the Commons again, after Bentley's death, to have the case debated and again he was fobbed off by the obfuscation of the Speaker and the system.

Paget's book raised five arguments why Maxwell-Fyfe should have granted a reprieve. First, the question of Bentley's age. Eighteen was the threshold and due consideration was given to those close to that age. In the ten executions prior to Bentley's, the average age was 27 years and 2 months. The last time a 19-year-old was hanged was in December 1951 when Herbert Mills was executed for the brutal murder by battery and strangulation of 48-year-old Mabel Tattershaw in Nottingham. There could hardly have been more of a distinction between Bentley and the devious oddball Mills. Albert Pierrepoint had done the honours in this case too.

Paget's next argument raised the issue that the 'leading actor' on the rooftop had been Craig. Nobody disputed this. William Bentley had said that, by comparison with the swaggering gangster-wannabe, his son was 'like water' and all the trial testimony bore this out. If Craig could not face the death sentence, neither should Bentley.

Third was the vexed issue of Bentley's intelligence. Various policemen had commented vaguely on this, but the only medical evidence heard in court referred to the nature of Miles's death, Fairfax's wound and the drugs administered to Craig in hospital. There was nothing about Bentley's IQ, his reading age or his ability to understand what was going on, because Goddard would not allow it. Dr Matheson had said that Bentley was sane, fit to plead and fit to stand trial. We have already read Matheson's summation and it would be difficult to find a more biased and objectionable report. The doctor seems to have been horrified by Bentley's 'marcel-waved' hair and 'very gaudy flower-pattern shirt'. Clearly, along with Goddard, Matheson believed that the country was going to the dogs! He also went so far as to blame William Bentley for Derek's situation. He was a 'poor type – very satisfied with himself, very confident and will not admit that there is anything evil in his son.' Ninety-nine per cent of parents think the same. What we see here is a medical snob appalled by the supposed arrogance of the working class.

Paget's next argument was an historic one. Twice, in 1839 and 1878, parliamentary commissions had looked into cases like Bentley's where death had occurred without malice. Both commissions recommended that the law be rewritten – it had not been.

Finally, the precedent in British law (and *all* British law is based on precedent) is that wherever there was a 'scintilla' of doubt over guilt, a reprieve should take place. Maxwell-Fyfe had ignored all this. That was because Home Secretaries are, first and foremost, politicians. Justice and right routinely take second place to the political mood of the day. And the political mood was to crack down on juvenile delinquency by supporting the police at all costs.

As Paget says in his closing paragraphs:

> Among the questions which the Bentley case forces us to ask are these. Is it right that the prerogative of mercy should rest upon the sole discretion of the Home Secretary – the Minister responsible for the Police Force? Is it right that in this matter

> alone the Minister should be irresponsible either to the Cabinet or to Parliament?
>
> For my part I believe the morale of the police force would be better maintained by some provision for Mrs Miles superior to the miserable pension of £2 16s a week than by the sacrifice of a drooling dim-witted Bentley. His execution was a supreme indecency.

The next book on the scene was William Bentley's *My Son's Execution* (W.H. Allen 1956). John Parris had already approached Iris about a book on the case which was to be ghosted by the journalist Leonard Parkin. Nothing came of it, but W.H. Allen contacted William in September 1955; was he interested? Since the execution, William had been appearing regularly at Speakers' Corner at Hyde Park – in those pre-social media days about the only opening for an ordinary man to make himself heard. Inevitably, his audience was dwindling and William accepted the offer of £125 advance (not a bad sum at the time). The book is a harrowing read, ghosted by a Mr Roberts and it spells out just how much the fates had it in for the Bentley family. In her own book, Iris blames Roberts for the mistakes in her father's book. As I wrote in *Let Him Have It, Chris*, Bentley's book 'should be compulsory reading for anyone with a child growing up in dangerous and hostile world. And for anyone who wants to see a return of the rope.' Today, that figure stands at an estimated 40 per cent of Britain's population.

Parris finally went into print, without Iris, in 1960. *Most of My Murders*, like the Paget/Silverman book, covered other cases from the man's career. By this time, although he made little of it in print, Parris had been disbarred for being an active member of a trading company, then illegal. He had also been temporarily suspended soon after the trial for a careless, defamatory comment against Lord Goddard, which most readers of this book today would find perfectly understandable.

In January 1953, Parris stood as the prospective Socialist candidate for Bradford North. During his speeches, he attacked Goddard who had backed the reintroduction of flogging, via his seat in the House of Lords. 'I cannot say anything,' he said, 'about the manner in which Lord Goddard conducts criminal trials, but I am entitled to say that many of his utterances [in the Lords] are sensational and untrue nonsense, so much so that many of the members of the House regard them with complete contempt.' Parris was actually suspended, by the Bench of Gray's Inn, because he had implied that Goddard's handling of criminal cases was equally contemptible. In the same year, C.G.L DuCann's book, *Miscarriages of Justice* appeared. It dealt with the case in eleven pages, half of which got bogged down in arcane points of law which cannot have much interested a general readership.

The first full-length book on Craig and Bentley was David Yallop's *To Encourage the Others* (1971) which caused a storm. Iris did not like Yallop, for reasons I could never fathom at the time but she explained it in *Let Him Have Justice*. Yallop was a floor manager for television and had written scripts. He had read *My Son's Execution* and visited the Bentleys, gaining access to all the material, newspaper clippings and so on that William and Lilian had collected. These included court papers given to William by John Stevens, Derek's solicitor. Yallop promised the Bentleys money but all they got was a cheque for £100 when the drama-documentary was shown on BBC2. The book was dedicated to the Bentleys – 'Let any who seek a definitive example of courage look no further than these three people.' Presumably, because of his age at the time, Denis was excluded.

In fact, Yallop's book opened a can of worms which at the time the Bentleys did not realize. As with Ludovic Kennedy's *Ten, Rillington Place*, the televised/film version reached a much wider audience than the book ever could. Both Parris and Yallop's books were deeply flawed. In *Most of My Murders*, Parris contended that there was a third boy on the Croydon rooftop. He did not name him in print but told me that he was Frank Fazey. Yet *no one* had seen a third boy on the roof. Fairfax, McDonald, Harrison, Jaggs and Pain, all of them in a position to see the roof area clearly, made no mention of a third boy. Neither did anybody on the ground, one of whom would surely have seen Fazey get off the roof by the only safe(ish) means – down a drainpipe. It is unlikely that Christopher Craig would have kept Fazey's presence a secret and, bearing in mind his limited intelligence, surely Derek Bentley would have let something slip about him.

Yallop's contention, which caused the furore, was that Miles was accidentally killed by a trigger-happy police sniper armed with a rifle on a roof adjoining the Barlow and Parker warehouse. Because the BBC version followed the trial transcript so closely, there was no mention of this (which rather negated its purpose) although extras in police uniforms were seen on adjacent roofs in the shooting recreations. Whereas when I wrote *Let Him Have It, Chris*, nearly forty years after the shooting, I was working blind, denied access to relevant material and putting perhaps too much of my faith in Claude Pain, Yallop had access to the leading players and all credit must be paid to him for doing so. He found and interviewed Christopher Craig, by 1971 a free man living in Clophill, Bedfordshire. The Bentleys wanted Craig's address, but Yallop would not release it. The author spoke to Frederick Fairfax, then retired from the force and living in Yeovil, and to Frank Cassels. Even Lord Goddard agreed to see him. And, because of his television links, Yallop knew how to chase publicity. He arranged what the Bentleys believed was a meeting with the prime minister, Edward Heath. They got no further than the lobby behind the famous black door. Yallop passed a copy of his book to a lackey there and that was it. Harold Wilson, as leader of the Opposition, was more forthcoming. Iris's daughter Maria went along as well and the whole thing had been arranged by a junior shadow minister, Anne Kerr. Wilson was concerned and sympathetic, sitting Maria on his knee. He promised a full enquiry when he got into power. When he did, surprise, surprise, nothing happened.

Iris was in hospital following an operation for bowel cancer when the BBC drama was shown. Alan Clark, the director, had borrowed the Bentleys' furniture and ornaments for realism. The actress Barbara Willmot who played Iris got involved with the family and visited her in hospital. The script made 'Iris' more strait-laced than she really was, something of a 'flibbertigibbet' at 21. The real Iris lent the fake one the clothes she had worn at the trial. Both the actors playing Derek and Christopher Craig called in on the family too; they were both well known to television audiences through the sit-com *Please Sir* starring John Alderton. An awkward moment was avoided when the Bentleys were invited to the studios to see a scene being made. There, too, although they were unaware of it until years later, was Albert Pierrepoint, off set as technical adviser.

Yallop's 'startling new facts' were actually mere hypothesis. In an italicized passage, he wrote, 'The fact is that there was not at any time, either before, during or after the trial, any ballistic evidence to prove that Craig had fired the shot that killed PC Miles.' This statement comes from page 173 of the first edition and is not alluded to again. In his account of the rooftop gunfight, Yallop makes his case – that Miles's death was a result of an accidental shot by the police. Given that Craig was no marksman and that his sawn-off Eley and wrong ammunition made the gun inaccurate, Yallop contends that Craig could not possibly have hit him. Yallop says that at least six police marksmen were in position overlooking the Barlow and Parker roof. Taking the testimony of Fairfax, McDonald and the bullet count, Craig had only fired four times, yet Fairfax claimed there had been nine and McDonald six. Rather like the infamous (and nonsensical) three shots in Dealey Plaza, Dallas eleven years later, shots fired are very much in the ears of the listener and are often at variance with reality. Yallop's claim is that the additional shots were fired by the police. The occupants of Nos 26 and 30, on either side of the warehouse, had said that armed police came through their houses and went into their rear gardens. They were not called to give evidence at the trial. Other than Fairfax's

.32 automatic, there was no information available at the time about firearms issued to the police.

Into the mix in 1971 stepped Philip Lee. He spoke to a reporter from *The People* on 21 November and claimed that he watched the Croydon rooftop shooting via the back bedroom windowsill of a house next to Barlow and Parker's. For this to have had any credibility at all, that is likely to have been No. 30 Tamworth Road. Lee's real name was Huxley and he had already given the police a 'long, rambling' account of what he saw. The two accounts differed considerably, including the vantage points from which he saw police marksmen on adjoining roofs. He claimed to have offered his story (presumably to the defence) at the time of the trial, but there is absolutely no evidence for this.

According to a police report in the Archive, Lee and Yallop had 'exchanged cross words' and Lee's own background was highly suspect. He had a Borstal record and seven previous convictions. Everybody has dismissed Lee as a fantasist.

Yallop interviewed the pathologist Dr David Haler (but not the ballistics expert Lewis Nickolls) who told him that he believed the bullet that killed Miles (which was never found) could have come from a gun that fired anything from .32 to .38 calibre bullets, not from a .455 calibre Eley. So outraged was Haler when he read Yallop's account of the interview that he threatened legal action.

The police enquiry into Yallop's contention says, 'Dr Haler's behaviour over this book seems to have been rather odd.' Haler claimed that he saw Yallop after a great deal of pestering, yet he was happy to give publishers W.H. Allen access to his post-mortem report on Miles and his diaries for that time. His wife even provided a photograph. Haler had agreed with the book's contents without reading it! According to John Parris, however, Haler sued both Yallop and the *Guardian* newspaper and won both times.

In the case of Yallop's interview with Fairfax, the officer was wary of him from the start. He believed that Yallop wanted his help in casting actors for a play and as he had no papers from the time to refresh his memory of twenty years earlier, he could not confirm or deny the details on the roof. He denied telling Yallop anything that deviated from his trial testimony and that there were no other policemen with firearms on any roof that night.

Craig's testimony to Yallop made no sense at all. 'What I've never been able to understand,' he said, 'is how I shot him between the eyes when *he was facing away from me and was going in the opposite direction.*' (Yallop's italics). This made no sense because Miles was supposed to turn *left* out of the door (on Fairfax's instructions) and would have been running in Craig's direction. Why, then, did the killer, twenty years later, claim that the opposite was true? Yallop, like so many others, has confused left and right – and perhaps in 1971, Christopher Craig saw an opportunity, even after all those years, to be cleared of murder.

In the summer of 1972, partly as a result of the uproar caused by Yallop's book, the House of Lords held a debate on the safety of the convictions of Bentley and James Hanratty, executed ten years later for the murder of Michael Gregston. Briefly told, the A6 killing on the appropriately named Dead Man's Hill, was a cause célèbre for years. Gregston and his mistress, Valerie Storie, were canoodling in his car, parked ironically near Christopher Craig's future home at Clophill, when an armed thief told them to drive with him holding a gun in the back. The attacker shot Gregston twice and raped Valerie Storie before putting five bullets in her. Astonishingly, she survived, and eventually, James Hanratty was found guilty and hanged for Gregston's murder. Because another man, Peter Alphon, insisted that *he* was the killer and that Valerie's testimony was full of holes, campaigners urged a review of the case. Since 1972, DNA evidence from Valerie's underwear has confirmed Hanratty's guilt, but the verdict at the time was a dodgy one.

The Lords' debate focused, not on Yallop's theories, but on the conduct of the trial. Lord Goodman was polite about Goddard but admitted it was 'not one of the most creditable performances of a distinguished judge'. I would personally contend that 'distinguished' and 'Goddard' should never appear in the same sentence. Goodman rightly criticized Christmas Humphreys' definition of when the 'joint enterprise' came to an end and Goddard's irrelevant reference to the knuckleduster. As for the Appeal Court, he said, 'How any experienced judge, reading the summing up, could have arrived at the conclusion that there was nothing to criticize in the summing up passes my understanding and I venture to suggest, passes belief.'

As a result of Yallop, the Home Secretary, Reginald Maudling, had set up a secret inquiry, the findings of which are in The National Archive and to which I have alluded above. Lord Arran went for specifics. Why was the inquiry secret and carried out by that most interested of parties, the Metropolitan Police? Why was David Yallop not questioned, nor Christopher Craig nor any member of the Bentley family? What about the statements of Constables Pain, Bugden [Beecher-Brigden] and Alderson? Why wasn't John Parris interviewed? And Frank Cassels? And Professor Denis Hill? What about Bentley's limitations? Why did neither Haler nor Fairfax actually take legal action against Yallop?

'Either Mr Yallop is the biggest rogue unhanged and is guilty not only of deceiving myself ... but of causing me to deceive the High Court of Parliament ... or he is telling the truth, the whole truth and nothing but the truth.' I do not personally believe that either extreme is true of Yallop. In trying to find the truth behind a carefully constructed wall of lies, he took a wrong path, but the Bentleys and all of us, owe him a debt of gratitude for exposing the injustice of the case as far as he could. In the context of the debate, the government's point of view, as closed as ever it had been in the days of Goddard and Maxwell-Fyfe, was that justice had been served and, in police parlance, 'Nothing to see here. Move along, please.' The conclusions of the secret Met report were that 'the "startling new facts" produced by Mr Yallop have no foundation at all.'

Throughout the 1970s and 1980s, Iris Bentley, increasingly supported by Maria, visited schools all over the country, backing plays about Derek and talking to teenagers who had never heard of the case. One long-running show that travelled was *Example*; another was *Lullaby for Mrs Bentley*. In 1982, the folk singer Ralph McTell recorded a song about the case, a tape of which he sent to Iris. I included the lyrics in *Let Him Have It, Chris* and he performed his hit *The Streets of London* at Iris's funeral. McTell's mother had worked in Timothy White's, the chemist shop in Norbury, so the links went way back.

As happens so often in the true crime world, there was a flurry of Craig/Bentley publications as I was writing *Let Him Have it, Chris.* In January 1990, Christopher Berry-Dee and Robin Odell wrote *Dad, Help Me, Please*, the despairing plea to William Bentley from his son shortly before the execution. Odell was a distinguished (this is the correct word this time) true crime writer but Berry-Dee was an ingénu (as of course, was I). He claimed to have seen hitherto unpublished Home Office papers by accident, but these had in fact been in Iris's possession for some time. The book is riddled with errors although the Appendix on the ballistics evidence in the case is the most detailed I have seen. Berry-Dee had contacted Iris in May 1987 to tell her that he was writing a film script on the case and that a production company had put up £2.5 million. Over the years, the family had been constantly plagued by oddballs claiming to have new evidence (I know – I became one two years after Berry-Dee) and they had learned to take everything with a pinch of salt. Iris may have been suspicious, but she contacted the family solicitor, the crusading Benedict Birnberg, just in case there was something in it.

I got to meet Birnberg later – a tall, aristocratic-looking man who had a reputation for lost causes. He spoke for the underdog and was one of the first civil rights lawyers before that sort of thing became fashionable. One of his colleagues was Paul Boateng who went on to become one of the first black MPs in the Commons. A bit of detective work on Birnberg's part established the fact that Berry-Dee's film company, Filmscreen International, was genuine.

Iris did not take easily to people. Perhaps because all her adult life she had been fighting Derek's corner and because nobody really understood, she had become suspicious by nature. She did not like Berry-Dee any more than she liked David Yallop. They fell out at the meeting with Birnberg, Berry-Dee claiming that he did not need permission to make a film about Derek (technically true) and asked Iris to leave. In February 1988 everybody signed a contract. Iris was a consultant, her fee being a donation to the Royal Marsden Hospital which was treating her cancer. That summer, another film company, Vivid Pictures, was in touch intending to make a film based on *My Son's Execution*.

By Christmas of that year, Filmscreen had gone into liquidation and its assets bought up by United Artists. Iris had already signed a 'living persons' release' so she in effect became the property of a huge American corporation. The rest would be movie history.

The following year, a heavyweight entered the contest. Ludovic Kennedy had a reputation par excellence as a journalist who sought the truth. *On My Way to the Club* was an autobiography, but it outlined the many criminal cases that he had investigated. Among these was the appalling miscarriage of justice in the case of Timothy Evans (*Ten, Rillington Place,* 1961), *The Trial of Stephen Ward*, 1964, and the probably wrong conviction of Bruno Haptmann in the Lindbergh baby kidnapping case of 1936 (*The Airman and the Carpenter,* 1985). Kennedy and his wife, the ballerina Moira Shearer, were outraged by Maxwell-Fyfe's decision in 1953 and Kennedy wrote *Murder Story*, a play based on the Bentley case. Despite rave reviews in the West End, the Bentleys did not like it and the run was short. As Kennedy observed, London audiences do not like their consciences being pricked.

I have dealt with those books because two of them (and my own) appear in a Home Office review, locked away in The National Archive until recently. Yallop's *To Encourage the Others* is an updated paperback version of the hardback in my collection. Yallop complained that

Reginald Maudling's review did not take into account everything in the book and Yallop, says the report, 'picks holes in everything'. Aren't we annoying, we true crime writers? The lack of evidence from his three wise monkeys was explained by the fact that PC Alderson's statement had nothing to add. Beecher-Brigden was on the ground at Tamworth Road on the night in question. PC Pain's statement I will discuss later. The Home Office report dismissed Yallop's pleas, re Bentley's epilepsy and backwardness, relying instead on Matheson's dismissive – and, I would say, controversial – decision that he was fit to stand his trial. As to Yallop's contention that armed police went through the adjoining premises, the report dismisses this by claiming that no firearms were issued until Miles was shot and that Christopher Craig did not mention armed officers other than Fairfax. The other points trot out the lame excuse that they were dealt with at the original trial.

Most depressingly of all:

> We have adopted the line that there is no point in our considering criticism of the conduct of the trial, i.e. the manner in which the judge, prosecuting counsel and defence counsel handled the case, nor the conduct of the Court of Appeal, since it would not be appropriate for the Home Secretary to seek to intervene simply because of an opinion that one or more of the parties did not do their job very well.

Could there be a more damning indictment of the system? Lord Goddard did not merely do a bad job at the trial, he actively behaved as prosecuting counsel, breaking every rule in the judicial handbook. A man's life was at stake and Rayner Goddard was, at least in part, responsible for ending it. How stupid and naïve he must have been to tell a colleague later that he never expected that Bentley would actually die?

'Similarly,' the report went on, 'it is fruitless to consider criticism of the Home Secretary [Maxwell-Fyfe] deciding not to recommend a reprieve since the reasons for the exercise of or failure to exercise the Royal Prerogative *are not a subject for public discussion.*' (my italics).

If the life of a British subject and whether the state has the right to take it away is not a subject for the public, then what is? Cliché though it may be, in 1953, David Maxwell-Fyfe worked for the public. He worked for *us.*

Dad Help Me Please was likewise dismissed by the Home Office report, on similar grounds. It was up to the protagonists at the trial etc. Etc. And inadvertently criticizes Parris and Cassels for not challenging the ballistics or producing their own medical practitioner to counter Matheson's damning report on Bentley.

Then, the report comes to *Let Him Have It, Chris* by M.J. Trow …

Chapter 9

Walking on Eggshells

It is an odd experience reading two accounts of the same thing. In essence, this is what historians do all the time; not merely two accounts but several and they try to make sense of it. In this instance, however, things are a little different. One account of the summer of 1990 is Iris Bentley's; the other is mine.

You have already read in the Introduction how I met Claude Pain and my attempts to back up his story through official channels, the channels that were, at the time, completely closed. As part of that, I contacted Iris Bentley. Luckily, despite marriage and divorce, she still kept her maiden name and she was there in the phone book, living in Collier's Wood, West London.

'Around about May 1989,' Iris remembered:

> I had a call from someone called Mei Trow. For a long time, I thought his name was Mike, but it wasn't. He was Welsh and it was short for Meirion. He was writing a book about Derek, he said, and wanted to come and talk to me. He had new evidence. There had been another policeman up on the roof, he said, that nobody knew about. Not only that, but he'd talked to him and this policeman said that Derek had never said the words 'Let him have it.'

Very kindly, Iris did not regard me as 'one of those nutters' who haunt families like the Bentleys. New to true crime writing as I was, I had no idea of the weirdos who are desperate for their fifteen minutes of fame.

This was pre-Internet days and trolls in those days were misshapen little creatures who ate inoffensive animals like the Billy Goats Gruff! I had no idea that David Yallop and, at more or less the same time as me, Christopher Berry-Dee, had already contacted Iris and left her less than enchanted.

Iris remembered that I called to see her and Maria on a perfect June day. Driving up from the Isle of Wight is always a haphazard venture and I'd got there early. I nipped into a local coffee shop and saw Iris (whom I recognized from various newspaper articles) walking past with Maria and shopping bags – our lunch. In *Let Him Have Justice,* Iris records faithfully my explanation of the whole chance meeting with Claude Pain. 'And now, after all these years, like a voice from the grave, someone else. And not just anyone. A policeman. A policeman who was up on the roof. A policeman who had been invisible for nearly forty years.'

I told Iris not to tell anyone at that early stage. I was already aware that an odd conspiracy of silence was going on. In 1988, it was the centenary of Jack the Ripper and, as one of my novels was based on that, I got involved in the whole Ripper circus, of serious researchers mixing with obsessives who call themselves Ripperologists. At a crime symposium, a Ripper expert and I talked about the Craig and Bentley case, and he told me that he had seen the documents I had been looking for. Cryptically, he did not elucidate, but the fact that sealed files were available to some people and not others screamed cover-up.

'Mei was always straight with me,' Iris wrote. 'The idea that David Yallop or Christopher Berry-Dee would take advantage kept me silent as the grave. I hadn't even told Ben [Birnberg] about him or about Claude Pain ... When I promise something, I keep my word. I told Mei Trow I wouldn't tell anyone, and I didn't.'

Iris looked Pain up in Yallop's book and there he was, four mentions in the index. He was one of the three monkeys whose testimony was never heard in court. Berry-Dee's book came out early in 1990, claiming that he too had seen Home Office documents, which Iris had also been trying to get hold of. Yallop, who always regarded the Bentley case as his, threatened to sue Berry-Dee over intellectual theft and misuse of photographs. As Iris pointed out, Yallop's pictures were actually hers anyway.

January was a bad time for Iris and on the 28th, as usual, she went to Wandsworth prison to lay a wreath. There was always a crowd of well wishers and only Iris and a few chosen friends and family could go through the electronic gates which now covered the old Victorian entrance. Thames Television (now defunct) had been in touch days before, wanting to do a story. The presenter was Carole Peters, a vivacious blonde I would meet later, and Iris invited her back to Colliers Wood. They got on like a house on fire and Iris gave her a copy of her father's book. It was Carole's first assignment for Thames.

Iris is under the impression that I contacted Thames with Claude Pain's evidence. I suspect it was the other way around, with that arcane ability that television companies have of tracking people down. I took part in a twenty-minute piece for Thames, the first time I had appeared on television. It was a blisteringly hot day in the summer of 1990 and I remember walking along Tamworth Road in Croydon with Carole discussing the case. Barlow and Parker's warehouse had long gone and an anonymous new housing estate covers the site now. I pointed out (off camera) that the .45 'Eley' revolver they gave me to use was actually a Webley, which did not please the producer/director very much. His name was Roger Corke, who told me that he was famous in the business for the speed and accuracy of reporting – 'One Take Corke' they called him.

In June, Iris met him for the first time and he asked her, 'Iris, how many people have walked through this door and told you that they can get Derek his pardon?'

'Hundreds.'

'Well, I'm afraid we can't promise you that.'

I had interviewed Claude Pain twice, both times at my Isle of Wight home. I recorded his evidence and kept that tape for years. He was honest, straight-talking and upright, despite his eighty years. But he was talking about a different time, when there was open animosity between plainclothesmen of the CID (Fairfax) and the uniformed branch (Pain et al.). He intimated the same thing to Carole Peters, who interviewed him more often than I did. The problem was that Pain had suffered a stroke by then and I did not want to push him further. In fact, I doubted whether anything he said after that could be trusted. If it ever came to a court of law, he would be destroyed by opposing counsel.

None of that deterred Thames Television. Corke and Peters had decided that my *Let Him Have It*, released that summer by Constable, 'hadn't begun to scratch the surface' (Iris's version of what Corke had told her) and the real story was one of fabrication in relation to PC McDonald. What bothered Roger and Carole was what had bothered me too – Claude Pain's story of the rickety old ladder that a local offered him to get to the roof. Thames, on the spot and with far greater resources than I had, could find no one who remembered it.

Inevitably, Carole asked Pain why he hadn't spoken up earlier. He had sat at Craig's bedside in hospital; he had helped wheel him in to Croydon Magistrates' Court. He had had years to open up to the media. 'Reasons,' he had told Carole, tapping the side of his nose. 'You don't want to get involved.' This was after the stroke and Carole wondered how accurate Pain could be as a result. She showed him a plan of the Croydon rooftop and he pointed out where he reached the roof and where he had sheltered.

'Then you would have seen Derek and DC Fairfax and PC McDonald,' she said.

'I didn't see them,' he said three times in answer to her questions. That was what he had told me too. Roger and Carole, according to Iris, played 'good cop, bad cop', trying to get the truth out of the old man. He would not be moved. With their background as newspaper journalists, Roger and Carole enlisted the help of the *Croydon Advertiser*, asking for help in the making of a documentary. Iris and Maria turned detectives too, looking up electoral rolls and knocking on doors. But forty years is a long time and the Croydon of 1990–1 was unrecognizable in terms of buildings and inhabitants. When I had visited Tamworth Road in 1989, I could only count two terraced houses that would have been there in 1952. Where John Ware's house stood opposite Barlow and Parker's was a car park.

But Thames came up trumps. They found three independent civilian witnesses who *should* of course have been interviewed by the police in 1952, who *should*, had they had the time and resources, have been interviewed by John Parris and Frank Cassels and made to appear in court. After forty years, some kind of justice and common sense appeared to be on the scene. John Tennant, who I met and interviewed as a result of the television programme, was a calm, mild-mannered man, with perfect recall of that November night. His testimony was vital, because he was the occupant of No. 31, the house next but one to the warehouse alongside the alley via which Craig, Bentley, Fairfax and, according to him, McDonald, got to the roof. Another witness was Douglas Barlow, whose father owned the premises. As one of the keyholders, he had been called on to open up by the police. His colleague, another keyholder, was Dennis Woodcock. Thames did not tell any of them the direction that the programme would take and, astonishingly, none of them had read any of the books on the case. They drew plans of exactly where they were on the night in question. The vital evidence of all three will be examined later.

Roger Corke interviewed John Parris too, the last legal man standing from the original trial. I was there too and arrived ahead of Roger. We spent an amiable hour or so, but Parris was clearly more comfortable with Roger (who has a law degree) and regarded me as something of an ingénu (which, of course, I was). His opulent house, his furniture, his extensive library, it all oozed Establishment and did not fit with the Northern 'honest lawyer' who had been dragooned into defending Christopher Craig forty years earlier.

As a result of the Thames Television programme, events moved on apace. While my wife and I spent an uncomfortable summer walking on eggshells, concerned that Constable Harrison or anyone would sue me and Claude Pain for defamation, I had a phone call from Superintendent Graham Seaby of Scotland Yard. He told me that he intended to interview Pain and asked if I knew of anyone who could be present because it was 'likely to be an uncomfortable interview'. I only knew of Ray Pain, Claude's son and by this time had lost touch with him.

On 20 December 1991, according to papers that I saw in The National Archive in December 2023, Seaby wrote up a report of an interview with Pain at his home on 22 November:

> He is a very friendly old man with treasured memories of his police career and a loyalty to the Service that still persists. He did not appear to be as badly affected by his stroke as the papers from Thames Television suggest. He was quite clear in making points and did not unduly ramble. He gave the impression of being utterly convinced that what he said he knew to be the truth.

Three days later, Seaby spoke by phone to Dennis Woodcock, who was as 'frosty' as Pain was friendly. He did not want to criticize the police and 'gave the impression of being a rather pompous individual with little sense of humour and a rather stern attitude to life'. He told Seaby that he denied his testimony to Thames Television and that he found Roger Corke and Carole Peters 'bossy and opinionated with a tendency to forming their own viewpoint'. Seaby believed that Woodcock was unhappy with the police version of events on the night in question but would not say so 'officially'.

What transpired from Thames Television's interview with Woodcock is that he and Frederick Fairfax were, years after the Croydon shooting, members of the same Masonic Lodge. Fairfax told Superintendent Seaby, following up on all this in 1991, that he was not a friend of Woodcock – in fact he called him a 'pompous oaf' – and he categorically denied that he had ever told Woodcock of a police conspiracy to frame Bentley. Woodcock said the same (minus the 'pompous oaf' quotation!) In a statement to Seaby – 'The comment [from Thames Television] that officers came to the warehouse "to rehearse their stories" is complete rubbish.'

Woodcock was clearly rattled by Thames Television. In a written statement now in the Archive, he wrote:

> During hours of questioning by Thames TV and in the process of concocting their story, they speculated widely and inventively on the background, putting forward innumerable suppositions and theories, mostly with sinister imputations quite novel to me – and ultimately, I began to feel with the purpose to inveigle me into fabrications rather than realities.

On 16 December (Seaby was a very busy man!), he interviewed Roger and Carole in Victoria. 'Both are forceful personalities and Peters is an aggressive talker' (which is not how I remember her at all!). Woodcock's comments were made off camera and they had no taped record of what he said. The implication was that it all came out after the interview and that 'generous portions of scotch whisky, supplied by Woodcock, were being drunk'.

The first of two programmes by Thames was broadcast on 11 September and all relevant evidence was sent to David Waddington, the Home Secretary. In the official Home Office report concerning the programme, I apparently wrote a letter (of which I have no memory) to the Home Office explaining that discrepancies between Claude Pain's account to me and subsequent ones to Thames 'stem from assumptions made' by me and not any actual discrepancy from Pain himself. I can only assume that I was trying to make sense of what was happening, especially as Pain's later interview diverged ever further from official police accounts. For example, at one point he claimed that Norman Harrison had not travelled with him, Fairfax and Beecher-Brigden to Tamworth Road as Harrison had testified, but that he got there on his bike! I can see no possible reason for Harrison to lie about how he arrived; neither is it likely he forgot his mode of transport.

That month, Christopher Craig surfaced again. He had spoken to David Yallop eighteen years earlier and was now complaining to the Home Secretary that he and his wife's lives had been made a misery by the media. Unlikely to respond well to a police interview, an arrangement was made for Craig to talk to Home Office officials. He declined, but did take part in a second Thames Television programme in September 1991. Craig came across as honest, relaxed and a pillar of society, but his evidence strapped to a polygraph machine took us no further than 1972, when Yallop talked to him or indeed 1952 with his trial testimony. Bentley was sent across the rooftop by police to talk him (Craig) down, although Bentley did not make this claim at the trial. And Bentley did not say, 'Let him have it, Chris.' Since polygraph tests are notoriously unreliable, they are not allowed in British courts and the Home Office was very sniffy about them.

This second programme also looked at the veracity of Bentley's statements to the police. Thames Television had found two linguistic experts to examine it. Dr Coulthard was a linguistics professor at Birmingham University who had helped evaluate the unsafe prosecution of the Birmingham Six 'terrorists', and the Reverend Morton had undertaken textual analysis in a number of cases. The Forensic Science Service did not, the Home Office report says, regard him highly.

Coulthard's conclusion was that Bentley's words were not recorded verbatim without questions being put to him. Morton believed that as many as four people may have contributed to it; none of it is pure Bentley. The Home Office report concedes that this is likely – in fact, it was hinted at in the trial itself. It was nevertheless possible that the police fabricated the statement, including the damning evidence that he knew Craig had a gun from the outset and was prepared to use it. Astonishingly, the Home Office report says, 'The possibility that parts of Bentley's statement were fabricated would not in itself constitute grounds for a free pardon.' But as John Parris told Thames Television, conviction can only happen if there is no reasonable doubt. As Iris put it, 'The fact that [the police] were lying at all, about anything, meant that all the rest of the evidence had to be taken with a huge pinch of salt.'

The second television programme produced John Tennant who told his viewers that while he watched the action from the garden of No. 31, an officer standing with him was James McDonald. He was not struggling up a drainpipe as he had said in court and no one was helping him. Claude Pain had made a similar observation. The Home Office found this identification unlikely, since there were many policemen at the scene and Tennant had only seen a photograph of the four medal recipients. This seems to be a particularly weak argument.

Carole Peters, still new to the television game, was apprehensive to say the least about interviewing Craig for that second programme. Her hands were bruised where her nails had dug into her palms. Craig admitted on camera that he had burst into tears at Wormwood Scrubs when his cell door slammed shut at 9 o'clock on the morning of Bentley's execution. As Carole wrote:

> Here was someone who at the age of sixteen had committed a terrible crime and knew he had committed a terrible crime and yet saw an even worse crime being committed in front of him and knew he could do nothing about it ... There was this incredible sadness and resignation and incredible venom. At the policemen who'd lied.

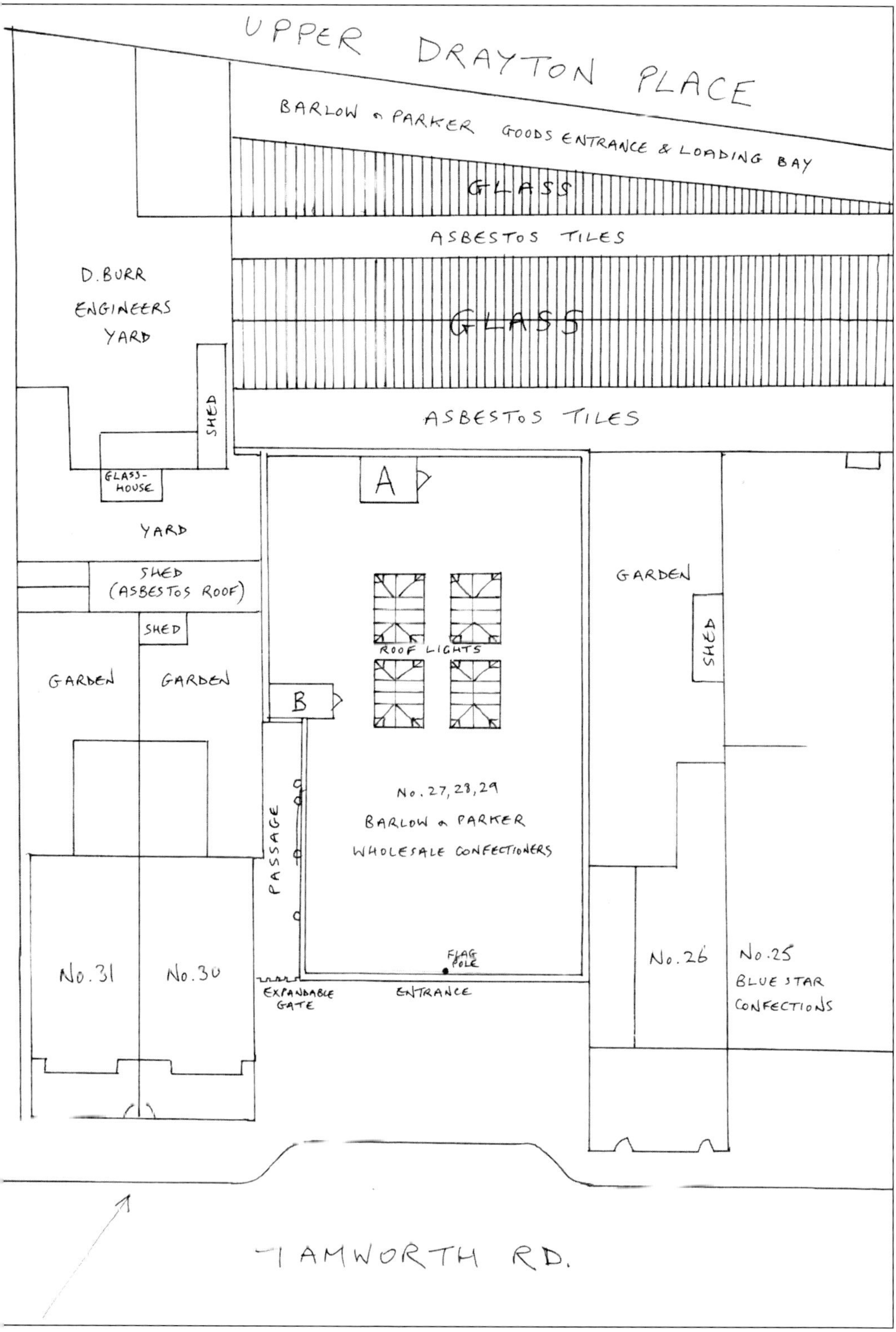

The rooftop plan of Barlow and Parker's warehouse, Croydon, as produced in court by PC Bernard Beard. (*Redrafted by author*)

Above left: Derek Bentley, the 'three-quarter witted boy' who went to Croydon 'just for a ride'.

Above right: Christopher Craig, the 16-year-old swimmer and gangster wannabe was a bad influence on people like Bentley.

Left: The 'man with a ton of guts'. PC Sidney Miles was shot dead by Christopher Craig on the Barlow and Parker roof.

Above left: The Lord Chief Justice, Rayner Goddard, was a dinosaur who wanted to retain hanging, bring back the birch and defend the police at all costs.

Above right: Christmas Humphreys QC was the lead counsel for the prosecution in the Craig and Bentley trial. He became a judge and a Buddhist.

Scene of the crime. The premises of Barlow and Parker in Tamworth Road, Croydon as it was in 1952. Craig, Bentley and several police officers reached the roof by climbing up drainpipes to the left of the building. (*Alamy*)

Above left: *Scapegoat*, the book by John Parris who defended Craig, was rushed into publication in 1991 in a wave of interest in the Craig and Bentley case. It is riddled with errors.

Above right: 'The man who rations mercy', David Maxwell Fyfe was the Home Secretary who could have spared Derek Bentley's life and chose not to.

Albert Pierrepoint, the landlord of the Poor Struggler pub, was also Britain's public executioner. It took him an estimated 15 seconds to hang Derek Bentley.

William and Iris Bentley with just some of the letters supporting Derek's cause. Iris spent the rest of her life trying to clear her brother's name.

The 'conspicuously brave' officers were given medals for facing Christopher Craig's bullets. Two of them 'swore away the life of Derek Bentley'.

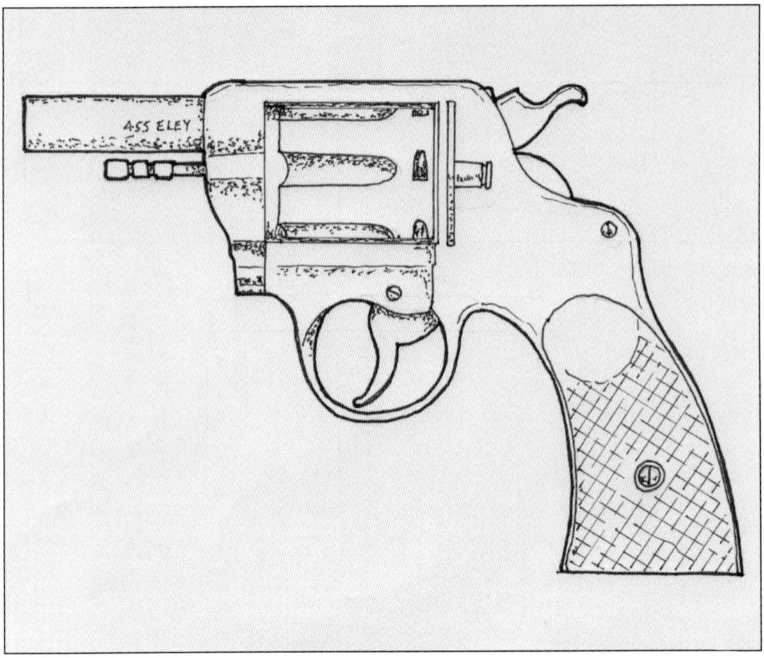

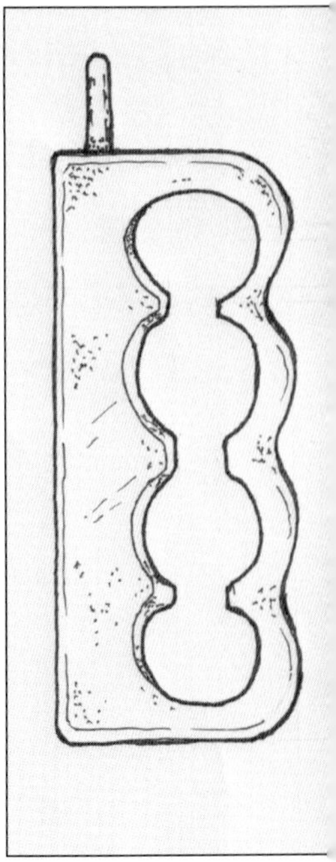

Above left: Christopher Craig's .455 Eley revolver. He had sawn off the barrel so that it fitted more neatly into his pocket.

Above right: The knuckleduster made by Christopher Craig and carried by Derek Bentley. Lord Goddard called it 'a horrible weapon' but it played no part in the case at all.

A crowd gathers on the morning of 28 January 1953 outside Wandsworth Prison on the day of Bentley's execution. Even though the death penalty was abolished in 1965, the mechanism inside the prison was still in place in 1991 in case parliament changed its mind.

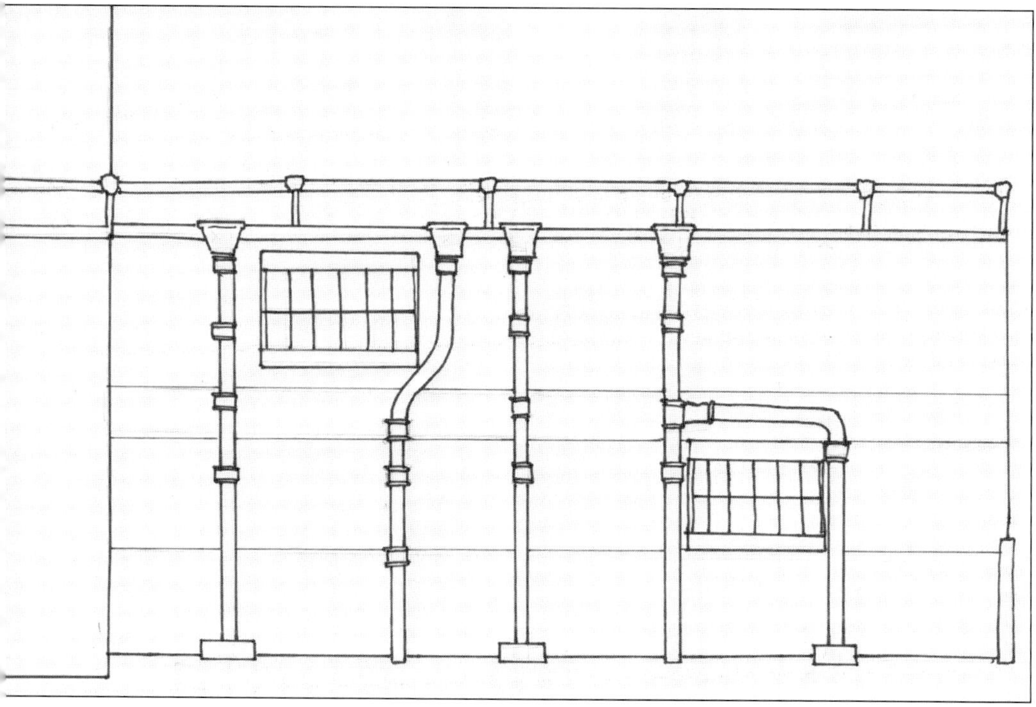

Above: The west façade of the Barlow and Parker warehouse, taken from the alley that ran alongside it. Craig, Bentley and several police officers climbed the gate shown on the extreme right and reached the roof via the drainpipes. The staircase head is shown in the top left-hand corner.

Below: The rooftop of the Barlow and Parker warehouse, from the Tamworth Road frontage. This was the view that Claude Pain told me he saw on the night of the shooting. The staircase head is on the left, with the roof lights on the right and the lift shaft ('the stack') behind them. Beyond that is the sloping asbestos and glass roof along which Norman Harrison crawled.

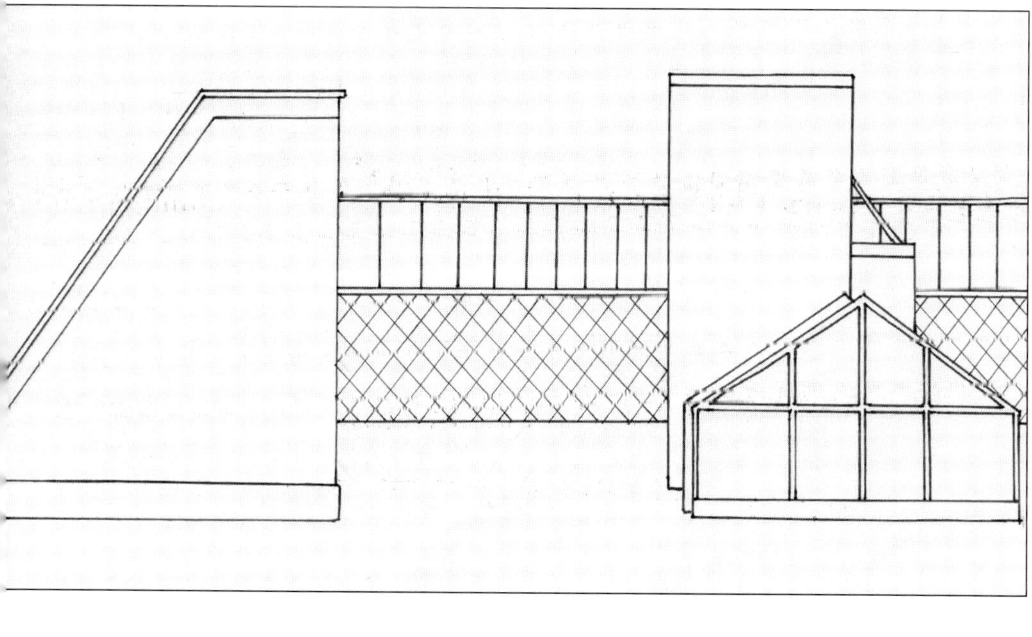

Above left: Derek Bentley under arrest and on his way to Brixton Prison. Note the damage to his right eye – was this caused in the rooftop clash with Fairfax or the beating given to him during police interrogation?

Above right: The dustjacket of my *Lett Him Have It, Chris,* written in 1990 contained all the facts I was able to obtain at the time.

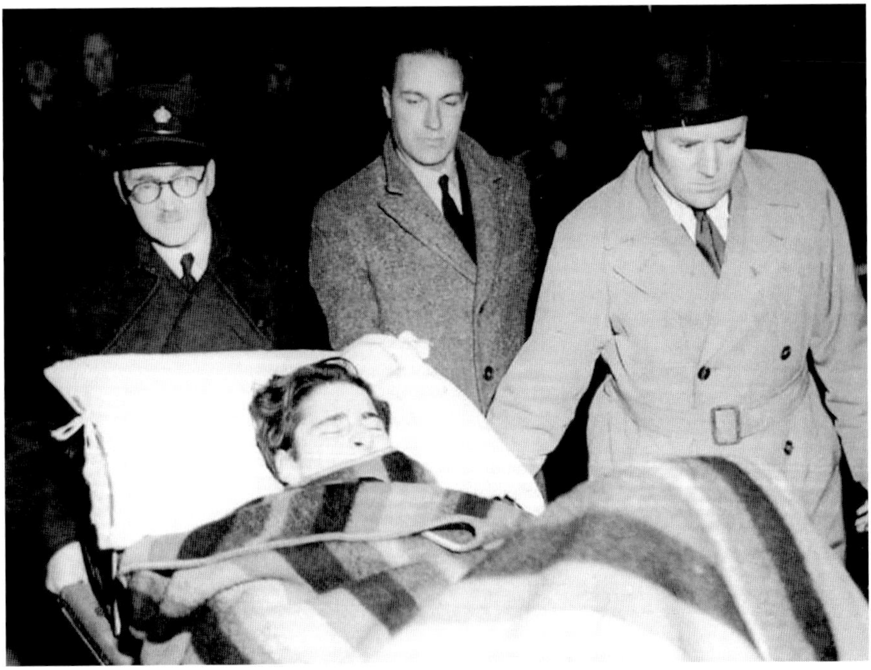

PC Claude Pain (centre) helps wheel the injured Christopher Craig into Croydon Magistrate's Court.

Carole asked Craig why he had taken so long to come forward. Actually, of course, he already had, in talking to David Yallop, but Yallop's insistence over the police shooting had somehow detracted from all that. 'Because I have to,' Craig told her. 'I saw three officers swear a man's life away. As sure as I killed PC Miles, they killed Derek Bentley.' There were five hours of film, but only fifteen minutes were used. Iris barely recognized the balding, bearded middle-aged man in the broadcast. The last time she had seen him was in the Old Bailey, sitting in a wheelchair alongside Derek.

Roger Corke was outside the room where the polygraph test was being carried out. He was so tense he took up smoking again, even though he had given it up long before. Carole Peters was chain-drinking coffee. The tests were done twice, once *in* camera and once *on* camera. 'Mr Craig,' said the expert administering the test, 'you have answered all the questions truthfully. And the machine doesn't lie.'

While the second programme was in production, a movie, *Let Him Have It*, was in production too. I went with my agent to see Robert Warr, the producer, to tell him about Pain and the new evidence. Roger and Carole had been to see him too, although neither of us knew this. I did not expect miracles. Warr shrugged and said he had a human-interest story enough, there was no need for more. Considering the time and money already invested by Vivid Productions, I was not surprised. Many people believe that because my book and the film had virtually the same title, that the movie was based on the book or that I was technical adviser. Neither is true, although I did attend various showings of the movie around the country to discuss the case with the audience.

Iris was 'special consultant' for the film, which was directed by Peter Medak after the original director, Alex Cox, resigned because he wanted to film exclusively in black and white. Shooting began in November 1990 and Vivid was faced with the same problems that any writer on Craig and Bentley has to face; the Croydon of 1952 has gone.

For the purposes of the film, Sidney Miles's funeral takes place in Liverpool, Croydon is nearby Wallasey and Fairview Road, where the Bentleys lived, is Reading! The scene of the crime, Barlow and Parker's warehouse, was actually that of George Payne and Co in Beddington, Surrey (although Iris remembers it as Perivale in West London). The rest was internal studio shooting.

Iris and Christopher Ecclestone, playing Derek, became very close. Ecclestone was 25 and immersed himself into the part, even talking with doctors about the effect that epilepsy has on individuals. All the more disappointing than that he was quoted later as saying that the film was 'liberal crap' and that he was 'crap in it'. I met the co-writers, Neal Purvis and Robert Warde, whom Iris called 'Pinky and Perky'. They were charming and enthusiastic but far too young (in their mid-twenties) to get the *sound* of the 1950s. One line that jarred for me was Craig's question to Bentley before the shoot-out – 'Are you keeping a low profile, Derek?' Pure 1990s. Ecclestone and Medak disagreed over Bentley's character and the script made him seem too streetwise and able to cope. This was not, of course, how Iris remembered him and, not for the first or last time, the advice of a technical consultant was ignored because of other considerations.

The rooftop scene was filmed in winter and the wind was a major problem. Filming was erratic because of passing traffic on the road below. Iris, who had seen so many films at the Streatham Astoria had no idea how complicated actual filming was. She remembered the standoffish attitude of Paul Reynolds playing Craig. His performance, like Ecclestone's, was excellent, but he kept away from Iris until she pinned him down in a bar. He felt she would hate him for who he was playing, but she told him that wasn't the case and they became friends over a brandy. Derek's 'Marcel wave' was natural, but Ecclestone had to have it done by a hairdresser – another example of fakery that annoyed Iris. She had little to do with Clare Holman (now better known for

Lewis and other television series) but they did talk and she felt that Clare had caught her 1952 'bounce' very well.

For my part, I was not impressed by Tom Bell's DC Fairfax. He had been given a moustache for reasons I could not fathom and was too snide for the real man. Michael Sheard in the Yallop/BBC2 version was far more accurate. It was a touch of genius, however, to cast Michael Gough as Lord Goddard. The villain in umpteen movies (he had murdered the princes in the Tower, for instance in Olivier's *Richard III* in 1955) he oozed malevolence from the Bench (and of course, all his dialogue came from the trial transcript).

The only media contact I had, apart from appearances on radio and television chat shows, was with David Bromley, of the Wakefield-based Telling Tales Theatre Company. His *Blue Murder* was a harrowing one-man show seen entirely from Bentley's viewpoint and based on William's *My Son's Execution*. It was a monologue with music and it broke Iris's heart. Bromley attended the Edinburgh Festival opening of *Let Him Have It* and in the question and answer session that followed ripped into Peter Medak for the errors in the film.

What irked him, Iris and me about *Let Him Have It* was a completely invented scene in the courtroom where counsel are arguing over the meaning of 'Let him have it'. Cassel's defence on Bentley's behalf was that he never said it, so there was never any such discussion.

As David Bromley had told Iris, *Let Him Have It* was building on popular mythology. 'Mythology's no good when it comes to getting a free pardon.' I would once have agreed with that, but while I was writing this book, a four-part drama was produced by ITV on the injustice done to innumerable sub-postmasters around the country. Called *Mr Bates vs the Post Office*, it starred Toby Jones and was a huge success. In the wake of it, after far too many years, the government is at last taking action to right those wrongs. *Let Him Have It*, however, did not have the same effect and is not listed in the Home Office report on representations requesting a pardon or even an enquiry into the Bentley case.

The media hoo-ha was even greater in 1990–1 than it had been for David Yallop's researches twenty years before. Director Peter Medak waltzed Iris off to New York and Los Angeles where she gave interviews without number. Perhaps because of all this, John Parris rushed into print with *Scapegoat* (Duckworth 1991). 'Rushed' is the operative word because, sadly, the book is riddled with errors. At one point, Z Division becomes J Division, Carole Peters is routinely referred to as Carole Priest, Dennis Woodcock is Widcock. As an insider, however, Parris's book was useful. He told me at our meeting – and reiterates it in *Scapegoat* – that after the shooting, DCI Smith convened a meeting of all those on the rooftop and they agreed what the line taken should be. He knew this at the time because an unnamed informant had told him, but without that testimony, he could prove none of it. The Home Office merely stated Parris's case and made no comment on it.

In January 1992, pressure from the media forced Kenneth Baker, the Home Secretary, to act. All correspondence to the Bentleys went through a junior minister, Chris Patten. I was in London, having been contacted by the papers and in those days, before mobile phones or the Internet, I had to liaise with Fleet Street via call boxes. Time, for the media, was of the essence and I had to give my response to Baker's decision in both ways, one in jubilation that he had granted a pardon and the other in gloom because he had rejected it. Luckily, the old 'am-dram' training kicked in and I did both.

The dithering, the walking on eggshells, went on until August. By that time, Ben Birnberg, acting for Iris, had submitted a dossier on the case to the Home Office which included the Reverend Morton's analysis of Bentley's statement to the police and Claude Pain's version of events. Birnberg had, however, opted not for any new evidence but a rehash of old ground, which was probably a mistake. As a lawyer, he knew perfectly well that British law was based on precedent and in this case, the precedent was anti-Bentley. He pointed out that the notion of constructive murder and joint enterprise were wholly artificial and contrary to common sense, as Yallop and I had both said in our respective books and which the Lords had debated in 1972. He also highlighted Goddard's outrageously biased handling of the trial and the fact that the 'conspicuously brave' policemen were handed medals six days before Bentley's appeal, to a great fanfare in the press. No attempt had been made, at the trial or the Court of Appeal or to the Home Secretary, to establish Bentley's severe limitations. Matheson's 'inaccurate and prejudicial' report was cited too. None of this cut any ice with the Home Office; they had heard it all before.

On 1 October 1992, Roger Corke rang Iris. It was early in the morning and Radio 4 had broadcast that Kenneth Clarke, now Home Secretary, was about to announce a decision. The usual press mob descended on the Bentleys and Iris was whisked to central London to wait for the verdict. Ironically, she had clashed with Ken Clarke before, long before he became a 'great beast' of the Conservative Party. She had championed the cause of underpaid nurses at a time when he was running the NHS and knew that he was, in her words, 'so pompous and full of himself'. The appeal had failed.

The rejection filled the papers the next day, forcing everything else off the front page. 'Kenneth Clarke,' Iris wrote in *Let Him Have Justice*, 'Maxwell-Fyfe. Spot the difference.' The whole decision was political, just as it had been in 1953. A police spokesman told the *Daily Mail*, 'We believe the conviction of Bentley was correct and we are pleased that Mr Clarke has rejected the totally unfounded allegations that police gave false evidence at the trial.'

John Parris was seething and pushed Ben Birnberg to demand a judicial review. Kenneth Clarke's sixteen-page explanation as to why he had turned the appeal down included the opinion that Maxwell-Fyfe's decision had been wrong; yet here was Clarke doing exactly the same thing. Déjà vu all over again! Without money and even with the celebrated QC David (now Lord) Pannick working pro bono for Iris, nothing was likely to come of a judicial review. But at least Iris was able to see the classified documents that all of us had been denied for so long. Or, at least, some of them. Iris had been told, as we all had, that papers were sealed in capital cases for seventy-five years. In the White Paper on Open Government in July 1993, the seventy-five years had vanished and 'sensitivity' had taken their place.

The documents released to Iris included a letter from Lord Goddard to Maxwell-Fyfe. It contained the same contentious tripe he had come out with at the trial – '[Bentley] was armed with a knuckleduster of the most formidable type that I have ever seen [irrelevant to the case] and also with a sharp pointed knife [equally irrelevant] and he called out to Craig when he was arrested to start shooting [denied by both Bentley and Craig and their respective counsels].' One has to wonder what planet Goddard inhabited. Had he never seen the knuckledusters made and used by British troops in both world wars? I have and I have handled Bentley's – there is no comparison. Among the papers too were a number of letters, from Philip Allen, Permanent Under Secretary, at the Home Office and Frank Newsam, his boss and Maxwell-Fyfe's chief adviser, recommending leniency. Maxwell-Fyfe was not listening. At the bottom of all this correspondence are the initialled words 'Let the law take its course.'

We have to remember Harold Macmillan's decision on Maxwell-Fyfe that he was 'stupid' and look no further than that for his reasoning. It was clear that the Home Secretary was pandering to popular demand (even though by January 1953, that demand had swung in favour of Bentley).

But there is more to it. Ann Clark (later Kerr) was a supporter of Violet Van der Elst and she, along with Desmond Donnelly, Labour MP for Milford Haven, Barbara Castle, a possible future Labour leader, and John Parris went to see Maxwell-Fyfe virtually on the eve of Bentley's execution. He assured the 'gang of four' that he had not intervened to disallow the debate on the issue by parliament and, insisting he not be quoted, explained why Bentley had to die. Firstly, he knew that Goddard and the entire judiciary would demand his head if he gave in. Goddard had told him, both verbally and in writing, that Bentley should hang, irrespective of the jury's recommendation to mercy.

Secondly, Maxwell-Fyfe believed that the whole of the Cabinet, including Prime Minister Winston Churchill would be 'at his throat' (Parris). Thirdly, he would have 'a near insurrection of the police force on his hands'. Maxwell-Fyfe admitted as much in his later autobiography. We shall look at the role of the police in a later chapter. The escaping of the death penalty of Donald Thomas for the murder of PC Nathaniel Edgar in 1948 had led to a similar outcry – 'There is little doubt that the decision of the House of Commons is being received with grave apprehension by members of the Police Service,' said the *Police Chronicle*. Maxwell-Fyfe's last argument was that if Bentley did not die, feral gangs of teenagers would go on to kill policemen with impunity. The Home Secretary ended the meeting, ignoring Barbara Castle's eloquence with '[Bentley] is a young man that society can well do without.'

Kenneth Clarke's assurance that every available witness had been consulted in his decision was just so much baloney. And by now, Claude Pain was dead. So was Thames Television, but the company had been bought up by Carlton, and Roger Corke and Carole Peters persuaded them to make another documentary. Carole was working for the BBC in Suffolk at the time, but lent a hand nevertheless. *The Case That Won't Die* aired on 10 February 1993. The Home Office had not interviewed Christopher Craig, nor Dennis Woodcock, nor the Tennants, nor Dr Coulthard. Exactly who they *had* interviewed remains a mystery because there is nothing about this in The National Archive or indeed on the Internet. Tony Blair, then shadow Home Secretary, took part in the programme; Ken Clarke and the Home Office did not.

This time, a judicial review was granted, after months of complex legal wrangling. David Pannick and Ben Birnberg had moved mountains, but it was still a long way from a pardon.

Iris was at the hairdressers when Birnberg rang her with the news and he read the queen's letter over the phone. 'Now know ye that we, in consideration of some circumstances humbly represented unto us, are graciously pleased to extend our grace and mercy and to grant the said Derek William Bentley our pardon in respect of the said sentence.'

This, despite the wording, was not a complete pardon. Derek was still guilty in the eyes of the law and that was not enough for Iris or her army of supporters. In November of that year, Iris, Ludovic Kennedy and Anthony Scrivener QC spoke at the Cambridge Union to the Motion 'That this house has no confidence in British justice'. Against them was Barbara Mills QC, Director of Public Prosecutions (the forerunner of the Crown Prosecution Service) and Lord Woolf from the High Court. Iris, Kennedy and Scrivener lost.

It was in 1992 that I had the first inkling of the Metropolitan Police's attitude to my book. *The Scotland Yard Files* by Paul Begg and Keith Skinner was published by Headline and covered 150 years of the CID. Both men were experienced researchers, with excellent books on, among other criminals, Jack the Ripper. I got to know them both in the years ahead and regard them as friends for whom I have the highest regard.

Knowing the police attitude from my visit to Scotland Yard's Black Museum and the line taken by Bill Waddell, its curator, I was half expecting the excoriation on page 225:

> Trow suggests that PCs Fairfax, Harrison and McDonald invented 'evidence' to ensure that Craig and Bentley were found guilty; that PC Pain made a written statement which contradicted the Fairfax, Harrison and McDonald story and that this was suppressed; and that the Metropolitan Police are still operating a cover-up.

Given the stonewalling that I outlined in Chapter 1, my conclusion was hardly surprising.

> [Trow] has also cynically suggested that when the Craig and Bentley case papers are opened to public inspection the deposition by PC Pain will be missing. Trow's cynical views of the police force actually puts him and PC Pain in an 'every which way win' situation whatever the files are found to contain when they are opened.

Two paragraphs follow explaining why case papers are not made available, none of which pertain to the Bentley case. 'There is no evidence we know of to support Pain's claim that he was on the roof at any time. As far as is known he was on the ground throughout.'

The other point that Begg and Skinner make is my lack of reference to Bentley being sent by Fairfax to persuade Craig to surrender. It was not raised in court and Pain did not mention it to me either.

Seven years later, Keith Skinner wrote *The Official Encyclopaedia of Scotland Yard* (Virgin, 1999) with Martin Fido, another Ripper expert for whom I had the highest admiration. This time, Claude Pain got an entry all to himself. His career is outlined (even though I was not given any such details by the authorities) as follows. He was born in 1908 and worked as a cable jointer before joining the Met in 1929. Posted to J Division (Bethnal Green) he was transferred to H Division (Whitechapel) in 1933 and Z Division (Croydon) three years later. He earned three commendations for good work on theft cases. Skinner and Fido claim that Pain was a dog handler, but I remember Claude telling me that he took this role on later in his last two years with the force.

The authors acknowledge that I was refused access to the MEPO files now in The National Archive and mention that I believe, because Claude assured me that this would be the case, that his original deposition might well be found to be missing. As we shall see, it is.

> In fact [say Fido and Skinner] the deposition is still on file [see Chapter 13] and it shows that Pain reported at the time that he had been on the road at ground level throughout the incident, in

> no position to hear what was or was not said on the rooftop. It is not known how his later misrecollections came about.

It is this 'misrecollection' which is, in a way, the whole point of this book.

On 30 July 1998, the 'walking on eggshells' was finally over with the decision by Mr Justice Bingham in the High Court in the Strand. Iris had died by this time, unable to see complete justice for her brother. Maria was there and so was I. I met Denis Bentley, far removed now from the diffident 9-year-old with curly hair he had been at the time of the case. The courtroom was crowded with Bentley supporters and a bewildering army of wigs and gowns. The court had told Maria the outcome the night before, but she had been sworn to secrecy and the rest of us had no clue how it would go. The Lord Chief Justice, Lord Bingham, Lord Justice Kennedy and Mr Justice Collins sat on the raised dais under the royal coat of arms. We all stood up and bowed appropriately and the decision was made.

The speech – and the written summary – were very lengthy and will be discussed in detail in the next chapter, but the verdict, which was music to the ears of every Bentley supporter and advocate of justice and fair play said:

> Since the trial judge [Goddard] in his summing up failed to direct the jury on the standard and burden of proof, to give sufficient direction on the law of joint enterprise or adequately to summarise the defence case, made prejudicial comments about the defendants and their defences and indicated that the police officers' evidence, because of their bravery on the night in question was more worthy of belief than that of the defendants, Bentley was denied the fair trial to which he was entitled and his conviction was in consequence unsafe.

Derek had already received a royal pardon in 1993; now the murder charge was quashed. On the bench in front of me, I heard a junior counsel murmur to his colleague, 'We've shafted Goddard at last!'

Christopher Craig's official statement on the back of all this is as follows:

> Today, after forty-six years, the conviction of Derek Bentley has been quashed and his name cleared. While I am grateful and relieved about this, I am saddened that it has taken those forty-six years for the authorities in this country to admit the truth.
>
> I am truly sorry that my actions on 2 November 1952 caused so much pain and misery for the family of PC Miles who died that night doing his duty.
>
> Also, for the Bentley family, I regret that Iris, Derek's sister, who fought all those years for Derek's pardon, died recently before this appeal was concluded.
>
> Finally, I apologize to my family, who have had to endure Press attention over the years. At the end of the day, the lawyers decided that it was not necessary for me to give evidence at the appeal hearing but I was ready and willing to do so in the interests of justice.
>
> A day does not go by when I don't think about Derek and now his innocence has been proved with this judgement. Now, at last, the case is over. My gratitude goes to those who have fought so tirelessly for justice.

It was all over. Well, not quite …

Chapter 10

The Ass That is the Law

In 2002, that indefatigable fighter for British justice, Ludovic Kennedy, went into print with *Thirty-Six Murders and Two Immoral Earnings*. He had written the introduction to my *Let Him Have It, Chris* over ten years earlier, but my only direct contact with him was over the phone at that time, to thank him for his input.

In the prologue to his book, Kennedy writes of himself as a teenager that:

> I never doubted for a moment … either the integrity of those taking part [in criminal trials] or the correctness of the verdict. That policemen in the witness box could lie through their teeth and suborn witnesses to do the same, that judges could show bias, never occurred to me.

That could have been me writing.

Kennedy is outspoken in his attitude to the court system and to judges. The law, mercifully, has changed since 1952 and anybody under the age of 40 today will not recognize the system I am talking about. Today, policemen stand by while protestors disrupt everyday life. They dance with revellers in Notting Hill. Judges, like chief constables, all appear to have sociology qualifications rather than law degrees and are increasingly liberal and even left wing. No one who was an adult at the time of the Craig and Bentley case would recognize any of this.

Let us turn again to *Dixon of Dock Green*. The television series, broadcast on BBC early on Saturday evenings, ran from 1955 to 1976, by which time its star, Jack Warner, was 81 (almost exactly Claude Pain's age when I knew him). Its 376 episodes constituted the longest-running police series on television. The whole thing (almost all of it in black and white) looks very tame today, but the folksy charm of Sergeant Dixon, smiling benignly at the camera at the end of each episode, was rooted in the public's attitude to the police. Fiction it may be, but it was rooted in fact.

As we have seen, the Dixon character was imported from *The Blue Lamp*, the 1949 Ealing Studios film in which Dixon is shot and killed by a young thug (Dirk Bogarde). The Metropolitan Police commissioner Harold Scott acted as consultant for the film and it was based in part on the murder of PC Nathaniel Edgar in the previous year. As we shall see in the next chapter, the reality was very different.

The late 1940s and early 1950s was a time of extraordinary uncertainty, perhaps because of the trauma of the Second World War. Children who lived through the war have been described as the most delinquent in history. Their fathers were away fighting, their mothers coping as best they could. Most major cities had bomb damage, gaping holes where houses, churches, schools and hospitals used to be. Rationing persisted until 1953, keeping desperate families on the breadline. Vast numbers of otherwise honest people became used to pilfering, fiddling coupons, 'cooking the books'. In that atmosphere, people turned to the law and to the police for comfort and security and, in the weekly television dose provided for them by George Dixon, they got it.

A policeman was an 'oasis of calm in a sea of troubles'. He provided the certainty that was missing everywhere else. He knew his beat backwards. He knew the time. He knew everyone in the area, the villains as well as the 'good guys'. He could be trusted. The detectives even more so, even though few people had access to them. We saw in Chapter 3 that trilby-hatted, lantern-jawed men like Ted Greeno, George Hatherill and Bob Fabian, were the leaders of a group of stalwarts who could be relied upon to bring nasty criminals to book.

Gordon Cummings, Neville Heath, John Christie, Ruth Ellis – through ten years of brutal murder – the litany of names of people caught by the law and facing the executioner have become part of the fabric of society.

Beyond the front line of crime and policing came the criminal courts where the concept of justice was routinely betrayed. Judges, from the Lord Chief Justice to the newest arrival on the Bench were almost exclusively the product of public schools and Oxbridge. The journalist Bryan Magee says of such men:

> Their general demeanour was like that of elderly clubmen determined that it should be clearly understood that they were men of the world, fully alive to all the tricks of your Tom, Dick and Harry; yet their actual questions and comments revealed that they had not the remotest notion what sort of world it was that … East End people … actually lived in, or how to evaluate their characters and the plausibility of what they said.

The case of Lord Goddard is an extreme one, but if he was the tip of an iceberg, we must not forget that there *was* an iceberg beneath him. Arthur Smith, Goddard's clerk, went into print on him in 1959, only seven years after the Craig and Bentley trial and while the old goat was still alive. After his death, of course, Smith let slip the little peccadillo concerning Goddard's sexual excitement at sentencing people to death, but the 1959 version has nothing but praise for the man. In his discussions of Craig and Bentley, Smith says, 'One could not imagine [this sort of] crime having been committed before the war,' conveniently ignoring the cold-blooded murder of PC George Gutteridge in September 1927. What Smith was *really* talking about was the assumed prevalence of teenaged delinquency, which rattled middle England in the 1950s. Goddard's clerk says that the case restarted the controversy over capital punishment and provoked discussion on the 'doctrine of implied malice and of constructive murder'. 'It also,' he writes pompously, 'subjected the Chief to a barrage of criticism, most of which was ill-informed and extremely unfair.' The snobbery of men like Smith, as a minion of the court, is apparent in his line 'Both Mr Cassels and Mr Humphreys were the sons of distinguished members of the high court bench' as though that places both lawyers beyond reproach. Smith was of course in the Old Bailey for the trial, but, nevertheless, believed that Craig came from 'an excellent home' (allowing for the fact that both his parents and his older brother had criminal records). His summation of Bentley was better – 'groping, monosyllabic answers to questions put to him … gave the impression of someone on the borderline of feeble-mindedness'. In the space of two paragraphs, Smith writes three mistakes into Humphreys' opening remarks, which cannot fill his readers with certainty as to his accuracy. Two patrol cars had arrived, he says – actually one of them was a police van. Harrison had arrived in the second car, says Smith, which was actually that of Miles and McDonald. In the case of Fairfax's wound, Smith implies that a *second* bullet fell out of his braces, rather than the only one that grazed Fairfax. There was no other bullet in his wound because there was no bullet hole in his body.

'In the witness box,' Smith wrote, '[Bentley] agreed with almost every suggestion which was made to him,' *except*, of course, that he ever said 'Let him have it, Chris.' As would be expected, Smith's account of Goddard's handling of the case and his summation are quoted verbatim (with certain vital omissions) and all appears sweetness and light; justice was served. Goddard, Smith assures us, was 'profoundly distressed' when David Maxwell-Fyfe refused to grant a reprieve. We know, of course, and it is difficult to believe that Smith did not, that Goddard had actually pressured the Home Secretary into his decision. 'The Chief was attacked by a public who knew nothing of his opinion of the case, as though he himself had tightened the noose.' He might just as well have done; that it was not just Harry Allen assisting Albert Pierrepoint, but the Lord Chief Justice of England too.

Smith's eulogy is little short of nauseating. At Goddard's retirement in 1958, universities and professional bodies queued up to honour him and invite him as their guest. More fool them!

Fenton Bressler continued in much the same vein, even though Goddard was no longer Chief Justice and times had changed. According to Bressler, himself a lawyer and part of the Establishment, Goddard was descended from Vikings and part of a landed family in Wiltshire. Far more likely is that his original family were German Jews who settled in London and changed their name from Gottlieb. Goddard's father, Charles, was a solicitor able to afford to send his son to Marlborough where he became a notorious bully. At Trinity, Oxford, he only passed his Bar examination at the sixth attempt. He rose under one of the worst Chief Justices in history, Lord Hewart, in the 1930s, worked with the Appeal Court until 1946 and then, unaccountably, was chosen by Clement Attlee as Chief Justice. For those who questioned Attlee's sanity anyway, this was proof positive; Goddard loathed the working class and Socialism with a passion.

When he tried his hand in politics in 1929, his opponent got 28,009 votes; Goddard 6,365. When John Parris spoke to Attlee about the man's appointment, he told him, 'I knew nothing about Goddard. [Hartley] Shawcross [the Attorney General] persuaded me that the judiciary had become slack and inefficient; Goddard, he claimed, would discipline them and "tone up the system".'

We have already heard Parris's observations on Goddard and they form a perfect foil to the adulation of Smith and Bressler. He was not knowledgeable in the law (despite his wind-bagging in the Craig and Bentley trial), did not grasp subtleties of common law or have the firm grasp of principle that Lord Denning imputed to him after his death. He was simply an old Marlborough bully in an eighteenth-century wig. 'What harm can there be in the brief?' he asked magistrates in the year of Smith's gushing biography. When Labour suspended capital punishment in 1947, Goddard spoke vehemently in the Lords against it. David Napley wrote of him, 'He was contemptuous of psychiatrists, social workers and probation officers.' And, we might add, junior lawyers like John Parris.

If Arthur Smith found the criticism of Goddard over the Craig and Bentley case unfair, let us look at it in detail. The phrase 'rush to judgement' could have been made for Rayner Goddard. He crammed a vast number of cases into his schedule which meant that neither prosecution nor defence counsel had sufficient time to prepare. As it was, Parris had to meet the Chief personally in his office and plead for more time. He was given an extra two days. In *Let Him Have It, Chris*, I slammed both Parris and Cassels for not doing their job well enough and I stand by that. However, it was very difficult for either counsel to make much headway because of the time factor, imposed upon them not merely by the system but by Goddard's hard-line interpretation of it. In tightening up what some saw as a lax judiciary, he was actually denying Craig and Bentley a fair trial. What was done about this? Nothing. Humphreys and Bass had a welter of police testimony on which they relied as well as the medical evidence of Drs Haler and Jazwon and the ballistics evidence of Lewis Nickolls. Paris and Cassels had Craig and Bentley. In 1990, Thames Television found Douglas Barlow, Dennis Woodcock and John and Jane Tennant who were all in or next to Barlow and Parker's warehouse on the night in question. All of them challenged the official police testimony. How many more locals could have been found by defence counsel had they been given time? Christopher Craig told Thames that he watched as 'three policemen swore away the life' of Derek Bentley. Rayner Goddard was also a huge help in that respect, and for him to be 'profoundly shocked' by Bentley's death, as Smith contends, defies belief.

Goddard's first interjection of any significance occurred on the first day of the trial when Parris was cross-examining Niven Craig Snr. He told the court of the 'captain's' conviction for firearms possession.

'To what issue is this going?' Goddard asked. In terms of counsel's questioning, this was none of the judge's business, but he claimed that it was necessary to 'keep within some bounds'. What Parris was probably trying to ascertain was that the younger Craig grew up in an atmosphere of 'gun culture' which was regrettable then as it would be today. Goddard's interruption about Craig running away to Hove is odd. 'Well, he went off on a sort of frolic on his own?' Perhaps it was because of this that Reginald Paget in the first book on the case in 1953 wrote, '[Craig] ran away from home, but was recovered in a week or so. This was a minor escapade.' Being in possession of two firearms is hardly 'minor'.

During the testimony of Fairfax, Goddard intervened several times to make it clear to the jury who was where and when. This was acceptable if Fairfax had not made it clear, but he had. All Goddard was doing was underlining the prosecution testimony. When Cassels cross-examined the detective, he caught him out. 'You see, I do not want to take advantage of any slip; but you did agree with my learned friend Mr Humphreys that Bentley broke away after the shot was fired; you said "Yes" to the question he asked.' Fairfax replied that that was a mistake on his part, that Bentley had broken away *before* the shot. Goddard pointed out, correctly, that Fairfax had said that Cassels pointed out that that was not what Fairfax had said in response to Humphreys' question and the Chief Justice, beaten, let it go. When Fairfax floundered on whether it was Craig or Bentley who said he had a .45 Colt, Goddard was there to bail him out. 'That is why I asked whether the word "he" or "I" was used.'

When James McDonald was trying to do the right thing and referred to Craig as 'the man on the roof', Goddard broke in and told the officer to call him Craig. It was a small point and accurate, but it all helped to establish guilt in the minds of the jury. Unhappy that John Parris was rattling McDonald in the context of Craig's shooting at Harrison, the Chief leapt in again. 'He says they were aimed at Harrison, but he does not know where they [the shots] went. Is that what you mean?' 'Yes,' a grateful McDonald answered.

One of the most damning remarks, sadly reiterated by another Lord Chief Justice forty-six years later, Goddard said, 'I wonder how anybody could be expected to be accurate on a matter like this, on a night like this when those men are being fired at, in fear of their lives, and now they are being asked weeks afterwards to count how many shots were fired.' But this was precisely the point. The police case was a pack of cards – if one fell, they all did. And a man's life was at stake. If the police could not be certain of the number of shots fired or the direction they were fired in, what was the point of a trial at all?

McDonald was undoubtedly a problem witness for the prosecution. His weight and lack of fitness meant that he was up and down the drainpipe like a struggling yo-yo and it was important to establish exactly where he was when he claimed to hear 'Let him have it, Chris.' Bass asked him how long it took him to get down the pipe. 'Minutes,' McDonald answered. Goddard, the extra prosecution counsel, sensed danger. 'Do you think you could have counted sixty?' 'I am not sure that I could.' Smugly, the Chief said, 'People can always say minutes when they mean seconds in these cases.'

For reasons best known to himself, the judge had a go at Sergeant Edward Roberts. 'Do you not remember without your notes, officer?' Roberts admitted that he did not. This, of course, despite Goddard wondering how anybody on that terrifying roof could have been accurate about the shots fired.

We have already seen how outraged Goddard was that Dr Jazwon had been brought 'all the way from Manchester' to give his evidence. Parris, by now nearly past caring how rude he was to the judge, snapped back, 'I thought the jury might like to appreciate it.' It was not, of course, Parris who had called Jazwon – he was a prosecution witness. And Goddard was completely out of line when he said 'The doctor is here to give medical evidence, not to speculate on the flight of bullets.' But medical evidence relating to gunshot wounds (Jazwon was talking about Fairfax's wound) was *directly* linked to bullet trajectory. It was not speculation, but medical fact.

Perhaps it should have surprised no one that a 76-year-old public schoolboy should know nothing about drugs. They were not at the forefront of public discussion as they are today, but Parris was doing his best to establish that Craig was off his head on painkillers for much of his time in hospital. 'What bearing,' Goddard wanted to know, 'have the drugs got on this case?'

As if to underline his contempt for 'three-quarter-witted' people like Bentley, Goddard asked to see a copy of his statement to the police. He looked at the misspelt signature. 'Well, it might be anything.' The statement, of course, and how it was obtained, became a burning issue in later appeals. To get DS Shepherd, who took it, off the hook, the judge asked for clarification. 'He would say a sentence, you would write it down, and as you wrote it, you would read the sentence and see that you had got it right?' 'Yes, my Lord.' This was at variance with the expert linguistics testimony used by Thames Television in 1991, but nobody in the Old Bailey had access to that sort of testimony.

On the second day, when DCI Smith was in the witness box, Parris complained that Humphreys was putting a leading question to him. This was contrary to the law as well as court procedure and Humphreys accepted that. Goddard did not. 'I do not think it matters one way or the other.' The Chief was anxious to cut to the chase in respect of the ballistics evidence. 'This revolver [the .455 Eley] if it is fired off, and even if it is fired indiscriminately, is quite capable of killing people?' 'Yes,' came the reply. Job, as far as Goddard was concerned, done.

When Craig was in the witness box, the Chief showed the utter contempt he had for him. He had already spoken at length about 'cosh boys' in the Lords, demanding a return to flogging and the birch. 'Did you know that firearms could kill people?' he asked. When Craig answered 'Yes, sir,' Goddard replied, oddly, 'Let us get on to something that matters.' When he asked Craig how many times he had fired and that he had reloaded, the judge underlined the point for the jury's benefit. 'Reloaded it.' Goddard's interruptions increased at this point. He was clearly incensed by Craig with his sullen air, even though, on paper at least, his answers were perfectly polite. Why, Goddard wanted to know, did Craig carry a knife? What was the spike for on the knuckleduster? It was 'a dreadful weapon'.

In what John Parris refers to as guilt by brotherhood, Goddard, wholly against the rules of law, referred to Niven Craig. 'The police had arrested your brother, had they not?' 'Yes, sir.' 'And has he been committed?' 'Yes, sir.' 'And he had a gun?' 'Yes, sir.' Goddard was establishing that the Craig brothers were a vicious, trigger-happy pair, yet when Parris had questioned Niven Snr the day before about his firearms convictions, Goddard expressed his disappointment. The judge also went so far as to put words into Craig's mouth. 'Well, "come on, you brave coppers. Think of your wives." "Your wives will be widows, if you do come on." That is what it means, is it not?'

And the barely literate 16-year-old calmly replied to the Oxbridge-educated bully, 'It was to frighten them away.' He also got the better of him in the judge's petty and facile question, 'How did you know where you landed if you were unconscious?' 'Because I am quite a good diver and I have been off lots of heights.' When Craig claimed to be 'hardly conscious' at various times in hospital, Goddard had had enough. 'Hardly conscious! Don't talk such nonsense.'

When Bentley was in the dock, Goddard pursued an entire line of questions by himself, even though Cassels was doing a perfectly good job of establishing the facts. Goddard wanted to know why Bentley went to Croydon that night and clearly did not understand the answer. 'Just for the ride, sir, an ordinary ride.' Men like Goddard never went anywhere for no reason. And he had people to drive him.

About the only time that the Chief showed a glimmer of understanding was when Humphreys fatuously asked Bentley to look at Exhibit No. 15, his statement to the police. 'He cannot read it,' Goddard pointed out.

When Goddard sent the jury out before the closing speeches, it was because Parris was seeking to point out that his client had no *intent* to murder anybody. This was a weak argument by any standards, but Parris probably thought it worth a try. Because British law is based on precedent, he cited Rex v Appleby 1940 and Mr Justice Brett's decision in 1873. The issue was whether the crime amounted to murder or manslaughter, which carried a lesser sentence. If Parris had won this one, it would have saved Bentley's life. He could not have been convicted of murder if Craig was not.

'The law is stated very carefully by Foster,' the Chief pointed out.

'And Hale, my Lord,' Humphreys chipped in.

Goddard went into details in the case before Judge Brett and got it spectacularly wrong. It was not a policeman who was killed in this instance but a passer-by, which made the whole thing a very different proposition. Did Parris or Cassels correct him? No. We have already seen the Chief's woefully inadequate summing up, in which he states Bentley's defence in two and a half lines. We have seen him make a *huge* amount of the irrelevant knuckleduster. We know that he refused to accept the pernicious influence of gangster films and violent comics. And that Bentley's limitations made absolutely no difference to the outcome of the case.

When I wrote *Let Him Have It, Chris*, I pointed out that the average juryman – like the average cinemagoer – has an IQ equivalent to what was then Grade 4 CSE (there is no real modern equivalent, but essentially a fail GCSE grade). How, I asked, could such average people cope with bullying dinosaurs like Goddard? I received an anonymous and deeply unpleasant letter after publication from a juryman (whether an actual member of the jury at the Craig and Bentley trial was not made clear) accusing me of ridiculing the average Joe. But this is precisely the point. Both Lord Goddard and Frank Cassels made reference to common sense, that just because each man wore a wig and appeared in court did not mean that common sense was left at home. But that is *exactly* what happened in the case of Regina v Craig and Bentley.

The entire legal system is biased against appellants who are, under the law, innocent until proven guilty. Ludovic Kennedy, writing in 2002, slams the British legal system even after it had been reformed, amended and improved. He rightly attacks the adversarial system where one team of lawyers out-argues another. The better orator, the better *actor* invariably wins, which is why a barrister like Edward Marshall-Hall in the early twentieth century won so many cases. It was not because his clients were necessarily innocent, but because he knew how to win juries to his way of thinking. The adversarial system is in use in the United Stats, but many countries, including those in the Commonwealth, have abandoned it in favour of the French system which is infinitely fairer. Why, Kennedy asks, do we persist in the fancy dress of the eighteenth century? When Lord Chief Justice Mansfield did his best to hang the outspoken reformer John Wilkes in the 1760s, long wigs and knee-breeches made sense; everybody wore them. By 1952 they were ridiculously obsolete, kept out of a ludicrous obsequience to tradition for tradition's sake.

Then there was the language of the court. Both leading counsel opened their closing remarks with the time-honoured 'May it please you, my lord'. This was just a formality many (especially lawyers) will say, but it is *so* much more than that. That there should be law lords at all is debatable. How could Goddard execute justice and fairness when, as a member of the House of Lords, he supported hanging and flogging? Where is the impartiality in any of that? It was not the job of Humphreys, Parris and Cassels to please his lordship, but to put the case for their clients to the jury. When John Parris remonstrated with Goddard over the interpretation of the law (and was overruled) he could only go so far because, had he protested, he would have found himself in contempt of court and that would have been the end of his career. It is noticeable that when he *did* criticize Goddard, outside the courtroom, for his handling of criminal cases, he was punished for it. Frank Cassels, who made no such noises, went on to become a judge himself.

Lawyers then, as today, see their profession as noble and a vocation. In reality, of course, it is a job, an obscenely well-paid one and everybody has their eye on promotion. This is why Cassels missed opportunities to challenge Goddard and why David Yallop and I criticized him in earlier books. For Parris to defend the man, while at the same time admitting he was no orator, makes no sense at all.

The whole system, says Ludovic Kennedy, reeks:

> Corruption … runs like a thread through the pages of [his 2002 book] of the police fabricating evidence to make a conviction stick, of judges believing police evidence and emphasising that belief to juries, who mostly regard the police as society's guardians, accepting their word in preference to that of defendants.

The pomposity of the legal system is exemplified by its terminology. *Ex parte'*, *res ipsa loquitur* and many other Medieval terms were still in everyday use in courts in 1952. A friend of mine, who himself became a high court judge, once told me that when he was a junior barrister defending a client, a judge harangued him in Latin for nearly four minutes. My friend had no idea what he was talking about. He merely smiled and said, 'Quite so, m' lud' and hoped that was the right reaction!

If British law is based on precedent, why is there so much disagreement over it? Why was Goddard's interpretation of the manslaughter/murder conundrum different from Parris's when both men were citing the same precedents? The woeful truth is that laws are made by men and are full of non sequiturs (there is that Medieval Latin again!) That ought not to exist. We will look at the role of parliament in the Craig and Bentley case below.

Moving on to the Court of Appeal, we have an action replay of the same thing. Cassels should have argued far more forcefully than he did about the bias and incompetence of Goddard. He did not. Why? Perhaps because he aimed for the Bench himself, but more probably because he knew it was pointless. In ancient Rome, the Praetorian guard was all powerful; it made and destroyed emperors. As Juvenal asked, '*Quis custodiet ipsos custodes*?' – Who guards the guards? So it was with the Court of Appeal in 1953. Three *judges* were asked to comment on the performance of not just another judge, but effectively, the man who was their boss, the Lord Chief Justice. And the principal was David Croom-Johnson, an actual mentee of Goddard.

So, chances of a fair trial were denied to Bentley in the Old Bailey and again at the Court of Appeal. The men (and by now a tiny handful of women) who actually made the law now had the opportunity to see justice done. On 27 January, the day before Bentley's execution, Sidney Silverman MP raised the issue of a Motion he had placed the day before. His opening line, the straitjacketed tradition of 700 years of history, is just as stultifying and wrong as that of the courts themselves: 'I desire your indulgence, Mr Speaker.' Again, just a form of words but taken literally, Silverman had to go cap in hand to the chairman of debates, as Parris and Co. had to go cap in hand to Goddard, merely to have the debate heard. Such decisions should not have been in the hands of one man, especially a Conservative MP who was no more impartial to debate on capital punishment than Goddard was. William Morrison had decided the previous day that the Motion should not be on the Order Paper. As Silverman pointed out, of the fifty MPs who had backed him, there were ten Privy Councillors, a former Solicitor General and an Under Secretary of State for the Home Office. Silverman had lodged the Motion shortly after seven in the evening and at a quarter past ten was told in a phone call that the Motion had been dropped. Silverman told Morrison that he had checked the protocols for this, and, just as Goddard had tried to deflate Parris by throwing precedent at him,

Morrison did the same – 'I think that perhaps the Hon. Member will find what he is looking for on page 384 of Erskine May.'

Erskine May is one of those terminally boring collections of House rules, just as the seventeenth-century jurist Edward Coke was regarded as some sort of plaster saint-cum-Moses in pontificating on the law for barristers. Like John Parris, Silverman was polite, referring (as lawyers always do) to his 'honourable and learned' friends, although in the case of the Commons, very few are learned in much at all and honour, in 1953 as today, was an extremely rare commodity. In fact, Sidney Silverman had done his homework and was able to quote chapter and verse from Erskine May as to why the Motion should not have been removed from the Order Paper. He cut to the chase. 'Is the House to wait until Bentley is dead before it is entitled to say that he should not die? No, sir.' Silverman had received over 200 telegrams, all but one complaining that the Home Secretary's decision to hang Bentley was wrong. He ended by ripping into Morrison. 'I say in these circumstances *with great respect* [my italics] that you exceeded your authority to withhold this Motion from the Order Paper last night.'

In reply, Morrison fell back on the old Goddard ploy of precedent. Because previous Speakers had interfered with Motions, so could he. In that case, why did he not go back several centuries, to a time when the Speaker was a royal servant, in effect snooping on the Commons on behalf of the king? Precedent is a two-edged sword, but Morrison ignored that fact. He simply said the Motion was out of order because that was what the previous Speaker, Douglas Clifton-Brown, had decided was the case in 1947 when a number of people faced the death penalty on the Gold Coast.

Silverman came back with the fact that the two cases were not remotely the same and reminded him of the strength of feeling in the country at large about Bentley's impending execution. Reginald Paget backed him up. 'The Ruling on which you have relied is based upon the decision of the Executive and not just on the decision of this House.' It was the old clash between the two principal areas of government, legislature and executive. Ever since the seventeenth century, the Speaker had been clearly in the legislative camp, so he had no right to enforce executive decisions over the Commons. Paget appealed to Morrison's sense of justice (if he had any):

'I think the great condemnation which was made of the German people [in 1939] was that they stood aside and did nothing when dreadful things happened.' And then came his brilliant 'A three-quarter-witted boy of 19 is to be hanged for a murder he did not commit and which was committed 15 minutes after he was arrested. Can we be made to keep silent when a thing as horrible and as shocking as this is to happen?'

Leslie Hale MP chipped in to remind Morrison what actually happened in the 1947 case. 'Before 1916 it was standard practice to raise questions in the House about the Royal Prerogative (the granting of mercy) and that this stopped then because 'we were executing so many decent Irishmen'. There was uproar at this, but it was true. The start of 'The Troubles' had been in 1916, with Southern Ireland trying to break away to form its own independent state. In the violence of what was, in effect, a Civil War, an unspecified number of innocent men were hanged, along with many guilty ones. The 1947 decision related to a Colonial governor, not the Home Secretary.

Hale smarmed around Morrison, saying that he was widely respected by all and sundry, but he nevertheless maintained that the Speaker himself was out of order (in the usual, lay sense of the phrase) to take the Motion off the Order list. Morrison countered with precedents going back to Victorian high-profile murder cases, that of Israel Lipski's killing of Miriam Angel and Mrs Maybrick's poisoning of her husband. There was no Court of Appeal then, but much discussion about creating one (that eventually happened in 1907). Florence Maybrick had her death sentence commuted to life imprisonment, but Lipski hanged. In the Lords, Lord Halsbury commented that 'such questions as these [the creation of an Appellant Court] are not appropriately discussed at times of public excitement about them'. His lordship was ignoring the notion of democracy (admittedly not fully achieved in 1890) if only because, as a member of the wholly unelected House of Lords, he had nothing to do with it. Interestingly, the new king in 1901, Edward VII, wanted more to do with the exercise of the royal prerogative, but the Home Secretary, Aretas Akers-Douglas, every bit as stupid and blinkered as David Maxwell-Fyfe, persuaded him otherwise. 'It is most important that the practice of the last eighty years [there is that obsession with tradition again] not be departed from.' He went on, 'it would be intolerable that Your Majesty's name should be dragged into the mire to serve the temporary progress of some wretched newspaper.'

Again, as with Goddard's and Croom-Johnson's decisions in their respective courts, where in any of this is the common sense that the law claims to have?

Then Aneurin Bevan took the floor. He conceded that Morrison's precedents were strong evidence, but that he had far from made his case, that he had in fact withdrawn the Motion because *in his view* (my italics) it was out of order.

Silverman weighed in again, assuring the Speaker that he was not accusing him of any impropriety and his request for a new Motion was turned down. So was that of Desmond Donnelly who followed with another version of it and that too was rejected.

As we have seen, even after Bentley's execution, the Motion did not appear on the Order Paper.

We must move on to David Maxwell-Fyfe. There is no doubt that Goddard reminded him, verbally and on paper, whose side the man was supposed to be on. The whole debate about capital punishment had become a political hot potato by 1948. Although there were exceptions on both sides, broadly the Conservatives backed the death penalty;

Labour did not. The Liberals, already consigned to their role as bit-players, dithered.

The Criminal Justice Bill caused uproar in both Houses of Parliament. It was one thing to abolish corporal punishment, the use of the cat and the birch. It was quite another to remove the death penalty. It had always been regarded as the only *real* deterrent against serious crime. The amendment to the Bill, which made the abolition of the death penalty temporary for five years, was carried by 245 votes to 222. The Home Secretary, Chuter Ede, announced that those currently under sentence of death, for example Donald Thomas for the murder of PC Edgar, should be given life imprisonment instead (although technically this was not necessary). The Lords were largely opposed to law reform, spearheaded by Goddard and with an estimated 80 per cent of the country backing him. The result in the Lords was 181 to 28 in favour of throwing out Silverman's amendment to the Bill. Goddard also pushed through a Bill to retain birching, passed by a majority in a House of less than fifty members. Chuter Ede held on, one of those rare parliamentary birds with a conscience as well as rationality. 'I was breaking the Bill of Rights, but it was a matter of common sense, that those reprieves should be granted.' Silverman et al. withdrew the amendment and here, even though the case had not happened yet, was another lost attempt to save Bentley's life. In 1911, after a constitutional crisis, the Lords had lost the power to veto or even delay financial Bills, but on all other issues, they could obstruct the will of the people as much as they liked. Here, under Clement Attlee was a chance to abolish the Second House or at least reform it so that it was not crammed with unelected hereditary peers. That chance, too, was missed. At least the Goddards of this world were no longer able to sentence criminals to the lash.

But Goddard fought back at every opportunity. In 1950, he sentenced two teenaged thugs who had robbed an old lady on a train. 'The sentence I am going to pass upon you may be a warning to others of like kidney. It is not for me to criticize the wisdom of Parliament that prevents me from doing what I might have done eighteen months ago, when I could have had you whipped.' He sent both boys to prison for seven years.

The return of the Conservative Party to power, with the superannuable Winston Churchill at the helm once more, saw a return of the death penalty, especially in the face of what was seen as an epidemic rise in juvenile delinquency. The cat and the birch were never brought back, but the rope was and the Pierrepoint family were in business once again.

At every stage since the Croydon rooftop, the legal system and its advocates, like the fates, had it in for Derek Bentley. Almost the only lawyer who stood up for him, indirectly, was John Parris, yet in 1991, Parris wrote, 'Not only was Bentley a moron but he was a lying moron.' That goes a long way towards Frank Cassels' comment when he first met Parris, that he thought, 'both little fuckers [Craig and Bentley] ought to swing.' MPs Silverman, Paget, Bevan, Hale and Donnelly also tried to do the right thing, but once again, the weight of the system, rigid, uncaring, covered in cobwebs, bore them down.

The judgement in the Court of Appeal before Lord Bingham of Cornhill ran to several pages. For the Appellant (Bentley, in the person of Maria) E. Fitzgerald and H. Blaxled covered all the arguments that you have already read. For the Crown, N. Sweeney and D. Perry retrod the 1952 prosecution position. Although the right decision was reached, that Goddard's handling of the case was unfair and prejudiced, their lordships essentially threw their hands in the air and said such was the tension and confusion of the rooftop shooting that it was not surprising that police evidence was contradictory. As to the notion of John Parris in *Scapegoat,* that DCI Smith had orchestrated a false and fabricated version of events, 'he did not make a very good job of it.'

In one respect, however, I believe their lordships got it wrong. I will return to this in Chapter 13.

There was one glimmer of hope. In 2015, a law firm called Just For Kids intervened in the case of Regina v Jogee, in which one teenager was accused of egging his friend on to murder another (essentially the situation in the Craig and Bentley case). The Supreme Court decided that this conviction was unsafe and the sentence was overturned. A group of academics from Cambridge University found from their extensive researches that children (anyone under the age of 18) are unlikely to have the cognitive ability to foresee dangerous situations that might escalate. With hindsight, of course, that fits Derek Bentley absolutely. But this new awareness came sixty-four years too late for Derek Bentley and, depressingly, the Criminal Cases Review Commission found in 2022 that the number of convictions involving the law of joint enterprise has actually increased.

So Lord Goddard is probably smirking in his grave. And the law is still an ass.

Chapter 11

A Gunfight in the Dark

Nathaniel Edgar, William Gibson, Alan Baxter, Duncan Fraser, Arthur Jagger – these are just some of the names of police officers killed in the line of duty between 1948 and 1951. Lord Goddard attributed this sort of violence, much of it carried out by young tearaways, to the Labour government's soft on crime stance. It hardly compares with prime minister David Cameron's much later 'hug a hoodie' mentality, but the removal of the cat and birch as deterrents convinced people like Goddard that the country was going to the dogs.

To set the record straight, Donald Thomas, who killed Edgar, was 22; Robert Smith who shot Sergeant Gibson, was 30; Alfred Moore who shot Fraser and Jagger was 36. Baxter's killer, Derek Poole, was 20. So all in all, the teenaged cosh-boy menace seems to have been largely illusory. Of the other officers from the Met who died in that period, the rest were the result of traffic accidents.

The problem for the police was that they were prevented from complaining. Occasionally, very senior policemen were interviewed by the press, but the rank and file, both uniformed and plainclothes, could say nothing. That does not mean that there was not considerable resentment among them, especially in the case of Thomas, who, were it not for the Labour government, would have faced Albert Pierrepoint one grey morning in 1948.

In the Craig and Bentley case, we are facing a stacked deck. In adversarial terms (with all the problems that that creates as outlined in the previous chapter) it was the word of twenty-four prosecution witnesses against two delinquents, both of whom had previous when it came to clashes with the law. Unless a miracle happened, Christopher Craig was bound to be found guilty; Derek Bentley, under the law at the time, was bound to die. In 1990, as far as I was concerned, that miracle was ex-PC Claude Pain, a man who had faced Craig's bullets, a man who had seen his friend Sidney Miles die in front of him, a man whose voice had never been heard until I, through sheer chance, found him.

Another miracle happened in 2000, although, like Claude Pain, its usefulness has been limited by the sheet weight of obfuscation and lies. As readers will know from Chapter 1 of this book, I was denied access to any official documentation on the case, even though there were people who told me they had seen the information that was classified and which I wanted to read. The Freedom of Information Act of 2000 should have changed all that and, to an extent, it has. For years, the Labour opposition had been pushing for more openness in government, resulting in a White Paper in 1997 called *Your Right to Know*. Before that, all papers, including the Metropolitan Police files in what was then the Public Record Office were housed there thirty years after a particular event. That meant that everything relating to the Craig and Bentley case was lodged in Kew in 1982. But those papers could not be opened to the public for fifty years, which would have taken us to 2002. The thinking behind this was that innocent parties would not want their names linked to, in this instance, the murder of a policeman. The arguments against this, I believe, are stronger than those for. Some of the names of people on the fringes of the case, like Frank Fazey and Norman Parsley, have appeared in print since 1971, in David Yallop's book. Others may well have had their names in print already, interviewed, as some people were, by the media of 1952–3.

The Freedom of Information Act, following the far more transparent American version enacted as long ago as 1967, was so full of exemptions and caveats as to be almost worthless. Lord Mackay at the time called it 'toothless', being far too wordy (as all legislation is) and too limited in its scope. It was not functioning properly until 2005. Tony Blair, who presided over it all as prime minister, called it 'one of the biggest mistakes of my career', not because it failed to deliver openness, truth and justice, but because it became a weapon in the hands of an ever-growing army of journalists going on what Blair's colleague Lord Falconer called 'fishing expeditions'. A recent apolitical study has pointed out that the UK Act has more limitations than any other in a free society and rightly criticizes the government's retained right to use a ministerial veto in relation to such information. What price freedom?

In fact, there is nothing 'free' about the Freedom of Information Act. Bringing an FOIA request against a public institution (private institutions are exempt anyway) may well involve lawyers and become very expensive and those in the know deny that same right to anybody else. As I write, a high court judge has demanded that the BBC hand over its emails in relation to the infamous Princess Diana interview by Martin Bashir. It had already cost £200,000 of licence fee money for the BBC hierarchy to fight this demand. Now that the relevant documentation has been handed over, it is full of redactions – the dreaded black felt tip cover-up that means, in effect, that the law is not being complied with. The BBC has all sorts of whingeing explanations, but essentially, it is breaking the law. It remains to be seen what the High Court and the Information Commissioner's Office intends to do about this.

So too with the Craig and Bentley case. In December 2023, as preparation for this book, my wife and I went to Kew with its modern, gleaming building and beautiful gardens. The staff could not have been more friendly and helpful, but my wife took a photograph of a buff-coloured folder in the files which was totally empty. What it once had in it, I have no idea, but it does not fill a researcher with hope. And, unaccountably, there are still papers relating to the case which cannot be seen until 2037. Is that to protect Frank Fazey and Norman Parsley, who, if they are not already, are certain to be dead by then? And are those the papers that are missing from that empty folder?

At least I have now seen, at last, the papers I asked for thirty-five years ago and I am able, for example, to fill in the details provided by Yallop's three monkeys – Beecher-Brigden, Alderson and, above all, Pain. What follows is an attempt to do what Lord Bingham said he could not do in 1998, restage the rooftop scene, the 'gunfight in the dark', using all available testimony. In Chapter 1, we looked at it exclusively from Claude Pain's point of view. In Chapter 4, we examined it from the evidence given in court, but that evidence, of course, contained nothing from Beecher-Brigden, Alderson or Pain, even though all three, I believe, were standing by, waiting to give their statements.

As you read what follows, have access to the roof plan in this book, drawn by PC Bernard Beard for court use. It may be inaccurate in two respects (see below) but in the absence of the actual building, it is all we have. Remember, too, that an incredibly fraught situation developed in which live rounds killed one man and wounded another, 22ft above street level on a night when the moon was often hidden by cloud. Defence counsel did not raise the issue of visibility in court, but perhaps they should have done.

In respect of witness statements, there are today twenty-seven in the current Archive file, only three of which refer to civilians. Two are the Wares who effectively kickstarted the whole thing by noticing Craig and Bentley behaving suspiciously and calling the police, and the third is that of Catherine Miles, whose brief account of her husband's leaving the house on 2 November is perhaps the saddest in the whole file. There was clearly no attempt by the police to find civilian witnesses to make statements, whereas there are many made by policemen who had no access to the warehouse roof or even a clear view of it.

DCI Smith, whose detailed and comprehensive report is in the Archive, makes reference to a number of witnesses whose statements are not present. There is nothing from Chief Inspector Percy Law, who took photographs of the crime scene the next day, nor from PC Bernard Beard who drew the roof plans, even though both men appeared in court. Both Wares made statements but only Edith stood in the witness box at the Old Bailey. The statements of Yallop's missing policemen are all there – Alderson, Beecher-Brigden and Pain – even though none of them was called to court. Other officers who made statements were also left off Christmas Humphreys' prosecution list – Inspector Thomas Bodley and a whole clutch of constables, several of whom we have heard from before in the context of Craig's time in hospital: Northeast, Lowe, Moore, Wells, Barrow, Stewart, Mitchell, Church, Carey, Harris, Gordon, Fenwick, Riding and Bastard.

Contrary to Yallop's contention – and mine after I had interviewed Claude Pain – there was nothing sinister or conspiratorial about this. Presumably, a complete list of officers present was provided by DCI Smith and it was up to Humphreys and Bass to make selections. The obsession with speed which was one of Goddard's watchwords was widely known and hearing the same evidence from an even larger number of policemen would have slowed proceedings down immeasurably.

Now that I have fuller access to records (there are several missing – see below) I can attempt to recreate what happened.

John Ware rang the Fell Road police station at approximately 9.25 p.m. Danny Watson, the desk sergeant who took the call, sent Pain and Harrison with the van driver Beecher-Brigden to Tamworth Road to investigate a possible break-in. Interestingly, in Pain's account, compiled the next day, there is no mention of Harrison. Neither is Pain mentioned in Lord Bingham's account of 1998. Pain later told Roger Corke and Carole Peters of Thames Television that Harrison must have got to the scene on his bike! According to his own testimony, DC Fairfax was writing up a report on a previous case when the Ware call came through and he decided to tag along. As I said in Chapter 1, this was not technically part of a detective's brief; perhaps Fairfax was bored.

The van journey to Tamworth Road took four minutes. Naively, I assumed that the vehicle pulled up at the *front* of the Barlow and

Parker warehouse, but the Archive evidence makes it clear that Beecher-Brigden drove around the rear of the premises, into Drayton Road that led to Upper Drayton Place (see map). Perhaps the police believed this was an easier access point to the roof than the front, especially as in his statement Beecher-Brigden says that there was an alleyway leading to the front. This is not at all clear from PC Beard's plan, but that may not be the only mistake he made.

There had been no shooting at this stage, but presumably the van had its sirens blaring as did the wireless car 7A driven by Sidney Miles with James McDonald alongside him. It is not clear from the statements exactly where the car stopped, but since McDonald and Beecher-Brigden were able to exchange words, it, too was at the back of the building. No one mentions a rear door to the premises. Craig and Bentley, on the roof by this time, had not looked for it and if the police did they found it locked. There had to be one because there was a goods entrance and loading bay to the south of Upper Drayton Place that clearly adjoined the building.

Whether under Fairfax's direction or not, the policemen split up to catch the culprits John Ware had reported. Fairfax checked doors and windows on the ground floor. All were locked and barred. Mills and McDonald had clearly arrived after Fairfax had gone on his search. Fairfax in effect followed Craig and Bentley by climbing the 6ft-high expanding metal gate to the left of the front of the building (west) and was told by McDonald that the suspects had been seen shinning up the drainpipes to the roof. Presumably, McDonald had found his way through to the passageway by those from Upper Drayton Place which Beard had not shown on his plan. How McDonald knew this is anybody's guess, but it may be that the inhabitant of No. 31, next but one to the warehouse, John Tennant, told him, as he later told Thames Television, that McDonald was in his garden.

Fairfax scrambled up a pipe, unaware that McDonald was trying to do the same, but, older, heavier and less fit, could not make the climb. Fairfax's statement (in the Archive) is set out below:

> I saw two fellows who I now know to be Craig and Bentley. They were about 15–20 yards away, in front and to my right.

The whole roof measured 90ft (30yds) so Fairfax's guesswork is likely to be correct and he probably climbed either the first or second pipe from the Tamworth Road end of the passageway.

> They both backed behind a brick stack [the head of the lift shaft where they would have been invisible to Fairfax]. I walked towards them and when about 6 feet from them I said 'I am a police officer. Come out from behind that stack.' One of them said, 'If you want us, fucking well come and get us.'

Clearly Fairfax did not know which of them had said that (he had never heard their voices before) but from what followed it is very likely to have been Craig.

> I said 'All right' and dashed behind the stack.

Fairfax does not stipulate whether he went right or left (the 1998 judgement assumed left). He had the darkened rooflights behind him and as far as he knew, he was alone on that roof facing, potentially, armed villains.

> I grabbed hold of Bentley and pulled him outside in the open and Craig went out the other side of the stack.

This was probably to the right of the stack as Fairfax looked at it.

> I pulled Bentley round the stack with a view to closing in on Craig and as we got round the other side of the stack, we came face to face with Craig.

Although Fairfax did not know it, Bentley was armed with a knuckleduster and sheath knife. He was also a couple of inches taller than Fairfax and possibly fitter, but he made no resistance. Neither did he try to break away from the detective's grip.

While this confrontation was going on, other officers were on the move. PC Harrison had gone to the right rear of the warehouse (east) having checked, with Fairfax, possible ways into the building. He reached the garden of 26 Tamworth Road and climbed onto an asbestos roof there and so on to its continuation that ran the width of the premises. No. 25 was unoccupied as it belonged to Blue Star Confectioners and was closed on Sundays, but the asbestos roof could be reached from 26. There is nothing in the Archive about the presence of occupants in No. 26 who could obviously, had they been in, given evidence of the evening's events.

Beard's plan does not do justice to the sloping roof on which Harrison now found himself. Neither do Percy Law's photographs. There was an asbestos-tiled guttering at the bottom of the slope, but the roof itself was glass and it was impossible for Harrison to stand upright here, especially since he was well within range of what turned out to be a maniac with a gun. Unlike Fairfax, Harrison had a torch and he did the detective no favours at all by pointing it at him, effectively lighting him up for Craig's first shot. He saw Fairfax grab Bentley and haul him round in front of the stack and called out to ask him if he was all right. Fairfax shouted, 'I've got the one but there is another one on the roof.'

> At this stage [Fairfax's account goes on] Bentley broke away from me and shouted to Craig 'Let 'em have it, Chris.'

Much was made later as to whether Bentley said ''em' or 'him', but in essence, it made no difference. As far as Fairfax was concerned, it was an incentive for Craig to start shooting.

> There was a flash and a loud report and I felt something hit my right shoulder.

This was exactly what Norman Harrison saw, lying on his back as he was. 'I then heard two shots fired from the direction of [the stack] where DC Fairfax had arrested the prisoner.' What is interesting about this moment is that neither Fairfax nor Harrison, the only two policemen in the immediate vicinity at the time used the word 'arrest'. The assumption was made in court, and has been ever since, that Fairfax's grabbing of Bentley was synonymous with arrest, but the lack of the word probably explains why Bentley did not believe he was under arrest. This would be exploited by the prosecution, judge and Home Secretary in the weeks ahead.

The sound of gunfire changed everything. By this time, PC Robert Jaggs had arrived. It was about 9.45 p.m. and Jaggs heard two shots. Like the others before him, he made for the drainpipes in the still dark passage. PC Daniel Wells was just getting out of his car when he heard those shots, but he does not say exactly where he was. Allan Beecher-Brigden, who had driven the van to Drayton Road, heard the shots too. He had seen Fairfax and Harrison climb over a garden wall (probably No. 30 Tamworth Road) and he stayed there to cover the rear of the premises. According to his testimony, Claude Pain stayed further back at Upper Drayton Place, probably not far from the van. From where he was, Beecher-Brigden could hear Harrison clattering up the wall to the asbestos roof. Sidney Miles turned up, still in Upper Drayton Place and said to him, 'There's two of them on the roof, are you all right here?' Beecher-Brigden told him that he and Pain had the rear covered and Miles sent him round to the front. It is not clear from this what right Miles had to give orders, but he may have been the senior officer in terms of years of service. Since my requests for these basic details were denied in 1990 and there is still nothing in the Archive, this can only be speculation.

There can be no doubt that it was Craig's first or second shot that hit Fairfax, so Beecher-Brigden's account does not quite tally with this. He believed the first shot sounded as if it came from 'the far side of the building' but since we do not know exactly where he was by now, this is unhelpful. 'A little time later I heard another shot fired and shortly after this PC Harrison, who was still on the [sloping roof] called out to me "Fairfax has got one," meaning a prisoner. "There's still another one up here."'

Bizarrely, a civilian whom Beecher-Brigden did not know came dashing into Upper Drayton Place to say he had a message from PC Miles that the keyholder had arrived 'and that they were going in'. This use of civilians to pass messages between police personnel seems amateur in the extreme and fraught with potential danger.

On the roof itself, Fairfax was on the receiving end of Craig's bullet. No doubt it hurt like hell at the time and subsequently, but there is no doubt from Dr Jazwon's evidence at the trial, however much Lord Goddard tried to rubbish it, that the bullet merely grazed the detective's shoulder and was travelling 'upwards' at the time, indicating a shot from the ground. Either Craig was crouching, kneeling or even lying (and why would he in the absence of any armed policemen?) or the shot was what he said it was, a ricochet caused by a bullet bouncing off the asphalt, a warning shot to keep police at bay. The fact that this bullet *fell out* of Fairfax's clothing at Croydon General Hospital implies that its energy had been spent, probably by striking asphalt first. As we have already discussed, a bullet hitting Fairfax directly, as in an attempt to kill him, would have shattered his shoulder blade and made an entry (and possible exit) wound in the shoulder itself.

Fairfax's statement went on:

> This caused me to spin round and fall to the ground. As I got up, I saw one man going to the left of me. I rushed at the man on my right [Bentley], closed with him and struck him with my

> fist, knocking him to the ground. At this stage there was a second report and I pulled Bentley up in front of me as a shield. I pulled him behind a large skylight and held him down and rubbed my hand over his clothing to try and find a gun.

The roof lights were 4ft 6in high at the apex but only 2ft 3in at the sides, so both Fairfax and Bentley must have been virtually lying down at this stage. They were now feet away from where Claude Pain had told me he was crouching, but his statement at the time puts him on the ground in Upper Drayton Place.

> I did not find a gun [Fairfax continued] but in his right-hand coat pocket was a knuckleduster which I put on, and in his right-hand breast I found a dagger.

Three things stand out about this part of the testimony. As we have established, Bentley was left-handed, so why should the knuckleduster be in his *right* pocket? The answer, it transpired later, was that Craig, whose weapon it was, had put it there earlier in the evening. Secondly, the emotive word 'dagger' which was repeated extensively by Goddard at the trial; the weapon was a standard sheath knife, of the type routinely carried by Boy Scouts and smaller than the one carried by Craig. The connotation 'dagger' had all kinds of sinister, assassination-type overtones. Third, how bizarre that Fairfax should put the knuckles on himself. Presumably, he hoped this would give him an edge in any further fisticuffs, although Bentley had offered no fight at all up to this point.

> 'That's all I've got, guv'nor,' Bentley said. 'I haven't got a gun.' [Fairfax told him he was going to work round the roof to that doorway, over there (he was pointing to the staircase head)] … and he said 'He'll shoot you.' I did not reply but pushed him out

> in front of me and worked my way round the roof to the door … I pushed him against the wall and told him if he stood still he would be safe.

Exactly where Fairfax and Bentley were by this stage is open to conjecture. The rational place would be the southern wall of the staircase head which rose to 7ft 6in and would provide safe cover for them both. The problem with this scenario is twofold. First, what did Fairfax mean by working his way round the roof? Presumably, this meant scuttling between the four roof lights, but again, this is conjecture. No one in the Old Bailey asked him for clarity. Secondly and more damagingly, is the clear evidence of John Tennant given to Thames Television and to me subsequently which was, of course, unavailable in 1952.

The Tennants lived in No. 31 Tamworth Road and the view from their garden across that of No. 30 gave them a clear sighting of the rooftop from the back of the building almost to the front. Taking his life in his hands though he was, John Tennant watched events from that garden and saw no one on the south side of the staircase head where Fairfax said he was. Tennant claimed that there was an alcove on the *north* side and that was where Bentley and Craig ended up. Its existence would explain one vital clue later, as we shall see. The evidence for Tennant's assertion is that he knew that view like the back of his hand, having seen it, presumably, on a daily basis for years. On the negative side, there is no sign of it in PC Beard's plan (but then, there is no clear ground access from Upper Drayton Place either, though clearly there was) and Percy Law's photograph of that side of the building does not show it either. As we have noted, the photographs are disappointing. There is no photograph of the roof from Craig's firing position, neither is the angle of 'Harrison's' roof obvious. Unsurprisingly, neither Parris nor Cassels challenged these photographs.

It was now that another contentious part of the police testimony arose. In his statement, Fairfax said:

> I then heard PC McDonald call up to me in a loud voice. [The constable was in the] passage below where I was standing. 'I have tried to get up the pipe but can't make it. Can you help me up the last bit?' I said 'Yes, I think so.'

Let us look at the situation now. Craig has already fired twice and hit Fairfax. Bentley has put up no fight and is now unarmed, but he is still a potential threat, especially as Fairfax has said that he invited Craig to fire with 'Let him have it, Chris.' We now have the bizarre situation where Fairfax leaves Bentley standing alone while he, Fairfax, apparently with a bullet in his shoulder, hauls McDonald the remaining feet onto the roof. All photographs of McDonald show an overweight, unfit man with a double chin. He must have weighed upwards of 15 stone. Yet Fairfax, with an injured right arm, can reach over a 2ft 6in rail and pull him up, albeit with McDonald's own help.

Fairfax now shouted to Craig to drop his gun, presumably feeling *slightly* more comfortable with a second officer with him. 'Come and get it,' was Craig's response. McDonald said, 'What sort of gun has he got, Fairy?' Bentley was being held, according to Fairfax, but he must have let go of him moments earlier to help McDonald. Once again, despite having the opportunity, Bentley made no attempt to rejoin Craig.

> Bentley then said, in a threatening voice, 'He's got a .45 Colt and plenty of bloody ammunition for it too.'

It was not, of course, technically a Colt .45 and Craig had eleven bullets, some of which did not detonate. Since Bentley did not know one end of a gun from the other, this must have been what Craig had told him, although *when* he did was not made clear. It was Bentley's contention that it was Craig who blurted this out, which would, of course, have been far more in keeping with his character.

There is no gap in Fairfax's testimony but there ought to be. Because it was now that Craig opened fire on Norman Harrison and now that Fairfax sent Bentley across the roof to try to talk Craig down from his ledge of insanity. Harrison, according to his testimony, was about halfway along the roof 'with my heels in the guttering and lying back on the sloping roof'. According to David Yallop, who was able to visit the Croydon rooftop himself in 1971, Harrison's view from the sloping roof would have been seriously impeded by the head of the lift shaft. Nobody raised this at the trial, even though the one thing that defence counsel had at their disposal was the crime scene. Craig went to the edge of the roof and looked down into the garden on No. 26. He saw Harrison and 'said something [no doubt unpleasant] about a copper'. Craig fired with his right hand and the bullet hit something behind Harrison [a chimney stack]. Realizing how exposed he was and probably within 15 feet of Craig, Harrison edged back the way he had come and, in the process, although he does not mention it, dropped his torch, which was found in the guttering by officers the next day. Craig fired again and again the bullet hit the chimney stack. There is only one chimney stack shown in PC Beard's plan and if Craig hit that twice, it is glaringly obvious how bad a shot he was. This in no way detracts from Harrison's danger or the cool courage he showed. 'Undaunted,' says DCI Smith's report, 'he rushed round and with other officers, including PC Miles, entered the warehouse which had already been opened up by the keyholder.'

In the version that Christopher Craig told to David Yallop in 1971, the gunman remembered that by this time there was a cacophony of noise. Police sirens and those of fire engines and ambulances shattered the Croydon night, punctuated, of course, by Craig's shots. Craig thought that Harrison was a fireman, unable to see him clearly in the dark. The comment about 'the copper' that Harrison had not quite heard was actually Craig asking if he was one. Craig says that his third shot in his direction made Harrison drop his torch. Yallop had no way to confirm this – Harrison, McDonald and Jaggs (only now arriving on the scene) had already refused his request for an interview.

It is odd that Fairfax does not mention Harrison's heroics, but perhaps, hiding where he is most likely to have been (despite John Tennant's later testimony) behind the staircase head, he did not see it. He certainly saw the next step, however, because he instigated it. Frank Cassels did not raise the issue in court, although he had every right to, skipping merrily from McDonald's arrival on the roof to that of Sidney Miles moments later. John Parris adopted this line of questioning too, although by doing so, both defence counsel missed a chance to catch the police out in a potential lie and Cassels failed spectacularly to save his client from the gallows.

'To me,' Craig told Yallop in 1971, 'one of the most terrible things that happened was Bentley turning against me. Helping the police like that.' First, when Fairfax had announced himself on the roof, Bentley had said to Craig, 'I'm going out.' This evidence was not heard at the trial. If it had been, it was cast-iron evidence that the joint enterprise, that ridiculous and unjust law that still stands, had come to an end; Bentley was, in effect, giving himself up. But, to 16-year-old tearaway Craig, 'worse' was about to happen. Fairfax and McDonald persuaded Bentley to go over to Craig to persuade him to give himself up. '"For Christ's sake, Chris, what's got into you?" I realized what he was up to and told him to stop or he'd get it too. "Get back, or I'll shoot you" … Then he turned and walked back to the police.' When Craig spoke to Yallop he was still bitter about what he saw as a betrayal. Derek Bentley had been dead for eighteen years by this time; what motive could he have for making any of this up? Yallop asked Craig why none of this evidence had come out at the trial. He said, 'It was bad enough that I was firing at policemen. If it had come out that I was prepared to shoot my mate, it wouldn't have done me any good at all.' But it could, of course, have saved Derek Bentley's life. When Yallop put all this to Frederick Fairfax in 1971, the ex-detective could not recall it. Surprise, surprise!

Parris admits, in *Scapegoat*, that Craig told him about the incident on their second meeting, the Sunday. He confirms what Craig had told Yallop, that it would not show him in a very good light and also, Parris contends, 'it was totally destructive of his own defence that he was only firing on the ground or over the garden of No. 30 Tamworth Road in order to frighten off the police and that the death of PC Miles was accidental.' It was, of course, no such thing. It was clearly obvious that Craig had already shot Fairfax, whether by accident or design and the fact that he was not willing to surrender his gun – 'If you want it, come and get it' – and Sidney Miles was not yet on the roof, still less dead. It would not have placed Craig in a worse light than he appeared already and it could only have been good for Bentley. According to Parris, he asked Craig's permission to tell Cassels all about it (presumably on the assumption that Bentley would fail to mention it).

At the interview with Cassels, Parris says that the man came out with his inexcusable 'I think both the little fuckers ought to swing.' Parris then had the sheer nerve to accuse me and David Yallop of criticizing Cassels for not doing his job. When Yallop interviewed Cassels in 1970, Cassels (by then a judge) remained as Goddard-like as he had almost certainly been in 1952 – 'anybody who carries a gun and kills a policeman ought to hang.' This was five years after capital punishment was abolished in Britain. The bottom line is that Cassels did not raise the issue in his examination of Bentley nor his summation on his client's behalf. Neither did he challenge Fairfax and McDonald on their lack of mentioning it.

Back on the roof on 2 November 1952 – or very nearly so, PC Miles was inside Barlow and Parker's and the lights were switched on. Nobody mentioned this at the trial, or even in police statements, but it must have made a huge difference. Craig could now see his targets clearly if they were in the open and they could see him. Only one gunman, not two and only, as he had told them, 16.

As Harrison said in his statement:

> PC Miles was in front of me [on the staircase to the roof]. He kicked the ... door open and I saw him fall to the ground as a shot was fired from the direction of the [lift] stack. I saw the young man I had previously seen on the roof [Craig] come from behind the [lift] stack. He still had a revolver in his two hands and fired another shot towards us and I thought it hit the brickwork of the doorway where I was standing. I leaned out of the doorway and threw my truncheon, a bottle of milk and a block of wood at him.

It is not clear where this assorted missilery came from. The truncheon was in Harrison's trouser pocket and presumably the bottle and the block were lying on the roof by the door. 'He shouted out,' Harrison's testimony continued, '"I'm Craig, you have just given my brother twelve years. Come on, you coppers, I'm only 16."'

Fairfax's version of the same event ran, 'It was at this stage that the door of the fire escape burst open and I heard police officers call to me. I shouted back that I was to the right of them and that the fellow with the gun was round to their left.' The extraordinary thing about this is not only does it conflict John Tennant's memory of where the police were on the roof, it is categorically *opposite* to the testimony given at the trial. Christmas Humphreys asked Fairfax 'Is the next thing you remember then the officers arriving from within the staircase head?' 'Yes,' Fairfax answered. 'What happened?' counsel wanted to know. 'The door marked B [on Beard's plan] burst open and officers called to me and I shouted back to them that I was round to their *left* [my italics].' This explains what was later incomprehensible to Craig. If this is what Fairfax *actually* said, rather than the version given in his statement, it explains why Miles was apparently moving left when he burst through the door, only to be hit head on by Craig's bullet. The challenge from those doughty defence lawyers Parris and Cassels? Nothing.

To be fair to them – although it was an appalling imbalance in the justice system as it was in 1952 – the prosecution was under no obligation to declare all evidence to the defence. It is therefore likely that neither Cassels nor Parris had seen a copy of Fairfax's statement before. Had they done, it would have exposed yet another hole in the official version of events.

Between them, Fairfax and McDonald dragged Miles's body behind the staircase head. 'I examined him,' Fairfax said in his statement, 'and found that he was beyond human aid.'

Harrison followed, joining the others, as well as Bentley, of course, out of the direct range of Craig's gun. Fairfax told the others he was going down the staircase and they should 'push the prisoner after me. I entered the building through the door in the roof and there as the officers pushed the prisoner, I dragged him into the doorway and he shouted "Chris, they are taking me down."'

Much was made of this at the trial. Either it was regarded by the prosecution as yet another incitement to fire (which it was not) or it was evidence of Bentley wanting to 'save his own skin' (Goddard). Fast forward to 1991 and we have a totally different sequence of events. The two keyholders of Barlow and Parker, Douglas Barlow and Dennis Woodcock, both contended to Thames Television that Sidney Miles's body was brought down *before* Bentley. As Superintendent Graham Seaby put it in his report of this evidence, 'Woodcock's account invests the police officers present with caution after Miles was shot [hardly unreasonable in the circumstances]. He describes an organized operation to get Miles's body off the roof.' Manhandling a dead body through a narrow doorway and down a flight of stairs is not easy. Doing it, whatever the exact sequence of events (and it is difficult to see why both Barlow and Woodcock would get it wrong) Christopher Craig made no attempt to shoot even though three or four policemen

– Fairfax, McDonald, Harrison and Jaggs (who had joined them via a drainpipe) – would have been easy targets.

There were a number of policemen on the stairs behind Miles and Harrison. One, 207Z Northeast, saw Miles glance to his left (according to Fairfax's instructions in his trial testimony) and then back to the others. It was as he turned that Craig's bullet hit him. Northeast had doubled back down the stairs, having heard 'about' four shots and did not see Harrison break out onto the roof, but he did see Craig jump off the roof moments later, presumably from the ground outside the building. PC 424 Lowe was not with them. Like Jaggs, he had climbed a drainpipe and saw Miles lying dead on the roof. He saw Fairfax, Harrison and 'another officer he did not know'. This could have been McDonald or Jaggs, but if Lowe is correct, one of them was not visible for reasons that are unclear. Lowe's statement includes Craig's conversation. 'Yes, it's a Colt .45. Are you hiding behind a shield? Is it bullet proof? Are we going to have a shooting match? It's just what I like.'

This was clearly in response to Fairfax's actions. Somewhere on the stairs or even on the ground inside the building, the detective was handed a .32 automatic by PC 722Z Barrett. At least four officers had been despatched to fetch firearms from Fell Road and Barrow was one of them, PC 121Z Gordon Stewart was another, as were PC 448Z Norman Mitchell and PC 779Z Arthur Church. Fairfax dashed back onto the roof, either with Miles's body still behind the staircase head (the official police version) or already down the stairs (Barlow and Woodcock). Fairfax shouted to Craig, 'Drop your gun. I also have a gun.' Craig's response was 'Come on, then, copper. Let's have it out.' Craig fired at him and Fairfax ran towards him in a semi-circle, firing as he went. He may or may not have used the now floodlit roof lights as cover and he fired twice, missing Craig both times.

Another officer on the stairs behind Miles and Harrison was PC 694Z Walter Carey. He too saw Miles lying on the roof and could not reach him because of Craig threatening to shoot. He and PC 428Z

Henry Harris kept the gunman talking for three or four minutes, during which he said that 'it would take more than four of us to get him'. Fairfax pushed past Carey armed with his pistol. He then says, contrary to Barlow and Woodcock, that he returned to Miles's body once Craig had jumped, knew that he was dead and helped carry the body downstairs.

PC 278Z James Gordon was on the stairs too. As Bentley was hustled down, he heard him say, 'I'm not the bloke who did it.' PC 481Z Harry Fenwick did not reach Upper Drayton Place until after 10 p.m. He had been handed two pistols by Sergeant Danny Watson and loaded them both. He checked vehicles at the back of the warehouse and handed one of his guns to Allan Beecher-Brigden before both of them left to return to the station.

The police evidence agrees that Christopher Craig threw himself off the north-west corner of the roof deliberately. Gordon Stewart wrote in his statement:

> I went through the back garden of an adjoining house [probably No. 30 Tamworth Road] climbed over a wall about eight feet high. From here I saw a man come to the edge of the roof … which was immediately above me, appear to overbalance and fall to the ground. As he fell I saw an object fall from him and this must have fallen on glass as I heard the sound of glass breaking. [The hole is clearly in evidence in Percy Law's photograph taken the next day] I then jumped from the roof I was on and made my way to a corner of the yard where I saw a man lying on the ground with PCs 424 Lowe and 161 Moore in attendance.

Twenty minutes later, Stewart and Sergeant Roberts found Craig's revolver lying on the greenhouse floor. Norman Mitchell was with Craig too and, with Fairfax, went through the house next door (again No. 30) and searched the garden. Mitchell 'found the prisoner lying on the ground, groaning … and crying "Oh, my back." The prisoner was then conveyed over the shed, through a garden and taken to Croydon Hospital by ambulance.'

According to Craig, shifting him to the ambulance was not the simple joy ride that Mitchell implied. He was dropped from the 8ft wall that Stewart referred to, with no regard at all for his injuries. James Ross had seen Craig jump. 'I saw a man silhouetted against the sky, standing near the edge of the roof. He was shouting all the time, but I could not understand what he was saying … He then turned round … and dived off the roof, as though he was diving into water.' Beecher-Brigden wrote that Ross had told him, 'He's committed suicide, he's just dived head first off the roof.'

Craig's gun was empty. He clicked the hammer two or three times. With his shout of 'Give my love to …' and it sounded like 'Pam', he brought his gunfight with the police to an end.

Years of cover-up and confusion would follow.

Chapter 12

The Wrong Arm of the Law

In his Introduction to my *Let Him Have It, Chris*, Ludovic Kennedy cites a number of murder cases in which miscarriages of justice have taken place. He cites the hanging of Timothy Evans in March 1950; James Hanratty in April 1962; the Luton Post Office murder in 1969; Patrick Meehan's case that dragged on from 1969 to 1976; the killing of Maxwell Confait in April 1972; and of the paperboy Carl Bridgewater in September 1978. He cites the murder of Met officer Keith Blakelock during the Tottenham riots of 1985 and the notorious (if understandable) overreaction that led to convictions for supposed terrorists the Guildford Four and the Birmingham Six in 1975. Not all the cases quoted by Kennedy were genuine miscarriages, but for the law to work effectively, it has to be just and be *seen* to be just. In all of the above, the doubts hover like Banquo's ghost.

Timothy Evans had the misfortune to become a lodger at 10, Rillington Place, Notting Hill, that was rented by John Christie and John Christie was a serial killer. Evans's wife, Beryl, and her daughter Geraldine were just two of the possible twelve victims (almost all prostitutes) killed by Christie over a ten-year period. He was not stopped – and hanged – until the summer of 1953. There are several similarities with the Bentley case, in that Timothy Evans was limited, with a very low IQ. He made four different statements to police, which did not help his case, but the Met was particularly lax in not searching No. 10 where at least two bodies had been buried in the garden. At Evans's trial in January 1950, the judge, Mr Justice Lewis, told the jury, 'Christie is a man who has told you that he is a sick man … he could not possibly have taken that woman [Beryl Evans] down the stairs.' But, as was apparent in Christie's own trial three years later, he did. I wonder what Mr Justice Lewis thought of that?

The Brabin inquiry, set up to investigate the Evans case, concluded that while Christie probably killed Geraldine (which he always denied) Evans probably killed Beryl. But Evans had been convicted and hanged for murdering them both and this was a clear miscarriage of justice. His was the first pardon granted in the twentieth century.

James Hanratty we have met already, hanged for the murder of Michael Gregston in August 1961. The evidence against him, apart from a pistol almost certainly 'planted' by somebody else on a bus, rested entirely on the eyewitness testimony of Valerie Storie, herself raped and shot by an assailant at Deadman's Hill, Clophill, Bedfordshire. Storie had clearly undergone a horrific experience but she failed to give an accurate description of Hanratty and testified that her assailant had not known how to drive a car and had to ask for her help. This was despite James Hanratty being an accomplished car thief! Tests carried out years afterwards, comparing Hanratty's DNA (from his corpse) with the semen stains on Storie's underwear were said to be a match. Over-reliance on DNA evidence is a story for another time, but Hanratty was not convicted on that (there were no DNA tests in 1961) but on the say-so of one traumatized woman. It did not help DI Robert Acott in charge of the case, that Peter Alphon admitted to the murder and that bullets of the matching calibre to the murder weapon were found in Alphon's hotel room. Alphon was never charged.

In the Luton Post Office murder, a sub-postmaster, Reginald Stevens, was shot dead by a gang of four in a car park, in their attempt to get Stevens' keys off him. One of the suspects, Alfred Matthews, turned Queen's Evidence (for centuries a cop-out clause to avoid the rope) and incriminated the other three – Patrick Murphy, David Cooper and Michael McMahon. Murphy was later freed when a belated alibi appeal was lodged, but the other two were sentenced to life imprisonment.

Their cases came Ludovic Kennedy's way and he investigated. 'By now [1969],' he wrote in *Thirty-Six Murders*, 'I thought I had plumbed the depths of police corruption and judicial incompetence, but this case exceeded them all.'

The villain in the case was a bent copper, Detective Chief Superintendent Kenneth Drury of the Flying Squad. Every London crook knew about Drury because of the many dodgy deals he had done with them. The superintendent bullied criminals in the days before PACE made this very difficult, with a mixture of threats and bribery. He was finally exposed by the *Sunday People* in February 1972 over allegations that he was in cahoots with James Humphreys, a Soho pornographer. Robert Mark, one of the most impressive of the Met commissioners, demanded an inquiry. His Number Two, Peter Brady, resisted, claiming that CID morale would be undermined and act as a green light to whistle-blowing criminals. In the event, Drury jumped before he was pushed, resigning from the Met. He was found guilty of corruption and sentenced to eight years in prison, reduced to five on appeal. Against his testimony in the Luton case, however, four courts of appeal turned Cooper and McMahon down, all of them acting with the same blinkered approach adopted by Croom-Johnson et al. at Derek Bentley's appeal and for the same reasons. If once a judge admits that other judges got it wrong or the police are found to be guilty of corruption, the rule of law – as it is laughingly known – floats out of the window. One of those judges, Lord Justice Roskill, wrote, 'The conclusion that each of us has independently reached is that Matthews was clearly telling the truth ... we see no justification in disturbing the verdicts which in our view were entirely correct.'

A fifth and final appeal court disagreed and Cooper and McMahon were allowed to step out into society again, free men after seven years in gaol for a crime they did not commit. Had the Luton case happened before 1965, given the ludicrous law of joint enterprise, both men would have hanged.

Our attitudes have changed in recent years, so that today, referring to murder victim Maxwell Confait as a 'transvestite' and 'cross-dresser' (both terms used in the media of 1972) would no doubt cause outrage. In fact, Wikipedia labels Confait as a 'sex worker'; in 1972 he was simply a 'prostitute'. His strangled body was found in a burning house in Catford, South London, in April 1972, and three males, Colin Lattimore (18), Ronnie Leighton (15) and Ahmet Salih (14) were arrested for the murder. None of them had adult supervision during their police interviews, as this was merely a recommendation at the time. Lattimore was sentenced to indefinite detention in Rampton Psychiatric Hospital, guilty of manslaughter due to 'diminished responsibility' a 'get out of jail' card which still causes controversy today and which became law in 1957. Leighton was given a life sentence and Salih, because of his age, was sent for four years to the Royal Philanthropic School.

A new government in 1973 saw Roy Jenkins, as Home Secretary, ordering a review of miscarriages of justice. Two of the great forensic experts of their time, Keith Simpson and Donald Teare, trounced the work of pathologist James Cameron, who had been the prosecution expert at the original trial. The case was sent back to the Court of Appeal (it had already been rejected once) and this time (October 1975) the convictions were quashed.

The Fisher enquiry looked into the police handling of the Confait case and revealed bad practice in the conduct of interviews. A Royal Commission into procedure in 1981 led to PACE three years later, the Prosecution of Offences Act in 1985 and the replacement of the Directory of Public Prosecutions by the Crown Prosecution Service. In theory, from 1984 onwards, all police interviews had to be conducted with a lawyer present and had to be taped. With the release of Lattimore, Leighton and Salih, the police conducted no further investigations and the case of Confait's murder remains open.

Six years after that killing, 13-year-old paperboy Carl Bridgewater was blasted with a shotgun during what was believed to be a robbery that went wrong at Yew Tree Farm, near Stourbridge, Worcestershire, in September 1978. Four men, Patrick Molloy, James Robinson and Michael and Vincent Hickey, cousins, all local burglars, were charged with the murder. Molloy, who claimed to be a witness only, was given twelve years for manslaughter (he died in prison two years later). Robinson and Vincent Hickey got life; Michael Hickey, detention 'at Her Majesty's pleasure'. The initial appeal (by now an automatic, knee-jerk process) was rejected, but in February 1997 the Court of Appeal overturned the original verdict. The police had coerced Molloy into his confession. The campaign to release the men was launched by writer Paul Foot, who had also worked on the Hanratty case and a prosecution was to have been bought against the policemen involved in those suspect interviews. Mysteriously, this was dropped in December 1998 and, like that of Maxwell Confait, the murder of Carl Bridgewater is still unsolved.

Every serious crime committed, especially that of murder, has a backdrop that is important to our understanding of the case. The mid-1980s saw an upsurge in violence between largely black communities in London and elsewhere and the police. One such upsurge occurred on the Broadwater Farm estate in Tottenham in October 1985. A black woman, Cynthia Jarrett, whose son was believed to be involved in criminal activity, had her home searched by Met officers and suffered a fatal heart attack during it. Immediately, there was an outcry in the area's ethnic community, with hundreds of black men, armed and hostile, taking to the streets. The Met's riot squads were dispatched and one unit, the eleven-man strong Serial 502, was sent in to protect firemen trying to put out a blaze at a supermarket, caused by the mob.

Outnumbered, 502 fell back, one of them, PC Keith Blakelock, stumbling in the process. The crowd of at least fifty leapt on him, hacking him to death with machetes and even axes. It was some time before the police could restore order and recapture the streets, by which time, any crime-scene evidence had been destroyed. One hundred and fifty officers under Detective Chief Inspector Graham Melvin arrested and interviewed 359 suspects over the course of the following days and weeks. Despite PACE having been set up the previous year, ninety-four of these were interviewed without the presence of a lawyer and without being taped. Eventually, three men were charged with Blakelock's murder; Winston Silcott, Engin Raghip and Mark Braithwaite. All three were found guilty and sentenced to life.

The case caused a great deal of unrest. The racial tensions of the United States, with its memories of slavery and the Civil War had floated across the Atlantic and had become a burning issue here too. It did not help that councils like Haringey had allowed places like Broadwater to become 'sink estates', cesspools of crime and drug-taking. The area was largely ignored by the police, anxious not to worsen an already dangerous situation and the whole affair was not helped by Bernie Grant, the rabble-rousing black leader of Haringey council who suggested that Blakelock may have been killed by another policeman! The rank and file of officers blamed their high command for the 'softly, softly' approach of community policing in the first place.

Again, police practice was called into question. Raghip was in the 'middle of the mildly mentally handicapped range' (not unlike Derek Bentley) but this was not put forward at his trial. Chief Superintendent Melvin struck a blow for genuine justice, however, when he claimed that 'the integrity of some firms of solicitors left a lot to be desired'. Much more recent events have proved this damning indictment to be correct.

The original appeal by Silcott et al. was turned down by the Lord Chief Justice, Lord Lane, in a decision condemned as unjust by Amnesty International. The media at the time had, rightly, been outraged at Blakelock's death, with banner headlines referring to 'hooded animals', 'packs of savages' and the 'beasts of Broadwater'. Not since the murder of Sidney Miles had Fleet Street gone so berserk.

But the Met's careless approach to the handling of interviews again proved their undoing. Raghip was defended by two of the most brilliant lawyers of their day, the solicitor Gareth Peirce and the barrister Michael Mansfield and the weight of public opinion, as with Derek Bentley, swung in his favour. Not only were the verdicts quashed, but Chief Inspector Melvin and his assistant DI Dingle were themselves put on trial, charged with conspiracy to pervert the course of justice. Both men were acquitted unanimously in July 1994.

The cases of the Guildford Four and the Birmingham Six are beyond the scope of comparison with the Craig and Bentley case. Undoubted miscarriages of justice though they were, and again caused by the incompetence and/or corruption of the police, they far exceed what happened in 1952. Suspects were routinely beaten in police custody, fabrications abounded. The Surrey police were blasted for their misconduct in 1989, but this was fifteen years after the event that led to the imprisonment of the Guildford Four. At an earlier appeal, Lord Justice Roskill had said, 'The new evidence … gives rise to no lurking doubts whatever in our minds. We are sure there has been a cunning and skilful attempt to deceive the court by putting forward false evidence.' Could there be a more damning indictment of the judiciary? As Ludovic Kennedy puts it, '"Never apologise, never explain for the monumental cock-ups our judicial system has made" should be the judiciary's motto as they repair to their cosy, privileged Inns of Court world.'

A short distance from Broadwater Farm, where Keith Blakelock was butchered, another police officer died in pursuance of his duty, trying to control a riot. In 1832, a miracle had happened. For the first time in British history, the electorate had been extended. Those now receiving the vote had doubled, but the reform only involved men of property, in effect excluding the working class. The early 1830s had seen waves of unrest and the Whig government of Lord Grey feared more of the same. Police spies had infiltrated the National Union of the Working Classes. The Met was only a few years old at the time and Commissioner

Charles Rowan took personal charge of the meeting that was due to be held by them at Coldbath Fields, Clerkenwell. The result was a ten-minute 'battle' in which Constable Robert Culley was killed. According to evidence at his inquest, he had become separated from his unit and staggered into the Calthorpe Arms pub where he died of his injuries. The jury were very anti-police and outraged that the Riot Act had not been read, which was standard practice as a preliminary to dispersing crowds. The police, witnesses contended, were 'ferocious, brutal and unprovoked'. The jury returned a verdict of 'justifiable homicide against person or persons unknown'. This was not a recognized verdict in a court of law and the Court of King's Bench threw it out.

Culley's widow was given £200 (£19,000 today adjusted for inflation) by the government. Contrast this with the feeble sum granted to Catherine Miles in 1952. The jurymen, however, were given medals, inscribed goblets and river trips by their peers.

The importance of all this is the change of attitude with regard to the Metropolitan Police by the public. To many ordinary Londoners in 1833, the 'New Police' were the baddies, equated with the political spies and snoopers set up by the thief taker Eugene Vidocq in Paris only a few years earlier. Contrast that attitude with Lord Goddard's defence of the police at the Craig and Bentley trial. In his summing up, he said:

> Miles, the dead man, was a police officer and the law for centuries – in fact, ever since there has been law in this country – has given special protection to police officers while in the execution of their duty … in the case of a peace officer who is killed, the law does not give the accused the same defences as in the case of other persons; it takes one away and I am going to direct you that this is the law.

Whether Craig intended to kill Miles or not, the charge was murder and not, as Parris tried to contend, manslaughter with its lesser sentence.

So pleased was Goddard with this situation that he said it twice. As David Yallop and many others have pointed out, creating a hierarchy of murder – that some crimes are worse than others – may be the natural reaction of many of us, but it should not be the reaction of the Lord Chief Justice of England. By virtue of the position he is in and the risks he takes, a police officer is far more likely to be killed than, say, an old lady or a child. The law should not be harsher on a 'cop killer' than any other kind of murderer.

It is worth noting, as we did in Chapter 10, that judges like Goddard were so steeped in the tradition of English law that he was able to cite Sir Edward Coke, a judge whose word was taken as something loftier than the Bible in 1644. That was a time when every word of the Bible was taken to be literally true and that devil-worshipping witches walked the earth, blighting crops and killing people. It would be refreshing to think that by 1952 the world had moved on just a little.

The public's attitude to the Met changed as time went on, until we reach the status quo as it was in 1952 and which is outlined in Chapter 2. Like all police forces, the men and women involved work hard to keep us all safe and their daily routines and triumphs rarely reach the front pages. When it all goes wrong, however, it inevitably creates a great deal of media attention. It did in 1833, 1952 and does again today. What went wrong in 1952 is still very much with us and it is a sad indictment on elements of the Met whose attitudes have changed little in the nearly 200 years of their existence. The Craig and Bentley case must be seen in the context of all that, because it very much forms a pattern.

The Detective Branch of the Metropolitan Police was only thirty-four years old when it was rocked by a scandal that almost destroyed it. In a complicated fraudulent betting scam run by two conmen, Harry Benson and William Kerr, a number of Scotland Yard detectives were involved in taking bribes. Bearing in mind the majority of the original 1829 intake of uniformed constables had been dismissed within three years for exactly the same offence, this should really have surprised no one. But by the

1870s, the British public had come to accept and trust their 'bobbies', if not exactly to love them. The 'trial of the detectives' at Bow Street court saw Inspectors Nathaniel Druscovitch, John Meiklejohn, George Clarke and William Palmer in the dock. Clarke was acquitted after a character reference from his boss, Chief Constable Adolphus 'Dolly' Williamson, but the others served two years in gaol. It was obviously the end of their careers. The Detective branch, reeling and trashed, was rescued by a bizarre intervention that could never happen today. Lawyer and soldier Howard Vincent suggested a compete overhaul, to be run by himself, called the Criminal Investigation Department.

As any number of police commissioners of the Met – and chief constables of other forces – have pointed out, there are rotten apples in anybody's barrel and the Met is no different. We have already come across Sergeant George Goddard, caught with his hand in the till in the 1920s, the decade in which Claude Pain joined the Met. The media of the day was apoplectic, especially since Goddard and a Constable Wilkins regularly escorted and protected prostitutes for a cut of the takings. Juicy stories sell newspapers and the 'white slavery' angle, of foreign girls shipped into London for immoral purposes, always made headlines. If the police appeared to be making life easy for those racketeers, so much the better as far as Fleet Street was concerned.

We should, of course, be wary of imposing the mores of our own time on to the past, but even officers regarded as upright in their day were a little on the shady side. DCI Ted Greeno who solved high-profile murder cases during the Second World War, was guilty of 'leaning' on Private August Sangret of the Canadian army, interrogating him for far longer than the law allowed. Greeno also had a gambling problem, spending a fortune on the horses. He also had an evening job guiding tourists around the East End's Cable Street 'where the negroes walked' as if they were some sort of exotic zoo exhibits.

It is with incidents *after* the Craig and Bentley case that corruption in the Met really takes off. Award-winning journalist Tom Harper has recently (2022) exposed the failures of modern policing in his *Broken Yard* (Biteback) but I would contend that his investigation has not gone back far enough. Criminals have, for centuries, contended that various police forces have 'fitted them up', planted evidence, obtained confessions under duress and much more. Ninety-nine per cent of the inmates in any prison in the world will tell you they are innocent of any crime. But sometimes, such assertions are true. In July 1963, Sergeant Harold Challoner, ex-SAS war hero and holder of the Military Medal, headed up a team to arrest protestors outside Claridge's Hotel in London. The purpose of the protest says it all about the idiocy of today's 'causes' (all of which, of course, the police are expected to cope with). Queen Frederica of Greece was on a state visit and apparently had pro-Fascist links. Cue confected outrage from youths who had it in for 'Queen Fred'. They were charged with carrying bricks in their pockets with which to pelt the queen. One of the arrested was an art teacher, Donald Rooum, who was also a member of the National Council for Civil Liberties. He passed the jacket he wore that day (untouched, as he was in a police cell overnight) to his solicitor and no traces of brick dust were found on it. The case was thrown out. There was an internal police inquiry (wholly worthless, of course, in terms of honesty, whatever the television series *Line of Duty* would have you believe about such inquiries) and those charged were compensated. Challoner and his officers were charged with conspiracy to pervert the course of justice. Challoner was deemed to be suffering from paranoid schizophrenia (or being as 'mad as a hatter', the phrase used by a psychiatrist) and sent to a psychiatric hospital. The others got three or four years in prison.

It emerged that Challoner took bribes and occasionally 'worked over' suspects in custody. How much of this was due to his illness and how much to the 1950s and 1960s culture in the Met is still open to debate. He had been examined by Detective Superintendent John du Rose, who spectacularly failed to catch the 'Jack the Stripper' murderer of women along the Thames in that decade, but the findings of the inquiry were never made public and led the new commissioner, Robert Mark, to root out all forms of corruption in his force.

After a long and varied police career and war service, Mark became commissioner in 1972, the year in which David Yallop's claim of police shooting on the Croydon rooftop reached the BBC and a very wide audience. As an outsider from Manchester (like John Parris from Leeds) Mark was resented by his Met colleagues and found little support at first. Even when promoted to assistant commissioner, he found that serious crime investigation was bypassing him to other colleagues. He was particularly concerned about internal corruption of the Drury/Challoner type and set up a Complaints Investigation Bureau called A10. This effectively took such investigations out of the CID's hands. *The Times* newspaper investigation into the Met's corruption, which highlighted Kenneth Drury's collection of dues from the Soho porn market was a clarion call for Mark to do something.

A10 discovered something that Claude Pain had known all along. The kudos of the detectives (no doubt going right back to Druscovitch and Meiklejohn) gave them an arrogance that was unjustified. 'Anything might happen, Mr Trow,' Pain told me. 'I might be run over by a car or anything.' At a meeting of plainclothesmen from the Police Federation, Mark told them that they represented 'the most routinely corrupt organization in London'. His message was simple – reform or inform. Back in the Victorian period, corrupt or under-achieving bobbies were routinely ordered back to inspecting horse troughs. Jim Callaghan, at the Home Office, was delighted. He telegrammed Mark, 'Quick, Decisive and Right! Congratulations.'

Under Mark, Soho prostitution was policed by a new Vice Squad ('The Dirty Squad') with a remit to crack down on an increasingly graphic pornography. Gilbert Kelland was brought in to head up No. 4 Area responsible for disciplining officers. Four hundred and seventy such men were dismissed, disciplined or took early retirement – one in six of the CID. The media railed that the Met was corrupt from top to bottom but Mark worked well with the press and was good at sound bites. By and large, he won them over.

In the Dimbleby lecture in 1973, he publicly attacked unscrupulous defence lawyers (and there were plenty) who effectively perverted the criminal justice system and often forced the police to use underhand tactics in order to secure rightful convictions. Contrary to the official line, say, in Claude Pain's day, policemen of all ranks were encouraged to let Robert Mark know what they felt about issues and he would engage with the public via the media. He was an outspoken critic of the system he ran because he could see its faults. He was equally outspoken about minority pressure groups who persisted in waving their banners and expecting the police to protect them. As one serving Met officer told me at the time, 'It was all about championing the cause of the unborn, gay whale.' As Martin Fido and Keith Skinner say in *The Official Encyclopaedia of Scotland Yard*, Mark was the man who cleaned up the Met.

But how long do such reforms last? Remember the casual comment I related in Chapter 1 from a switchboard operator at the Met's Press Office – 'There's some bloke here wanting to know about old crimes. That's peculiar, isn't it?' By 1990, the antics of Craig and Bentley were old crimes and I could tell from his voice that my co-conversationalist was probably not born when they happened. Now, a quarter of a century later, such crimes are older still. But such crimes continue.

It perhaps goes without saying that the police – and the Met in particular – have an impossible job and it is a job they are expected to do 24/7. Retired colonels and most of Middle England want the police to get heavy, catch burglars and knock seven bells out of street gangs and football hooligans. The pinko-liberals of the London 'bubble' want them to empathize with a bewildering array of minority causes, make cups of tea for eco-protestors and dance the night away with Notting Hill revellers, however much illegal substance hangs in the air at the time. Harassed chief constables, Met commissioners and divisional commanders try to make all this work and inevitably, they fail. Sadly, there have been too many cases in recent years when the Met has come up short. So bad had the picture become by 2022 that Scotland Yard, once the feared headquarters of crime busting, was placed in special measures, like an under-achieving infant school.

The recent shortcomings of the Met make depressing reading and critics will say that they have no bearing on the events of 1952, but they do. 'The Met,' a Home Office source told journalist Tom Harper in 2022, 'is like a horrible onion. You start peeling back [the layers] and you cry more and more.' And this is not something that has suddenly appeared out of the blue; it has always been like that.

We have to acknowledge two facts before we can make any judgement on the police handling of the Craig and Bentley case. First is that crime, like everything else, comes and goes as fads, fashions and mores change. In the early 1950s, the fad was the 'cosh boy', juvenile delinquency in which most juvenile crime was carried out for gain and most targets were older, 'respectable' people. The press, always barometers of public moods, jumped on this quickly, putting pressure on police forces and the judiciary to do something about it.

As early as 1933, with the passing of the Children and Young Persons Act, there was a growing tendency to bring more teenagers to court, rather than boxing their ears, which had been the norm for centuries. Many believed that lax parenting was the chief cause. Both the Craig and Bentley families were criticized for being too soft with their children and for allowing their little darlings to wander the streets unchecked and unsupervised – to get to Croydon, for example, 'just for an ordinary ride'. It was rather depressing that Sir Philip Game, commissioner of the Met, attributed the rise in theft to displays of goods in shops. This almost smacks of the old rapists' defence – 'She was asking for it.'

The solution was more boys' clubs, where, presumably, ping-pong was about as exciting as it got. Christopher Craig, of course, went to

Bible classes, but it did not stop him from shooting two policemen. Cyril Burt, an influential educationalist in the 1940s and 1950s, advocated corporal punishment and the use of the birch, singing from Lord Goddard's hymn sheet. Many authorities pointed to the effects of war and to the rise in wages paid to the young. Christopher Craig was only on £2 a week when the Croydon shooting happened, but before he lost his job, Bentley was on £6 a week – far too much, said the critics. It encouraged drunkenness (although Bentley did not drink) and bad behaviour.

The 'cosh boy' menace gave way by the late 1950s to Rock n' Roll and Teddy Boys. Youth now had its own uniform – winkle picker shoes, 'DA' haircuts and sideburns, ra-ra skirts for the girls. A couple of years later, 'Mods' and 'Rockers' were kicking seven bells out of each other, for no particular reason, and getting to their seaside battlefields each summer on noisy, fume-belching Lambrettas.

Drugs transformed young crime. Like much else, a whole range of narcotics was imported from the United States, not directly but in the sense of a culture associated with youth. 'Narcotics' in the pre-war period consisted of a tiny group of pseudo-intellectuals, the Bohemian set who used opium. The vast majority of the country was untouched by this.

More recently, other influences have gained ground. The rise of militant Islam, which began as a 'Dark Ages' problem, gave cause for concern, as did Irish terrorism in Britain. What struck me on the last of my three visits to Scotland Yard's Black Museum was the number of exhibits relating to terror. The Met now has a counter-terrorism unit, in common with other forces, an idea that would have been unthinkable in the days of Craig and Bentley. The media continues to monitor this, often (as with the *Daily Mail*'s fatuous 'Chicago' gun battle in Croydon in 1952) distorted and exaggerated to sell newspapers. The recent arrival of social media, with its irresponsible and unaccountable 'platform' has made this so much worse and, since the Met is the police force for the capital, it is under more pressure from this quarter than ever before.

So crimes come and go. Craig and Bentley belong to a bygone age. So, in time, will Russian agents poisoning people in Salisbury and pro-Palestinians taking to the streets to demand freedom 'from the river to the sea'. In ten years' time, few will remember what river and what sea they were chanting about.

One of the most repugnant crimes of the 1990s was the murder of black teenager Stephen Lawrence by a gang of white thugs in once-genteel Eltham, south-west London. Lawrence and his friend Duwayne Brooks were set upon by roughnecks as they waited for a bus and Stephen was knifed to death. Youth murders by youths and the rise of knife crime is now a major headache for London's authorities, as were the 'cosh boys' of the 1950s. The initial police investigation was woeful. The Met claimed that they met a 'wall of silence' from the local community, whereas in fact within hours of the murder, the names of all five killers had been given to the police by several unrelated individuals. The police seemed loath to believe anything Duwayne Brooks told them and he himself was pulled over several times in the months ahead. No charges were ever brought. Surveillance of suspects did not begin until three days after the murder and the crime-scene evidence was seriously compromised. The Met was convinced that drugs were involved, but this was not the case.

What the police had not reckoned with was the articulacy and tenacity of Stephen's parents, Neville and Doreen, who launched a national appeal for justice, much as the Bentley family had done for Derek. The initial case collapsed, despite the best efforts of Michael Mansfield QC and it would be eighteen years before the accused David Norris finally faced justice. The others were brought to book too but only because Paul Dacre, editor of the *Daily Mail* stuck his neck out against libel lawyers with a front-page headline 'MURDERERS', together with the names of the suspects and their photographs.

This was a pivotal moment in British crime and policing history, Jack Straw, at the Home Office under Prime Minister Tony Blair wrote that the Met 'were judge and jury in their own courts. When things went wrong there was no one ... who was able to hold them to account.' He ordered a public enquiry under a retired high court judge, Sir William McPherson, to investigate.

The McPherson report, 12,000 pages long, had interviewed 88 witnesses and involved dozens of lawyers. It found that evidence had been lost and chances had been missed. Scotland Yard's own internal inquiry had exonerated everybody, which has now become the norm in reviews of most institutions, but McPherson slammed everybody, from the commissioner, Paul Condon, down. When the report was issued in February 1999, not long after Lord Bingham's verdict on the Bentley case, the Met was found to be guilty of 'professional incompetence, institutional racism and a failure of leadership by senior officers'. Because McPherson had been less damning on actual police corruption, no single officer was disciplined for any failings. As Duwayne Brooks said in reaction to this, 'It takes six years to admit that a couple of lads had been neglected and mistreated by the police. Six years – followed by a conspiracy of silence.'

Three years before the murder of Stephen Lawrence, a private investigator, Daniel Morgan, was hacked to death in the car park of the Golden Lion pub, Sydenham, South London, in March 1987. The police investigation into the murder lasted for thirty years and still has no definite outcome. There were five separate police investigations but each one was dropped by obfuscation from certain officers and an infuriating lack of evidence. As with the Lawrence and Bentley families, interest was kept alive by a family member, Daniel's brother Alistair. As with the Lawrence murder, the crime-scene investigation was lamentable. The car park was not cordoned off, contrary to police protocols, evidence was removed from the scene and not logged and the senior detective involved went into the pub for a drink before he began work.

What emerged was that Morgan had been investigating major corruption in the Met that centred on his own partner, Jonathan Rees, and Detective Sergeant Sid Fillery. Despite the fact that Fillery had known the dead man, he was put in charge of the case, again breaking every rule in the book. 'My brother,' wrote Alistair, 'had been butchered because he was about to blow the whistle on police corruption. And what did we get from the Crown? Feeble, corrupted policing, wilful blindness and sleazy denial.'

Operation Russell in April 1987 and Operation Niagara in 1998 were both attempts to root out this corruption and may or may not have had a bearing on the Morgan murder. Both failed. Of particular interest were the links between Morgan's company, Southern Investigations, and the *News of the World* newspaper. Known as 'News of the Screws' to all and sundry, Rupert Murdoch's tawdry rag specialized in stories of sleaze, preferably of a sexual nature. In 1996–7, *News of the World* paid Southern Investigations, now run by Jonathan Rees, £166,000.

As for Sid Fillery, he was found to have child pornography on his computers and lost his job. His sentence? Three years' community service on account of his previous good character! The murder of Daniel Morgan remains unsolved. As Doreen Lawrence wrote in a letter to Alistair Morgan in 2005, 'This is a whole can of worms that you are opening … it is going to be a long struggle and a lot of people will be covering their backs.'

Derek Bentley had written a similar letter to his mother Lilian on the day before he was hanged. In a prison warder's handwriting, he related, 'as I said in the visiting box that one day a lot of people are going to get into trouble and I think you know who those people are.'

Ali Dizaei was the 'Teflon commander' because no allegations of corruption stuck to him. In 1999, Operation Helios investigated him after allegations of using drugs and prostitutes and taking bribes. The timing was fortuitous for Dizaei. Only the year before, the McPherson report had branded the Met a racist organization and here was an Asian officer under investigation. He played that race card and won, despite being charged with money-laundering and working illegally with various London-based embassies. It helped too that he was defended by Michael Mansfield, always a champion of noble causes. And by the 1990s, there was no more noble cause than the racial one. We now have the absurd situation where racism is regarded as one of the worst crimes on the statute book, to the extent that when Tom Harper wrote of the damning surveillance tape the Met had made of two men involved in the Lawrence killing, he had to write it this way – 'I'd go and kill every black cunt, every P**i, every copper, every mug that I know.' So the offensive 'c' word is acceptable in print today (Harper's book was published in 2022) but the 'P' word, which, after all, simply describes an ethnic origin from the country of Pakistan, is not. This is exactly what Dizaei was counting on. He was awarded £80,000 compensation, and got his job back. That was followed by promotion. Met Commissioner John Stevens told the press, 'Superintendent Dizaei is returning to the Met with his integrity demonstrably intact.'

It all fell apart for the Teflon commander however in 2008, when he was found guilty of assaulting an Iraqi businessman and attempting to frame him. Described as a 'criminal in uniform', he was dismissed in February 2010 for perverting the course of justice. Even Teflon wears off, eventually.

The case of Jean Charles de Menezes was more about cock-up than corruption, although there was an element of the latter too. The summer of 2005 saw a state of high alert in London over recent terror bombings and trigger-fingers were perhaps over-quick. I remember newspaper accounts of the time telling us what had happened when the Met's counter-terrorist snipers closed in on a suspect in Stockwell Tube station. He was carrying a backpack and wore a padded jacket, either or both of which could have contained a bomb. He behaved furtively and ran when he felt himself targeted, leaping over ticket barriers.

In fact, his jacket was thin denim and there was no backpack. He got on a bus (the vehicle of choice for earlier suicide bombers) and walked, rather than ran, into the Tube station. All of this was picked up on

CCTV. He was not a Muslim fundamentalist with a visceral hatred of the West, but a Brazilian electrician, Jean Charles de Menezes, on his way to work. He was shot at least five times by a panicky police unit that was trailing him, despite that fact that on at least that occasion, they had been told that they were following the wrong man. The commander running this operation from long distance was Cressida Dick, who, as a 5ft tall woman, stood out in the macho world of the Met. Of all the police officers mentioned in various records in the Craig and Bentley case, there is only one woman, a WPC, and her role is not specified. The leadership in the de Menezes case was later described as 'chaos, confusion and indecision'.

The new Met commissioner, Ian Blair, urged the Home Office not to let the IPCC (which investigated police procedure) become involved and went through the motions the next day of a press conference which regretted the actions at Stockwell. The Crown Prosecution Service said that there was insufficient evidence to bring any charges against individual officers, but after a five-week trial, the Met was found guilty over health and safety issues and hit with a huge fine. There were demands for Blair to resign but the commissioner had the backing of Gordon Brown, the prime minister, and his Home Secretary, Jacquie Smith. The press uncovered the fact that Andy Hayman, who ran the Yard's counter-terrorism unit, had had no previous experience of this sort of policing before his appointment.

Over a year later, an inquest on de Menezes was finally held in which the coroner, retired high court judge Sir Michael Wright, told the jury that their choice was either lawful killing by the police or an open verdict. Since the killing was clearly not lawful, the jury chose the open option. Wright's advice to the jury was within the bounds of a coroner's remit (as was Lord Goddard's in his interpretation of the law to the Craig and Bentley jury) but it left a nasty taste in the mouth. The ass that is the law was braying again. Individual officers, including Cressida Dick, were blasted for incompetence and she went on to become commissioner herself in 2017. As for Ian Blair, he was obliged to offer his resignation in 2008 when Boris Johnson became Lord Mayor of London and expressed no confidence in him.

Largely because of the rise of the #MeToo movement, both in the United States and Britain, there was a subtle change in police procedure. Too often in the past, the police in both countries and all forces had ignored the complaints of sexual assault victims, abandoning all hopes of sorting out the he said/she said accounts of events and, no doubt, letting guilty men go free. The #MeToo movement changed all that, with a powerful female lobby gaining public support for their side of the story.

Out of this came the notion that victims of sexual harassment should *always* be believed. Out of this came 'Nick', a sexual fantasist who reported sexual misdemeanours to the Wiltshire Constabulary, claiming that a number of prominent figures had abused him and other children from the age of 12. Into the frame went: Maurice Oldfield, ex-head of MI6; Michael Hanley, ex-head of MI5; Labour peer Lord Janner; the television celebrity Jimmy Savile; and 'Nick's' own stepfather. Wiltshire investigated, interviewing 'Nick's' mother, his former teachers and his doctor and concluded (rightly) that the man was making it all up, for whatever weird purpose. Of the accused, only Savile was actually a child molester and since he was dead, there was little that could be done.

Undeterred, 'Nick' used the same pitch to the Met, except that this time his targets were: Lord Brammall, a former general and D-Day hero; Leon Brittan, ex-Cabinet Minister; Harvey Proctor MP; and the late Edward Heath, prime minister. These men, 'Nick' claimed, had sexually abused him and killed three children in various prominent buildings in London, taking him there and home by taxi. Before 'Nick's' mother had been interviewed, Detective Superintendent Kenny McDonald held a press conference at which he claimed that 'Nick's' claims were 'credible and true'.

This went so far beyond acceptable police behaviour as to be unbelievable. It is for a court to decide what is true, not the Metropolitan Police. And it runs counter to the old police maxim – A, B, C: Assume nothing, Believe no one; Check everything. McDonald was part of Operation Midland, overseen by Cressida Dick, Deputy Assistant Commissioner Steve Rodhouse and Steve House (confusingly), Dick's right-hand man. All in all, twenty-seven officers were involved in Midland, which took fourteen months to complete and cost £2 million.

Officers assured Judge Howard Riddle that they had sufficient evidence to search the homes of Brammall, Britten and Proctor when in fact all they had was 'Nick's' word. The MP Michael Soames said 'no sloppy PR spin from the Met will ever disguise its repulsively dishonourable treatment' of those named, all of whom were subjected to long, privacy-invading searches of their homes, offices and computers.

In November 2016, Judge Richard Henriques led an enquiry into Midland and identified forty-three separate errors made by the Met and that officers had misled Judge Riddle to obtain warrants. Ex-Detective Superintendent McKelvey said to author Tom Harper, 'Why the fuck did they believe Steve Rodhouse who ran the job? If you'd gone back to the 1980s and 1990s, he would have been sacked. How the hell did he ever get that role?'

In fact, Rodhouse had already failed to stop Jimmy Savile's genuine reign of child abuse when he served with the Surrey Constabulary.

When the media got involved, 'Nick' was outed as Carl Beech, who had no links with any of the accused. What he did have was child pornography on his computer (in which he tried to frame his son) and he was jailed for eighteen years for this and perverting the course of justice. As Harvey Proctor said, 'It was a truly disgraceful chapter in the history of British policing.' The commissioner, Bernard Hogan-Howe, resigned over it and has ended up in the Lords. Steve Rodhouse, far from being charged with incompetence and possible corruption, was promoted to play a prominent role in the National Crime Agency,

Britain's (pointless) answer to the FBI. Not a single police officer has been charged.

But all this pales into insignificance against the case of the Met officer Wayne Couzens. On 3 March 2021, in the insane days of lockdown over the Covid pandemic, 33-year-old Sarah Everard was walking home across Wimbledon Common in London when she was stopped by an off-duty police officer, Wayne Couzens, who handcuffed her and put her in his car. No doubt he told her that she had contravened the government's draconian lockdown laws, which technically she had, but rather than take her to a police station, he drove her to a wood near Dover, raped her and strangled her with his police belt.

Couzens was a firearms officer responsible for parliamentary and diplomatic protection work and on the day in question had just finished a shift in the House of Commons. How he expected to get away with his crime is unknown. CCTV tracked him everywhere, from talking to Sarah Everard outside his car, to the journey itself. By the time cameras caught him at a service station, he had probably already killed her. Two days later, Couzens returned to the scene of the crime, burned Sarah's body in an old abandoned fridge and dumped the remains in builders' bags in a pond at Ashford, Kent. On 8 March, he reported sick, handing in his cuffs and belt, both items used in the kidnap and murder.

The next day, Couzens was arrested in Deal and told his interrogators that he was being blackmailed by an East European gang that had threatened his wife and children into providing girls for their prostitution racket. Two days after that, police found Sarah's remains 110 yards from land owned by Couzens. She could only be identified by her dental records. Because of the lockdown regulations, the Old Bailey trial was operated by Zoom, with Couzens giving evidence from Belmarsh prison. He was found guilty and sentenced to life imprisonment.

All this was bad enough, but such was the culture in the Met that two of his colleagues were also jailed for distributing 'grossly offensive' tweets in his support. Five had communicated with him before trial and several offered him character references while the trial was taking place.

On 13 March, a vigil was held on Clapham Common briefly attended by the Duchess of Cambridge and, again because of the anti-Covid restrictions, the police acted in far too heavy-handed a way. There were four arrests and women were forced to the ground by uniformed officers.

The media, as always, led the outrage, demanding that Cressida Dick, now commissioner, resign. The North Yorkshire force came under fire when their chief constable, Philip Alcott, told the press that women should be more street savvy in such situations. He had to go. When the information came out that Couzens had been improperly vetted by the Met and that he was laughingly referred to as 'the rapist' by his colleagues, there was a natural outrage. Couzens was subsequently convicted of flashing offences before the murder of Sarah Everard and crime experts doubted whether the killing was actually his first such offence. Despite the fact that he seemed to be unaware of the all-pervading presence of CCTV, the murder was carefully planned and calculatingly carried out.

A group of feminists formed the Sisters Uncut organization and set up advisory units on how to cope if approached by a lone male officer. Stung into reforms, Cressida Dick abandoned such policy anyway and promised a swingeing review of the Met's standards.

By the end of February 2022, various authorities were saying 'enough is enough'. A senior Home Office source said of the Home Secretary, Priti Patel, 'We have lost count of the number of conversations that the Home Secretary has had with Cressida and Steve House. They are not interested. It is institutional. They are very defensive. Policing is very defensive but the Met are absolutely the worst.' In that month, London's Lord Mayor, Sadiq Khan, told the press he had lost confidence in the Commissioner and she resigned. As Ray Raman, ex-commander of the Flying Squad, said, 'Cressida is unique in lots of ways but she's not the first Dick we've had as a commissioner.'

The tragedy about the litany of cock-ups and examples of corruption is the way the Met defends its own, standing together in the 'buddy-buddy' mentality we see all too often in American law enforcement. As Operation Countryman, looking into the Met's corruption, discovered in 1978 that there were at that time eighty-four officers being investigated for bribery, the planting of evidence and conspiring with known criminals. In that investigation, some files disappeared and almost everything took weeks to be passed on to the investigators. Of the eighty-four officers involved, only two were prosecuted. As Laurie Cork of the Flying Squad told Tom Harper in the context of evidence planting, 'Everyone does it. I'm not a rotten apple in danger of rotting the barrel. It's a fucking rotten orchard.' The Sheehy Report of 1993 was supposed to shake the Met out of its Victorian attitudes and blinkered mentality. The police attitude to it at the time was that Kenneth Clarke, the Home Secretary, demanding Sheehy was rather like putting 'King Herod in charge of Mothercare', which is just about as wide of the mark statement as you can find. There was a mass demonstration of at least 9,000 Met officers at Wembley Arena, complaining about the suggested reforms. One wonders what kind of field day London's villains had with so many officers off the street, but by 1993 officers had been off the street for nearly two decades – I doubt whether anybody noticed.

In case the reader thinks that the woeful list of wrongdoing by the Met is of recent origin, read this chapter again. It goes back at least to the trial of the detectives in 1877 and there are numerous examples of it since. On 26 January 1956, four years after the Croydon rooftops shoot-out, questions were raised in parliament about the number of Met officers who had been convicted over a five-year period (from 1951). One had been convicted of manslaughter, one 'using an instrument to procure a miscarriage', one for 'persistently importuning male persons for immoral purposes', three for shoplifting, sixteen for larceny, two for demanding money with menaces, four for false pretences, one for forgery, two for corruption, one for conspiracy to pervert the course of justice, one for common assault, two for permitting a ferocious dog to be at large, three for not paying rail fare, two for having no wireless licence and thirty-eight for motoring offences. The grand total was 140 charged and 87 found guilty.

The Craig and Bentley case, like other miscarriages of justice, must be seen in this context.

Chapter 13

Putting the Record Straight

This book has to end, as it began, with Constable 241Z Claude Pain. When Carole Peters of Thames Television interviewed me, she said in a voiceover that I had written a book about Pain. I had not; I had written a book about the Craig and Bentley case, although it is true that without Pain, there would probably have been no book at all.

If you have read Chapter 1 which explains the version that Pain told me and Thames Television, you will notice that it does not square at all with the evidence of the men on the roof, like Fairfax, McDonald, Harrison and Jaggs. In fact, none of those officers mentions Pain at all. Why is this? It is because, despite all his assurances and realistic memories, *Claude Pain was not on the roof at all.*

As Ludovic Kennedy wrote in his Foreword to my *Let Him Have It, Chris*,

> [Pain] had written a deposition in which he made no mention of Bentley shouting anything and one would like to think that, asked by his colleagues to join their club, he refused to compromise his integrity. Yet he, no less than they, had felt the death of PC Miles keenly; and police solidarity being necessary not only for their morale but their survival, there could be no question of his disassociating himself from their evidence. So, although a witness on the roof along with the rest of them, he does not feature anywhere in his colleagues' presentation of their case; indeed they denied on oath that there was any other officer on

the roof beside themselves. He was not cited as a witness, and soon after his notebook and his deposition 'disappeared'.

Er … not quite.

David Yallop has his three monkeys whose silence in the Craig and Bentley case he and I believed was deafening. In fact, all three officers – Pain, Beecher-Brigden and Alderson – gave their statements to CID officers (the standard procedure) that were duly typed up and signed. It was then at the discretion of either DCI John Smith in charge of the case or Christmas Humphreys for the prosecution, to decide who to call. For whatever reason, these three men were not called, but then neither were Daniel Wells, Leslie Moore, Charles Northeast, Thomas Bodley, Douglas Barrow, Gordon Stewart, Norman Mitchell, Arthur Church, Walter Carey, Henry Harris, Harry Fenwick, Reginald Riding and Archibald Bastard. There is nothing out of place in any of these officers' testimony, all of which is in The National Archive, but since Yallop made so much of the missing three, let us see what their original statements said.

James Alderson, in a deposition given on 2 November, hours after the rooftop shooting, to DC William Robson of Z Division, said that he was patrolling in police car 553T No.1Z with 773Z Stephens. They got a call at 9.52 for them to go to Messrs Barlow and Parker to 'assist in apprehending men who were shooting from the roof of those premises'.

When they got there two or three minutes later (9.55) they met Inspector Cook who told Alderson to take up a position in front of the building in Tamworth Road. After five minutes or so (10 p.m.) Sergeant Roberts came out of the building with 'the prisoner Bentley'. Alderson helped Roberts bundle him into the car and they drove for Fell Road. 'On the way … Bentley said "I knew he had a gun but I didn't think he would use it, he's done one of your blokes in."'

Bentley was searched at the station (Fairfax had of course already done this) 'but no firearms were found on him'. 'Whilst I was standing in front of the premises I heard about five or six revolver shots.'

As with Bentley's statement, this was clearly a question and answer session. Alderson's addition of the shots he heard sounds like a prompted afterthought. And I very much doubt whether the constable had the expertise to know what kind of gun fired the shots he heard. Alderson's testimony was probably deemed unnecessary because Sergeant Roberts gave the same version in court.

David Yallop got Beecher-Brigden's name wrong, calling him Bugden. This was almost certainly because that was how it appears in the version written by Met Commissioner Harold Scott in his book *Scotland Yard* in 1954. Such mistakes are unfortunate and do not make life any easier for true crime researchers. For the record, Scott's account of the rooftop shooting is an accurate reporting of the prosecution side of the case. He visited Fell Road on the morning after the incident and congratulated Harrison, McDonald and Jaggs personally. Later that day, he spoke to Fairfax too, still in hospital at that point. In H. Montgomery Hyde's *Trial of Craig and Bentley* in the *Notable British Trials* series, PC Stuart Stanley Lowe is listed as Stanley Lowe Stewart!

Beecher-Brigden's statement was taken on 5 November, three days after the shooting, by Christopher Rowe, a DS in Z Division. Beecher-Brigden left Fell Road at 9.21 p.m. driving the police van, with Claude Pain, Norman Harrison and Frederick Fairfax. They got to Drayton Road and Beecher-Brigden, Harrison and Fairfax ran up Upper Drayton Place. Fairfax and Harrison climbed over a garden wall at the west of the warehouse. There is no mention of a passageway that others describe. Beecher-Brigden waited by the wall, covering the warehouse rear. 'Pain stayed at the other end of Upper Drayton Place where it meets Upper Drayton Road.'

Beecher-Brigden heard 'clambering at the side of the warehouse and a few minutes later I saw PC Harrison on the warehouse roof at the West Croydon side. I had not heard any gunshots up to then.' This is very confusing. According to Harrison's account at the trial, he got to the sloping roof, *not* the warehouse roof, via gardens and walls to the *east* of the warehouse, not the west.

Beecher-Brigden told Rowe that PC Miles appeared from the Drayton Road direction and told him, still in Upper Drayton Place, 'There's two of them on the roof. Are you all right here?' Beecher-Brigden told him that they had the back and sides covered and he dashed back to the front of the building. 'Shortly after this I heard a gunshot fired and to me it seemed to come from the far side of the building.' It is not at all clear what Beecher-Brigden meant by 'the far side' and since he was not called as a witness, his testimony, like that of Alderson and Pain, was never questioned. 'A little later, I heard another shot and shortly after this PC Harrison, who was still on the roof, called out to me, "Fairfax has got one," meaning a prisoner. "There's another one still up here."'

From more than 20 feet below him, Beecher-Brigden can have had no idea where Harrison was, but clearly Harrison was in a position to see him, even though he was flat on his back negotiating the sloping roof.

It was now that the anonymous civilian arrived in Upper Drayton Place with a message from Sidney Miles. As we said earlier, this was highly irregular. In the absence of personal radios, messengers were essential to coordinate police movements, but messengers should have been policemen, not civilians. The keyholder had arrived, Miles had said, and they were going in to the building from the front. Beecher-Brigden heard four shots fired at intervals, then the back doors of the warehouse burst open and Sergeant Roberts and PC James Ross came through them and joined Beecher-Brigden.

The driver got back to his van and moved it in case a fire engine needed access. Beecher-Brigden went back to Upper Drayton Place and as he went he saw a man 'silhouetted against the moonlit sky' shouting something that Beecher-Brigden could not make out. He called Roberts and Ross over to him and heard another gunshot, this time seeing the 'flash of flame … about waist high on the man on the roof'. Beecher-Brigden believed he and his comrades were the target and then he heard another shot.

PC Ross's account is remarkably similar to Beecher-Brigden's which is not surprising bearing in mind that the two were together at various times and saw the same thing. Even so, Ross's 'I saw a man silhouetted against the sky but I could not understand what he was saying' is perhaps a little *too* similar for comfort. Ross made his statement on 6 November, the day after Beecher-Brigden and to the same CID officer, DS Rowe.

At the back door of the warehouse, Beecher-Brigden was handed a pistol by PC Fenwick and cocked it, ready for use. As he went back to Ross (he believed that Roberts had gone by then), he heard two more shots. When he reached Ross crouching by a wall, he realized that he could not see the man on the roof any more. Ross said, 'He's committed suicide. He's just dived off the roof.'

Beecher-Brigden stayed in Upper Drayton Place until 11.45 p.m. when he was told to take officers back to Fell Road. He took a second pistol from Fenwick and returned both to Sergeant Denny Watson at the station. 'No rounds had been fired from either of these guns.'

Had he been able to access Beecher-Brigden's statement, David Yallop might have thought twice about his police sniper theory. It is still not obvious exactly how many guns were issued that night and to whom, but another piece of evidence in The National Archive clears this up. Craig's gun, by the way, was stolen from the house of Ernest Roberts of 45, Riddlesdown Avenue, Purley, between 9 and 18 October 1952 along with four blank cheques, a paper knife and a pair of binoculars. It had not helped that after Roberts had reported a burglary, he had not missed the knife and binoculars and had not mentioned the gun because he had no licence for it. On 12 November 1971, in response to questions about the police use of firearms, DI G. Monger C2 (Legislation Unit) wrote, 'I must first point out that the time laid down for the destruction of the Occurrence Book, Crime Book, official messages and other locally held records is long past.' The 1971 response was undoubtedly because of David Yallop's accusations, and the disappearance of such records is, to say the least, unfortunate. The Craig and Bentley case had been controversial since 2 November 1952 and all records should have been maintained. In the recent improvement in technology, when all such information can be digitized on a memory stick, this is unacceptable. Monger was therefore reliant on police testimony in the case papers (which neither Yallop nor I were permitted to see). According to all available records, firearms were issued at Fell Road a minute or two after PC Miles was shot. Inspector Cook issued orders to get an ambulance, police surgeon, police dog and fire engine at 9.50 via R/T to the Information Room. Guns were given to PCs Stewart and Barrow. The latter gave his to Fairfax who fired his two shots at Craig. Monger underlines the fact that, 'when PC Miles was shot, no police officer at the scene was armed.' In all, five .32 automatic pistols were issued, each loaded with eight rounds of ammunition. All were returned unfired except Fairfax's gun which had fired the two bullets. This information, gleaned from the testimony of various officers, would have been written up by Cook in the Occurrence Book, although no statement from Sergeant Danny Watson has survived.

Monger estimates the distance from Fell to Tamworth Road as ⅜ of a mile by the most direct route, which would have taken at least three minutes by car. Barrow and Stewart must have been missing from the scene for about eight minutes.

The rest of Monger's report deals with the rounds fired on the roof. He points out that a .45 calibre bullet is much larger than .32, although it was this very point that Yallop quizzed Dr Haler on and quotes the pathologist as saying that a .32 *could* have killed Miles. Haler denied having said this and Monger's report backs that up. Altogether, Craig fired up to ten times (he would have had to reload his six-shooter) and Fairfax twice, making up the total of at least twelve shots heard by various police witnesses.

This information was collated after an urgent request from Assistant Commissioner J. Weston of Scotland Yard to make clear the issue of guns on the night in question.

Where, in all this, is Claude Pain? The deposition he made on 3 November 1952, far from being missing as he told me, was in The National Archive all along. Had I been permitted to see this document, there would have been no *Let Him Have It, Chris* by M.J. Trow and I would not have got involved in the case at all. It is worth quoting in full:

> On Sunday 2 November 1952, I arrived at the Police Station early at about 9.15 p.m. to go on duty at 9.45 p.m. (night duty).
>
> Shortly after my arrival at the police station, at 9.21 p.m. I was in the Reserve Room when a telephone call was received to the effect that some men had been seen climbing over the gate leading to the side of Messrs Barlow and Parker's premises at Tamworth Road, West Croydon.
>
> I went in the police van with the driver, PC 229Z Beecher-Brigden and Det. Constable Fairfax to Messrs Barlow and Parker's.

Note that there is no mention of Norman Harrison. In fact, he does not mention Harrison throughout his entire statement.

> We went to Drayton Road which leads to the rear of the premises. Actually, there is a small passageway at the back of Barlow and Parker's and I covered the rear entrance in this passageway. Det. Constable Fairfax climbed over a wall and went towards the factory premises.
>
> Several minutes afterwards PC 252Z Sid Miles who I knew was driving the wireless car, came up to me and informed me that there was two chaps hiding behind a stack on the roof and they were firing a gun. He told me to *stay where I was* [my italics] while he went round to the front of the building.

> I had heard a couple of reports [shots] before this, but I wasn't sure what they were. PC Miles then came back and asked me to phone for assistance as the men on the roof were armed. I went to a nearby public house and phoned the station asking for further assistance and then returned to the passageway.

This is odd. Miles had already told Pain that the men were armed – Pain had heard two shots himself – why come back to tell him the same thing? And why did Pain not use the R/T in Miles's car, parked in Drayton Road rather than find a pub? Perhaps the vehicle was locked or perhaps Pain could not work the radio. Either way, it would have been useful if his report had told us.

> While standing there I heard revolver shots, about 7 or 8 altogether at intervals.

If we include the first two, then Pain heard nine or ten of the shots fired. He must have been away from the scene making his phone call for a few minutes, but we have no way of being accurate about this. He does not give the name of the pub but it may have been the Robert Peel, mentioned by John Ware in his statement.

> On hearing this, I went to the front of the premises [he does not explain how] and was informed by PC 528Z McDonald R/T operator on the car 7Z that PC Miles had been shot in the head.
>
> I stayed in front of the building and kept the forecourt clear of people, as by this time a crowd had assembled.
>
> I later was sent to Croydon General Hospital to guard the prisoner Craig who had been detained and sent to hospital. Whilst there, he said to me 'Have I shot a policeman?' Later he said 'You made

mistakes when you were young.' I left the hospital at 2 a.m. for refreshments.

This statement has been read to me and it is true.

(Signed) Claude Pain
PC 241Z

The statement was taken down and witnessed by DC William Robson of Z Division.

There was no rickety ladder, no Claude Pain edging his way to the relative safety of the roof lights. He did not hear 'Let him have it, Chris' because he was not on the roof at the time. In fact, he was never on the roof. He did not see Sid Miles go down to his side 'like a ton of bricks' and he did not help carry him off the roof.

I have no doubt that he saw his dead friend – his description of the darts in his pocket and his head, exploded like a pig, was just too graphic to be anything but the truth. The rest of it, I am afraid, was fiction.

Fast forward to 20 December 1991. This was the day a detailed report was drawn up by Detective Superintendent Graham Seaby of SOI, International and Organized Crime Branch of Scotland Yard. In November, a number of issues had been raised with Mrs Mitev and Stephen Whitelegg of the Home Office, both by letter and on the telephone. These were in the context of Thames Television's programmes which, in turn, had been kickstarted by my book.

On 22 November, having rung me to see if someone could be with Claude Pain in what was likely to be a 'difficult' interview. Seaby visited Pain at his home. He found him to be a very friendly old man with treasured memories of his police career and a loyalty to the Service that persists. 'He did not appear to be as badly affected by his stroke as the papers from Thames Television suggest.' He was quite clear in making points and did not ramble. 'He gave the impression,' said Seaby, 'that what he said he knew to be the truth.'

At no point did he waver from what he had told Thames (which, in turn, was exactly what he had told me) and when Seaby showed him a copy of his 1952 statement (see above) he made three points. He doubted the veracity of what he read because it was a copy and he had nothing to compare it with. There are no police pocket books in the Archive and this would have been Pain's go-to document as a matter of routine. Along with the log books referred to by DI Monger above, such books have presumably been destroyed long ago. Secondly, Pain had never heard of DC Robson, even though he is on record as having taken the statements of several other officers. Thirdly, Pain accepted that the account while Miles was still alive is accurate 'but more of what he wrote is omitted. He wrote about going onto the roof.'

Four days later, Seaby contacted Claude's son Peter, known as 'Sonny'. It was Ray who had been my original contact, teaching my wife to drive, and I did not know Peter, not even his name. Pain junior told Seaby that his father was adamant that he had written a statement himself (not usually police procedure) and had handed it in together with his pocket book on the night in question. The old man was convinced that the copy that Seaby had shown him was not what he had written and not what had happened. Needless to say, there is no formal statement from Pain to Seaby. 'At this stage it would serve no useful purpose.' His version of events was already in the police dossier, both in my book and in the Thames Television programme.

So where are we left in the case of Craig and Bentley vis-à-vis PC Claude Pain? It seems to me that there are two possibilities. The first is that Pain told me, Thames Television and Superintendent Seaby the truth. And if that is the case, then there was a conspiracy among certain officers of Z Division to obscure the truth and to fabricate evidence. Sidney Miles had been killed by a 16-year-old who was too young to hang. His 19-year-old accomplice according to the law then – and to the law now – was equally guilty of murder. And in 1952, murder carried the death penalty. The police wanted to make sure that somebody paid in full for the death of one of their own – and that somebody had to be Derek Bentley.

One of the many mistakes that John Parris makes in *Scapegoat* is with reference to the Hulton and Jones murder of 1944, in which he states that, 'Hulton and Jones were convicted and hanged.' In fact, only Hulton faced the rope (via Albert Pierrepoint at Pentonville in March 1945). In its day, despite the fact that the war was still raging and newsprint was in short supply, the case caused a furore. 'Ricky' Hulton (whose real name was Karl Gustav) was a deserter from the American army stationed in Britain and, rather like Christopher Craig, adopted a gangster-like persona, even claiming to be part of the Chicago Mob (which he was not). He picked up 18-year-old Elizabeth Jones, who called herself 'Georgina Grayson' and the pair went on a Bonnie and Clyde wannabe series of robberies. There was a gun (like Craig) in Hulton's pocket. On 7 October 1944, the couple held up a taxi driver, George Heath, and Hulton shot him. Heath was bundled into the passenger seat and the trio drove towards Staines. On the way, the cab driver died of his injuries and Hulton and Jones threw his body into a ditch. They continued to drive around in the dead man's taxi and Hulton was arrested by police in Hammersmith.

Jones was not with Hulton at the time of his arrest, but she let things slip when talking to a War Reserve policeman and was herself arrested. She confessed to full involvement in the murder, but claimed that she had been under duress from Hulton. Two days later, the American made a fresh statement implicating Jones further, saying that she had egged him on.

Unusually for the time (American servicemen were routinely tried by US military courts) the United States waived this right and Hulton was tried at the Old Bailey. Jones was reprieved two days before her execution and was released in 1954.

The case was called in the press the 'Cleft Chin Murder' on account of the physical appearance of the victim, George Heath and the story filled the newspapers as much as that of Craig and Bentley eight years later. To add to the excitement on the front pages, Jones's barrister was a woman, Mrs Lloyd Lane, and this was the first time that a female had been so prominent in a capital murder trial. The press bench at the Bailey was enlarged to facilitate the army of American journalists who descended on London for the trial. Like the Craig family, Jones's parents had been brought down from Wales by courtesy of a Fleet Street cheque book. For the first time, Jones was allowed to appear hatless in court.

In this case too, the jury returned a recommendation of mercy after the guilty verdict in Jones's case. Interestingly, the public's attitude hardened after the trial and there were demands, especially from women, that she should hang. Writing the case up in 1945, the barrister C. Bechhofer Roberts told his readers that some people wanted them both to hang (reminiscent of Frank Cassels' 'I think both the little fuckers should swing.'). Others regarded them both as foolish children and should be let off with a warning. Still others wanted him spared and her hanged. There really was, at the end of a harrowing and exhausting war, no rational explanation of it all.

One of the bleeding hearts was Ernest Bevin, the cabinet minister of Labour, who pleaded Jones's case to the extent that she was a bright girl whose achievements were undermined by a lack of money in post-war Britain, the Britain of the dole and the means test. Furious, the chairman of her school governors produced her actual results in examinations in 1938. She got 28 out of a possible 150 in Maths; 62 out of 150 in English. Had she passed the exams, however, she would have received handouts to buy books and would have received free school meals.

When the obligatory Court of Appeal convened in February 1945, there, surprise surprise, was Mr Justice Croom-Johnson, Goddard's crony. The appeal was rejected.

One of the oddest responses to this case was a letter from George Bernard Shaw, the outspoken Socialist who in earlier days would happily have taken the government to task over anything. Shaw was not arguing that Jones should not hang but he found hanging itself outmoded (the government would agree with him twenty years later). Instead, he suggested some kind of euthanasia whereby the gangster's moll would be quietly put to sleep. Bechhofer Roberts found this idea 'grotesque'.

The day after Shaw's letter appeared, Jones was reprieved. Bechhofer Roberts finds this six-week wait for the Home Secretary's decision 'an abominable penalty'. He predicted she would spend fifteen to twenty years in prison (in fact, she served nine).

Why is the case of Hulton and Jones relevant and important to the Craig and Bentley case? Although there are obvious dissimilarities, there are common factors too. In both cases, the prosecution alleged that the shooter had been egged on by the aider and abetter. In both cases, the jury recommended mercy. In one it was granted; in the other, it was not. Why?

Firstly, in the Croydon shoot-out, the victim was a policeman. And in law and in the public's mind, there was something particularly heinous about killing a policeman. George Heath, in the meantime, was a mere taxi driver. In fact, he had no licence to drive his cab and there were rumours (as it turned out, irrelevant to the case) that he was a black marketeer (as were, I might add, thousands of others). Secondly, the war was over and the Conservative government could concentrate its mind on getting tough on crime. The waywardness of Britain's youth during the war (and partly as a result of it) was already known to the police, courts and social workers, as a detailed study of runaway girls in the Bath area in 1943–4 had shown. Thirdly, and perhaps most obviously, the actual killer was old enough to hang and the jury, the Home Secretary and swathes of the public, took pity on the silly little Welsh girl who had got in with the wrong crowd.

We have established already that British criminal law is based on precedent. What a pity that David Maxwell-Fyfe ignored this entirely in the case of Rex v Jones and Hulton.

But there is another earlier case that has even more relevance to Craig and Bentley. John Parris referred to it at the Old Bailey in December 1952, but not in the context he should have. Officialdom has continued to ignore it, even in the summation of Lord Chief Justice Bingham in 1998, who believed the suggested comparison 'far-fetched'. It has not been ignored, however, by John Parris (as writer rather than barrister), Ludovic Kennedy, David Yallop, Christopher Berry-Dee and me. Every other fair-minded writer on the story of Craig and Bentley has mentioned it too. It is the Appleby case of 1940.

On 29 February that year, Jesse Smith was cycling home in Coxhoe, County Durham, when he saw suspicious activity in a Co-operative store. It was 2.15 a.m. and no one should have been on the premises then, yet lights were flashing on and off. Smith pedalled to the nearest police station and PC William Shiell went back to the shop with him. With them was PC William Stafford. At the back of the premises, it was clear that bolts had been levered off the door so Smith and Stafford waited there (like Pain and Co in Upper Drayton Place) while Shiell went round to the front.

He had only just got there when someone crashed through a plate-glass window and ran for it, with Shiell in pursuit on foot. Stafford and Smith followed and heard a shot. When they reached some open ground at the back of Westly Road, they found Shiell dying. His 'last' words (always taken seriously – and I believe wrongly – as a dying declaration by the law courts) were that the shooter's accomplice had shouted, 'Let him have it, he's all alone.'

Constable Shiell survived to get to hospital where he told other officers that his killer had looked like a Spennymoor footballer called Fewsted and had an auburn moustache. Shiell died on 1 March.

Clues were everywhere for the police. A getaway car abandoned by the burglars was found and traced to a doctor in nearby Chester-le-Street who had reported it stolen. Three days after Shiell's death, police arrested Vincent Ostler and William Appleby. Appleby was all too ready to make a deal and told his interrogators that Ostler had pulled the trigger. As for 'Let him have it', he never said it. At their trial in Leeds in May, Mr Justice Hilbery presided and both men were found guilty of murder. As in the case of Jones and Hulton and again in the case of Craig and Bentley, the jury recommended mercy and presumably on the same grounds. The law of joint enterprise, in which everybody is guilty of a murder, made no sense to ordinary people in 1940, 1945 or 1952. It still makes no sense today. Only bewigged idiots, out of touch with reality, could see it any other way.

What about the laws of coincidence? What are the odds that two men, deemed not to be the actual murderers, in two separate cases, should have incited the gunman using *exactly the same words*? The point is that it is not a coincidence at all. The case judgement, as well as the basics, were written up in a variety of books available in every police station in the land in 1952.

John Parris told me, when we met after I had finished *Let Him Have It* in 1990, that in the small hours of the morning of 3 November 1952, the officers on the Croydon rooftop, as well as DS Stanley Shepherd, were called to a meeting at the Fell Road police station by DCI John Smith. There, still in shock and outraged over the death of Sidney Miles, they agreed the events of what had happened. As Commissioner Harold Scott observed, meeting the same men hours later, 'My impression, indeed, was that I had gone into a family home where one of the family had suddenly died. It is characteristic of the police that when one of them is in trouble, they give unstintingly whatever help is needed.' The result was what came out at the trial – twenty-four police witnesses for the prosecution; two criminals for the defence. Of course, not all those twenty-four, Parris told me, were lying, but three of them were.

Debunkers who routinely rubbish conspiracy theories will tell you that conspiracies are unreal, that they cannot work because of the sheer numbers involved. How can you be sure that dozens, scores or hundreds will keep quiet and not, in street parlance 'blow the gaffe'. The answer in the Craig and Bentley case is the tiny and finite numbers involved. There were only four policemen on the Barlow and Parker roof. Robert Jaggs had got there too late to have heard the infamous 'Let him have it' so he was not called to Smith's meeting. James MacDonald was but because he was up and down drainpipes like an out of condition yo-yo, he was only called upon to say that *someone* said 'Let him have it' but he could not identify who. That left Fairfax and Harrison. Both men were near enough to Craig and Bentley to hear much, if not all, they said. And the evidence of *two* officers in that respect would be better than one.

At the trial, Harrison nearly went too far by asserting that Bentley had used the words to incite Craig to fire, even though no one contended this. Whether DS Shepherd was at Smith's conference is unknown. As the DCI's number two it would make sense, but he was not absolutely essential.

Would an experienced and apparently upright officer like Smith orchestrate this sort of thing? Take a close look at the photograph of Bentley being taken away from his night in the cells at Fell Road and you will see the clear contusions to his forehead, which shocked a prison officer on Bentley's arrival at Brixton. Was this the result of Fairfax hammering him to the ground on the rooftop or the result of a kick that Derek told Iris that Smith had given him during interrogation? John Parris told me that he heard of this clandestine meeting from an inside police source. He did not divulge his name.

In *Scapegoat*, Parris was even more forthright. In his final chapter, he writes, 'Good God! How have accused persons these late years been punished when the Judges themselves have been such delinquents?' He was quoting the man in whose former house he lived, the Lord Chancellor (the highest legal authority in the land) Edward Hyde in May 1641. Parris was writing seven years before Lord Justice Bingham's decision to quash Bentley's murder conviction. At the time, Parris believed that an enquiry into the Craig and Bentley case would not work 'given the notorious corruption of the English criminal system'. This, despite the fact that two years after the Craig and Bentley case, F.T. Giles, Chief Clerk of Clerkenwell Magistrates' Court, wrote in *The Criminal Law* 'English law will probably be regarded as the greatest system of law the world has ever known.' Tell that to the Bentley family.

'What no judicial enquiry will ever accept,' Parris wrote, is that:

1. The police habitually commit perjury
2. They habitually fabricate evidence against accused persons
3. They usually fabricate it in cases where they believe the accused to be guilty, but they know perfectly well that the accused is innocent [and he goes on to cite, inter alia, the Guildford Four, the Maguire Seven and the Birmingham Six]
4. That they and previous Directors of Public Prosecutions and prosecuting counsel deliberately suppress and conceal evidence in favour of the defence [this was perfectly legal – and standard practice – in 1952]
5. [not relevant]
6. Judges are, and have always been, mere servile tools of the executioner
7. In many criminal trials, the judge's summing up is nothing more than a second prosecution speech, more effective because it professes to be delivered from a position of professional impartiality …

Ludovic Kennedy focuses on various aspects of the Craig and Bentley case – 'The first case I came across of the police putting words into the accused's mouth, with devastating consequences.'

Lord Goddard had posed the question at the trial in his address to the jury, 'Are you going to say they [the police] were conspicuous liars?

Because if their evidence is untrue, these three officers are doing their best to swear away the life of that boy [Bentley].' Kennedy answered that with:

> In my view, the short and regrettable answer is that, on the balance of probabilities, the three officers in question – Fairfax, Harrison and McDonald – did lie, although by this time they may well have deluded themselves into thinking that they had heard the words spoken (they had to believe it to maintain their self-respect) and there was no likelihood of the jury doubting them.

By the time Parris and Kennedy wrote their books, the testimony of Dennis Woodcock, George Barlow and John Tennant, all eyewitnesses to the Croydon events, were in the public domain. And they all contradicted the prosecution case in 1952.

The fact remains, however, that what motivated both Parris and Kennedy and what led to Thames Television discovering Woodcock, Barlow and Tennant was the story told to me by Claude Pain.

So this is the other possibility. On 3 November 1952, an exhausted and no doubt shell-shocked PC Pain went home to his family. The events of the night would soon be all over the newspapers and the radio. In the case of Pain and, I suspect, most of the officers involved, this was the most exciting and high-profile thing that had happened in their careers (I cannot know, because the powers-that-were in 1990 would give me no details of individuals' careers) and naturally, they talked about it. Human nature being what it is, Claude Pain was not just one of the dozen or so policemen on the ground around Barlow and Parker's, he was up there, on the roof, facing Craig's bullets. I have no doubt that he really did see Sid Miles's body from his graphic retelling of the memory. This was the story Pain told his wife and his children – and any friends who were not in the police force. This is the story that stayed with the Pain family, the little harmless exaggeration that

Ray Pain told my wife. The story that I believed wholeheartedly was true because no one in the know would give me any information at all.

Derek Bentley has had his murder conviction quashed, not on the unreliability of police evidence, but on the appalling miscarriage of justice perpetrated by Lord Goddard. That is right and proper, although it came too late to be of comfort to Iris who died January 1997, months before Lord Bingham's pronouncement.

But I have felt guilty about my own role in this story and annoyed with myself that I was duped (admittedly along with others) by an old man who probably found himself caught in a spotlight of his own making.

Are we talking about police corruption, which, as we know, has always been an issue in criminal cases? Or are we talking about police exaggeration, the little white lies that we all tell to make ourselves heroes, at least to our families?

You have read a great deal in this book about juries. Now, *you* are the jury. You have as many facts at your disposal as I can find.

You decide.

Let me end on this note. After months of wrangling with an uncaring state, the Bentley family won the right to have Derek's remains removed from Wandsworth to Croydon Cemetery. In 2008, someone removed the headstone and left it outside Streatham Police Station in London. Why? I have no idea, but perhaps it was a little reminder that the case is *still* not resolved, that the cover-up by some officers of the Met has not been fully exposed. And what did it say on that headstone? A line that Iris had to fight tooth and nail to have incised?

Here lies Derek William Bentley
A victim of British justice.

Bibliography

Books

Ascoli, David, *The Queen's Peace,* Hamish Hamilton, 1979

Bechhofer Roberts, C.E., *The Trial of Jones and Hulton,* Jarrolds, 1945

Begg, Paul and Skinner, Keith, *The Scotland Yard Files,* Headline, 1992

Bentley, Iris (with Dening, Penelope) *Let Him Have Justice,* Sidgwick and Jackson, 1995

Bentley, W.G., *My Son's Execution*, W.H. Allen, 1957

Berry-Dee, Christopher and Odell, Robin, *Dad, Help Me Please,* W.H. Allen, 1990

Bland, James, *True Crime Diary Vols I and II,* Futura, 1986

Bressler, Fenton, *Lord Goddard,* Harrap, 1977

Calder, Angus, *The People's War,* Pimlico (reprint), 2000

Cohen, Albert K., *Delinquent Boys,* 1956

Du Cann, C.G.L., *Miscarriages of Justice,* Frederick Muller, 1960

Duff, Charles, *A Handbook of Hanging,* E.P. Publishing, 1974

Eddlestone, John J., *The Encyclopaedia of Executions,* John Blake, 2002

Elsworth, Steve, *Acid Rain,* Pluto, 1984

Fido, Martin and Skinner, Keith, *The Official Encyclopaedia of Scotland Yard,* Virgin, 1999

Friedland, Martin, L., *The Trials of Israel Lipski,* Macmillan, 1984

Furneaux, R, *They Died by a Gun,* Herbert Jenkins, 1962

Gattery, Charles Neilson, *The Incredible Mrs Van der Elst,* Leslie Frewin, 1972

Gauté J.H.H. and Odell, Robin, *Murder 'Whatdunnit'?* Harrap, 1982

Gauté J.H.H. and Odell, Robin, *The Murderers' Who's Who,* Harrap, 1979

Harper, Tom, *Broken Yard,* Biteback Publishing, 2022

Jackson, Stanley, *The Old Bailey,* W.H. Allen, 1978

Kennedy, Ludovic, *On My Way to the Club*, Collins, 1989

Kennedy, Ludovic, *Thirty-Six Murders and Two Immoral Earnings*, Profile Books, 2002

Lewis, David and Hughman, Peter, *Just How Just?,* Secker and Warburg, 1975

Lock, Joan, *Blue Murder? Policemen Under Suspicion,* Robert Hale, 1986

Mark, Robert, *In the Office of Constable,* Collins, 1978

Maxwell-Fyfe, David (Earl of Kilmuir) *Political Adventure,* Weidenfeld and Nicholson, 1964

Mays, John Barron, *Crime and the Social Structure,* Faber and Faber, 1963

Montgomery Hyde, H. (ed), *Trial of Craig and Bentley,* Notable British Trials Vol 81, 1954

Moriarty, C.C.H., *Police Law,* Butterworth and Co, 1941

Morris, Terence, *Crime and Criminal Justice Since 1945,* Blackett, 1989

Morris, Terence, *The Criminal Area,* 1957

Paget, R.T. and Silverman, S.S., *Hanged – and Innocent?* Victor Gollancz, 1953

Parris, John, *Most of My Murders,* Frederick Miller, 1960

Parris, John, *Scapegoat,* Duckworth, 1991

Pierrepoint, Albert, *Executioner: Pierrepoint*, Harrap, 1974

Scott, Sir Harold, *Scotland Yard*, Andre Deutsch, 1954

Seabrook, Mike, *Coppers – An Inside View of the British Police*, Harrap, 1974

Selwyn, Francis, *Gangland*, Routledge, 1988

Smith, Arthur, *Lord Goddard,* Weidenfeld and Nicholson, 1959

Smithies, Edward, *Crime in Wartime,* George Allen and Unwin, 1982

Symons, Julian, *Bloody Murder,* Penguin, 1972

Trow, M.J., *Let Him Have It, Chris*, Constable, 1990
Trow, M.J., *War Crimes,* Pen and Sword, 2008
Wertham, Fredric, *The Seduction of the Innocent,* Museum Press, 1954
Yallop, David A., *To Encourage the Others,* W.H. Allen, 1971

Newspapers and Periodicals

Croydon Advertiser
Croydon Post
Croydon Times
Daily Express
Daily Mail
Daily Telegraph
Picture Post
Police Review
Sunday Pictorial

Index